The Busy Woman's Guide to Financial Freedom

VICKIE L. BAJTELSMIT, J.D., Ph.D.

AMACOM
American Management Association

New York · Atlanta · Brussels · Buenos Aires · Chicago · London · Mexico City · San Francisco
Shanghai · Tokyo · Toronto · Washington, D.C.

Special discounts on bulk quantities of AMACOM books are
available to corporations, professional associations, and other
organizations. For details, contact Special Sales Department,
AMACOM, a division of American Management Association,
1601 Broadway, New York, NY 10019.
Tel.: 212-903-8316   Fax: 212-903-8083
Web site: www.amacombooks.org

This publication is designed to provide accurate and authoritative
information in regard to the subject matter covered. It is sold with
the understanding that the publisher is not engaged in rendering
legal, accounting, or other professional service. If legal advice or
other expert assistance is required, the services of a competent
professional person should be sought.

Library of Congress Cataloging-in-Publication Data

Bajtelsmit, Vickie L., 1957–
    The busy woman's guide to financial freedom / Vickie L. Bajtelsmit.
        p. cm.
    Includes bibliographical references and index.
    ISBN 0-8144-7108-4
    1. Women—Finance, Personal.   2. Finance, Personal.   3. Investments.
    I. Title: Guide to financial freedom.   II. Title.

    HG179 .B282 2002
    332.024′042—dc21   2001034131

Printing number

10   9   8   7   6   5   4   3   2   1

My mother, Beverly Barwick Herring, was the classic "busy woman," the manager of our household as well as the extracurricular activities of five children, all while working a full-time job as an elementary school teacher. An aspiring writer of poetry and children's literature, she died in July 1998 at the young age of 62 before she could realize her dream of becoming a published author. I know that if she had had more time in this life, she would have eventually reached that goal.

Mom, this book's for you.

Contents

Acknowledgments

This book would not have been possible without the help and support of many others. Although I have been writing for nearly all my professional career, I have never before tackled a book-length project. Despite that, my husband Rich and our sons, Kristopher and Kyle, the three most important people in my life, never once doubted my ability to see this through. I am also thankful to have been raised by two wonderful parents who taught me to believe in the grace of God and in my own potential. I would be remiss if I did not acknowledge the Ladies Lunch Group, my terrific circle of women friends—Elaine, Alex, Nancy, Joan, Pat, Sue, Dawn, Diane, and Chris—who are an unending source of wisdom, humor, and love. I am incredibly blessed to have such wonderful family and friends. Last, I would like to thank the terrific people at AMACOM, who have been instrumental in getting this book to its present form: Ray O'Connell, Jim Bessent, and the many others who have added their time and skills.

You Can Do It!

You Have What It Takes to Achieve Financial Freedom!

If you are like me, you have many roles. You may be wife, mother, career person, and any number of other roles. In each of these roles, women are consistently proving themselves to be equal to or better than their male counterparts.

With so much to their credit, why do women so often rely on men to take care of their finances? Why are men more likely to have the responsibility for the household budget, retirement planning, and insurance purchases? In previous generations, we could point to our husbands' or brothers' greater experience and education, but that is no longer a sufficient explanation.

The answer lies in our *confidence* rather than our *ability*. Although men generally do not have any more knowledge of financial planning, women have less confidence in their ability to make correct decisions when they are not completely versed in the subject. Studies of male-female differences in decision-making styles have shown that this gender difference holds true in other areas as well. Female students are less likely to ask questions in class for fear of saying something wrong. In business meetings, men will express

1

strong opinions on topics they know very little about, whereas women will reserve judgment until they have had time to read supporting materials.

So why do I say that you have what it takes to achieve financial freedom—and to be financially successful? Because taking charge of your finances is *not* rocket science. Your success in your prior endeavors, whether those endeavors are managing your children, running a household, or running an office, proves that you have the basic intelligence to succeed at finance as well.

However, it *is* likely that you lack two components that are necessary to your financial success. You probably don't have the fundamental knowledge about financial planning and, being a busy woman, you probably don't have very much time in which to learn it.

Financial Knowledge: You Probably Don't Have Enough of It—Yet

Women commonly express concern that they don't know enough about their finances. The fact that you are reading this book indicates that you probably have similar feelings. This is nothing to be embarrassed about. Unfortunately, our educational system has never placed a high priority on teaching personal financial planning. Some high schools are now including a few of the basics in their curricula; I applaud this, but high school may be too early for most students to see the relevance of this material. In college curricula, financial planning is often an elective course, and, even for finance majors, some subjects such as insurance and retirement planning may not be covered at all. At Colorado State University, where I am a member of the finance faculty, I teach a survey course in risk management and insurance, but it is one of several electives that finance majors can opt for.

So where did all those people out there who are successfully handling their own finances get this knowledge? Most of them figured it out for themselves or turned to professionals for advice. In this book, I give you the tools to figure it out yourself, but I also recommend that you consult with professionals for specific tasks that require specialized expertise. Using professionals for certain tasks is an important, although not always a necessary, component of financial planning. The problem with hiring experts is that you need to know enough to tell them what you want and to judge whether they are doing a good job. And, too often, those who are holding themselves out as experts are also trying to sell you something at the same time, whether it be financial advice or a particular financial product. Turning over your financial problems to others costs you money and results in some loss of control, so having a little knowledge up front is essential.

Time: You Probably Don't Have Enough of It

A second problem you may be familiar with is lack of time. Whether you are a single career woman, a homemaker, or a working mother, it is an established fact that women have fewer "leftover" hours (or minutes) in the day than men have. In fact, studies have shown that, on average, working women spend twice as much time doing child-related and household chores as their husbands, even when they work equivalent hours outside the home.

Here's what my typical weekday is like (which should sound familiar to other working mothers): Up at 5:30 A.M. to feed the pets, wake up my two high-school-aged sons, and make sure they have their homework and any essentials they need for after-school activities. By 6:00 A.M., I'm in the shower; I have a precious half-hour to shower, dress, and apply a little makeup (sometimes I don't make it to the last step). Out the door at 6:35. Drop the kids at school and arrive at work around 7:20. My work schedule sometimes involves evenings, but typically I am home by 6 P.M., unless I have to stop for groceries on the way. Then it's time to make dinner, except on the rare days when I can enlist more than just "help" from my husband and sons. Of course, I also need to police the clarinet and saxophone practice, check math problems, read rough drafts of language assignments, etc. The boys are usually in bed by 9:30, so that's when I can finally put my feet up.

Does this sound familiar? Does the illustration below remind you of yourself? Women who don't have children usually aren't much better off because they typically put more effort into their jobs. Many women are choosing to put off motherhood in order to establish their careers first. Their work may extend into the evening hours or involve extensive travel. Or they may have additional obligations at church or volunteer work that takes up their time. Single women are also likely to have time commitments to relationships or dating.

Are you thinking that maybe it's a fair trade to allow the men to take care of the finances? The problem with this philosophy is that it makes women dependent when they should be independent. Most married women will someday be widows, given women's longer life expectancy. And it is still an unfortunate truth that many marriages end in divorce. You can't afford *not* to understand your finances. You can't afford *not* to allocate the time to this important task. So where's the time for dealing with your finances going to come from? Frankly,

Illustration by Kristopher S. Bajtelsmit

it doesn't take much. You will need to efficiently allocate a few extra hours to work through this book. Happily, the end result will be worth it. Once your financial plan is in place, it won't require a lot of upkeep and you will be able to sleep better knowing that you have taken care of your financial needs.

It's Not Because You *Can't* Do It

Some women say that the reason they don't have control of their finances is that they just aren't that interested. I've even seen studies that suggest that women are somehow less capable in finance. I don't buy this. I have been teaching finance for many years and, although I will agree that women make up a smaller percentage of our majors, they tend to do just as well as the men in our courses. Women are just as capable of doing a good job of handling their finances as men are. If anything, women tend to be more organized and detail-oriented than men, which aids in the process of decision making.

It is well established that people tend to like things that they feel more knowledgeable about. No one likes to feel stupid. There's nothing more frustrating to me than being at a social function and having the conversation turn to football. Everything I know (or want to know) about the game could be summarized in a paragraph. For some people, the same thing happens when the conversation turns to financial issues. And people who are successfully managing their investments love to talk about them! (You should always keep in mind that they never tell you about all the mistakes they have made along the way.)

My reason for writing this book is that I think there are a lot of women with similar problems. First, women don't have sufficient understanding of finance to feel confident in making decisions in this area. Second, women don't have very much time to devote to learning about or managing their finances. I think that most of you will agree with me when I say that men do not face the same constraints that women face in these areas. For whatever reason, men tend to have greater knowledge of their finances and more leftover time to deal with them.

So How Can You Do It All?

As a busy woman, I have never had the luxury of wasting time. At work, at home, and in school, I always look for the most efficient method of doing whatever task is set before me. There's nothing that bugs me more than to have someone else waste my time.

With this in mind, I have designed this book to be an efficient resource for you. I know that you don't have the time to read books on every financial planning subject (and if you've browsed the shelves at Barnes & Noble or Borders lately, you know that there are literally hundreds of such books to choose from). I have attempted to condense a wealth of information (no pun intended) into a small space so that you can get the most out of your valuable reading time. Of course, this means that you are getting only the basics—a "primer," so to speak. It should be enough to get you on the road to financial success, independence, and self-confidence. For some topics, I have provided citations to other useful resources in the appendix. For those of you who are Internet savvy, I have listed web sites that can provide useful calculators and supplemental information.

The Structure of This Book

Each chapter of this book covers a different aspect of your finances. Although you do not need to read them in order, I recommend that you do the organization and self-evaluation exercises in Chapter 2 before you go on to the later chapters, since many of the other chapters will require that you have an understanding of your net worth and cash flow. Once you have completed that part, you can use the book as a reference and look up the specific topics you need help with.

Each chapter other than this one begins with a checklist to help you identify your needs and to indicate the basic chapter coverage. Whenever I thought it would be helpful, I have created easy-to-follow worksheets that help you to work out some of the math. The only tool you will need to do any of the calculations in this book is a simple calculator that can add, subtract, multiply, and divide. I have provided shortcut tables for any more complex calculations (like compound interest and mortgage amortization). For those of you who want more, most of the topic areas include references to informational Web sites and Web site calculators for more in-depth coverage. Throughout the book, I also provide illustrative examples of women in circumstances that may be similar to your own. Although these examples are fictionalized, they are drawn from the life experiences of the many women I have known in the course of my professional career.

Do You Really Need to Read This Book?

If you are browsing through this book and think that perhaps you don't need to read it because your finances are in pretty good shape, ask yourself the following questions:

1. Do you know what your net worth and annual cash flow are?

2. Do you have and follow a monthly budget?

3. Do you have specific short-term and long-term financial goals, and are you taking steps to meet those goals?

4. Are all of your personal and family financial documents organized and easily accessible?

5. Do you have credit cards in your own name and, if you do, do you pay your balance in full every month?

6. Have you forecast your retirement income needs and established a savings program to meet those needs?

7. If you have children, have you established a savings program to meet the costs of their college education?

8. Do you understand the process of buying a car and financing the purchase?

9. Do you have a valid will that is up-to-date?

10. Do you understand the process of buying a home and financing it?

11. Have you considered the impact of estate taxes on your heirs and taken steps to minimize this tax burden?

12. Do you understand your investment options?

If you answered no to *any* of these questions, then this book will be worth its purchase price many times over.

Congratulations!

Before you go any further, let me congratulate you on your decision to begin the process of taking charge of your financial future. With a little help, you can do it! The evidence is clear that the financial condition of the nation's women is improving. In a recent academic study that I did for the Employee Benefits Research Institute with Nancy Jianakoplos, a professor of economics at Colorado State University, we found that even though there has been little improvement in the wage gap over the last decade (women on average still make significantly less than men), the difference between men's and women's retirement account accumulations (the pension gap) is improving at a much faster rate. Women are taking the hand they have been dealt and making the most of it. And the more knowledge you have, the better off you will be.

CHAPTER 2

How to Organize and Evaluate Your Finances

You need to read this chapter if:

✔ You do not have a simple and comprehensive system of organization for your household and personal financial information.

✔ You aren't sure what your net worth is or why it is important.

✔ You aren't sure what your monthly cash flow is or why it is important.

How Is Your "Fiscal Fitness"?

Do these excuses sound familiar to you?

"I don't have enough time."

"My New Year's resolution is to get organized."

Or my personal favorite (from Scarlett O'Hara):

"I'll think about that tomorrow."

You can't bake a cake without the right ingredients. You can't sew a dress without the necessary zippers, thread, and buttons. You can't play golf without your clubs and ball. And you can't take charge of your finances unless you are moderately well organized and you have a working knowledge of your current household wealth and cash flow. This may not be the most fun thing you have ever done in your life, but it's so important that you *must* make the time. Your future, and that of your children, depends on it.

In this chapter, I will help you to set up a *simple* organizational system for your household finances. You will also learn about several measures of financial well-being, what each of them measures, how to apply each of them to your own situation, and how to determine if your financial health is in jeopardy. The starting points for personal financial planning are actually the same ones that financial professionals use in judging the financial well-being of a business:

- Cash flow

- Net worth

- Future prospects

After you have gotten your information organized, figuring your cash flow and net worth will be easy and will help you to prioritize the areas of your financial health that need work. In later chapters, this information will be important for other aspects of your finances.

The First Step: Getting Organized

Before you can proceed with evaluating your finances, you need to have certain information at your fingertips. The time spent on this step will reduce your stress level, and today's organization will make your life simpler in the future.

For many women, this is the hardest step because it is a time-consuming task that is easier to "think about tomorrow." Although I believe it is easier to do it all at one time (maybe a Saturday morning when you can get your husband to take the kids to the soccer game), you can also split this task into a few smaller and more manageable tasks, as I will outline later.

Two Boxes or Many?

My husband likes to joke that when he met me in 1979, my record-keeping system consisted of two cardboard boxes that I had covered with lime green contact paper. One had yellow contact paper letters that said "Bills and Records." The other was labeled "Miscellaneous." Neither one was more than one-half full. We should all be so lucky as to have all our records and miscellaneous fit in two small cardboard boxes. (Of course, I long ago outgrew those boxes. I now find that my weekly pile of mail could fill a box.)

My grandmother, fondly known as "Gagee" Herring, was an example of the other extreme. Until she moved in with my father in 1998 at the age of 97, her small house was literally overflowing with boxes of "important papers," miscellaneous yet-to-be-opened junk mail, magazines, and newspapers that she could not bring herself to throw away. After so many years of this behavior, she was not likely to change her methods, but family members were known to take small piles with them after a visit for later disposal. She never noticed. If you are still in the small box stage of your life, then the organization process will be simple. Otherwise, plan to spend a few hours on this task, preferably without interruption.

Simple Is Better

Simplicity should be the primary rule for your system of financial organization:

- Don't keep unnecessary papers.

- Handle papers only once, if possible.

- Design your system to accommodate *all* of your financial needs (records, taxes, bill–paying) so that you don't need to duplicate the effort.

- Be sure that your system is easy for someone else to under-stand (in the event that something happens to you, and your spouse, sibling, child, or parent needs to step in and help).

- Design your system so that you can find a necessary document within a short time.

Keep as Little as Possible

The steps in setting up your organizational system are given in Table 2-1. Before you begin the task, you should carefully consider what you need to keep. Remember, the main rule of organization is to simplify your life. Do not keep anything unless you think you will need it in the future. I generally categorize my "keeps" in three ways:

1. Long term:

Records that I need to keep for taxes

Records that I want to keep for personal reasons (such as my kids' report cards, drawings, school assignments)

Copies of contracts (life insurance, mortgages, auto insurance, investments)

Table 2-1 Organizing Your Finances

You should have on hand:
  small file cabinet
  box of 25 hanging files
  box of 50–100 manila envelopes
  small portable file box (optional)

Steps:

1. Purchase a file cabinet and file folders.

2. Sort your old records into general piles and throw away the ones that aren't on your list.

3. Sort the larger piles into smaller piles and put them in the individually labeled files.

4. Decide on categories of records and papers that you need to keep.

5. If possible, put the filing cabinet in a place that is convenient so that you can regularly file new items as they appear.

Bank account information (including cancelled checks or checking statements)

2. Short term:

Things I need to keep temporarily to check on (such as credit card receipts and phone bills). Some of these I keep for only one month; others I keep for longer periods as I feel necessary.

Bank-related receipts (deposit slips and ATM receipts). I keep these until the bank statement is reconciled, preferably no more than one month.

Any other records that I need to keep for household budgeting purposes, generally for no more than one year.

3. Other

Magazines or articles that I want/need to read

Hobby-related items

Most women are inclined to keep too much. In fact, many books and articles on organizing yourself may actually suggest that you have files for nearly every aspect of your life. My recommendation is that you get rid of everything that you don't need for some purpose.

Examples of expendable records are monthly utility bills for which you pay a set amount each month. Since you pay with a check, you have evidence that the bill was paid and the payment was received. Once you have verification that the bill was paid in full for the prior month, there is no reason to keep the old record. For bills that vary from month to month, good household financial planning requires that you know how much you spend on a monthly and annual basis. Since many checking accounts now do not give you back your individual checks, you may want to keep these receipts for one year so that you can easily access this information in your file cabinet instead of wading through your old checkbooks.

In deciding what to throw away, keep in mind that if the filing becomes too much of a job, guess what will happen? You will put it off until tomorrow, and the pile will get bigger and bigger until it is impossible to face. The more papers that make it into the trash can on bill-paying day, the less clutter in your life. If you're like me, you have to be in a "throwing-away mood" to do this kind of task. I tend to do sorting and cleaning during these short bursts of inspiration. Wait for the mood to strike, and then be ruthless!

Your Tools

Although I am recommending that you downsize your record keeping by getting rid of a lot of unnecessary records, it is still advisable that you invest in a small filing cabinet (or a file box if you don't have a lot of records) and file folders. Hanging folders are a little more expensive, but you will find that they are the neatest way to store papers, since they do not slip down in the cabinet. The file cabinet will be most useful to you if you have a convenient place to put it where it is close at hand so that you are not tempted to put off your filing. However, if space is at a premium, you can store your long-term records in the attic or basement and keep a small portable file box for current information and bill paying.

Sorting Your Records

Keeping simplicity in mind, the first thing you need to do is divide your old records into piles for appropriate filing. You may want to proceed to step 4 and identify your categories before you make your piles. However, since everyone's situation is slightly different, starting with the piles will avoid unnecessary relabeling of file folders.

If you are like most people, you should be able to throw away a large percentage of the papers you are sorting. If you don't need a paper for some particular purpose, throw it away.

Even if an item is related to taxes, you do not need to keep it forever. I recommend that you keep all your old tax returns in full, but that you throw away the detailed receipts for older returns. The IRS recommends keeping records for seven years, but individuals are rarely audited after three. If you have a small business, you are more likely to be audited, so keeping records for a longer time is a good idea.

The division of piles is up to you, but they will probably fall into several logical categories. Items that do not seem to fit logically may be prime candidates for the trash can.

Once you have a set of general piles, you are ready to separate them into subcategories and put them in their respective files.

Label and File

Look over the list of file labels in Table 2-2 and compare them to your piles. You will probably need to make a hanging file for each of the general categories and a manila file for each of the subcategories that apply to you (and any others you have decided to add to my list). Each hanging file will hold several manila file folders.

What's Next? Measuring Your "Fiscal Fitness"

If you have completed this organizational process, then you have taken the first steps toward financial freedom. Most women feel a great deal of satisfaction when they can see the results of their work neatly labeled and filed. Now's the time to take a well-earned break.

The next step is to take stock of your current financial situation. You now have all the information that you need at your fingertips.

As I mentioned earlier in the chapter, the starting points for personal financial planning are actually the same ones that financial professionals use in judging the financial well-being of a business:

- Net worth

- Cash flow

- Future prospects

Let me take a moment to talk about the use of the computer and the Internet in the steps to come. Let's face it—I know that you are a

Table 2-2 Labels for Your File Folders

General Category (Hanging Files)	Subcategory (Manila File Folders)
Auto	Insurance Policy Title Information (original in safe deposit) Repairs/Expenses Auto Loan/Lease Information
Bank	Separate file for each account
Credit	Separate file for each credit card Credit Reports (if you have them) Applications for Credit
Home	Mortgage Homeowner's Insurance Repairs/Capital Improvements Rental Contracts
Investments	Files for each mutual fund/CD/other
Kids	Report Cards School Photos School Policies/Procedures Manual Child Care Expenses
Life	Life Insurance Policies Premiums/Bills Copy of Will (original in safe deposit)
Medical	Bills/Premiums Prescription Drugs Insurance Policy Health/Immunization Records
Pensions	Annual/Monthly/Quarterly Reports Employer Information
Taxes	Tax Statements from Employer(s) Tax Statements from Banks/Investments Tax Returns (for each year) Receipts for Next Tax Year

Illustration by Kristopher S. Bajtelsmit

busy person and that you do not have time to consult every possible resource in your quest for financial know-how. Since my intent in writing this book is to condense what you need to know into as small a space as possible, my assumption is that you would prefer to have the "short version" of the story rather than the epic-length mini-series. However, for those of you who want more, there are lots of available resources. Relevant Internet resources are identified in each chapter, and these resources are also collected in the appendix for easy reference. If you are computer savvy, you may find it helpful to use one of the commercially available personal finance programs. The two leading competitors are Microsoft's Money 2001 Deluxe and Intuit's Quicken 2001 Deluxe. Both of these offer easy tutorials and budgeting and financing tips, as well as connectivity with the Internet for easy downloading of information and updating of investment information.

What Is Your Net Worth?

The easiest way to think about your net worth is to picture what would happen if you suddenly had to get rid of everything you own and pay back all of your debts. Would you have anything left at the end? If so, then you have positive net worth. If not, then you have negative net worth.

Take a few minutes to fill out Table 2-3. You should be able to get this information from your most recent statements (in your newly organized file drawers).

To determine your net worth, take the final total of your assets and subtract the final total of your liabilities as indicated in the worksheet:

Table 2-3 Calculating Your Net Worth

Assets	$	Liabilities	$
Checking accounts	————	Credit card balances (list)	
Savings accounts	————	1. —————	————
Money market accounts	————	2. —————	————
CDs	————	3. —————	————
Treasury bills	————	4. —————	————
Cash value of life insurance	————	5. —————	————
		6. —————	————
Investments			
Mutual funds	————		
Stocks	————	Personal loans	————
Corporate bonds	————	Student loans	————
Municipal bonds	————	Car loan ————	————
Business interests	————	Car loan ————	————
		Life insurance loans	————
Pension fund value	————	Pension fund loans	————
IRAs/Keoghs	————		
College savings plan	————	Home mortgage balance	————
Other savings plans	————	Home equity loans	————
		Other real estate loans	————
Market value of home	————		
Market value of 2nd home	————	Alimony/child support owed	————
Other real estate owned	————		
Value of cars	————	Taxes owed (above withholding)	————
Value of home furnishings	————		
Jewelry	————	Other investment loans	————
Artwork/collectibles	————		
Clothing/personal assets	————	Other liabilities/debts	
Other valuables	————	1. —————	————
		2. —————	————
Total Assets	————	Total Liabilities	————

Net Worth = Total Assets − Total Liabilities = $ ————

$$\text{Net Worth} = \text{Total Assets} - \text{Total Liabilities}$$

If your net worth is negative or zero, then you are not in very good financial shape. If you were a business, your net worth would be the approximate value of the owners' dollar interest in the company. If this is not positive, then their stock investment, for which they paid good money, is worthless. Of course, your household is not a business, but there are still consequences to having too much debt and not enough assets. Lenders (other than high-interest lenders such as credit card companies) will not be willing to lend you money. You have no cushion against temporary job loss, death, or other unexpected needs for cash. These are serious problems that need to be addressed through short-term and long-term planning.

If you have positive net worth, then your household's finances look more promising. However, you still need to be sure that you have considered other aspects of your total financial plan.

Net Cash Flow

Cash flow refers to the amount of money that flows into the household each week, month, or year and the amount of money that flows out:

$$\text{Net Cash Flow} = \text{All Money Received} - \text{All Money Spent}$$

The next step in getting control of your finances is to understand your household cash flow. From there, you can create a budget to help you better allocate your family resources.

What Is Your Net Cash Flow?

Fill out Table 2-4. Again, this should be fairly easy, since you now can just look in your files for each item. I recommend that you do your cash flow on both an annual and a monthly basis, since there are usually some expenditures that occur only once or twice a year (like real estate taxes and insurance premiums). If you do it on a monthly

Table 2-4 Calculating Your Nondiscretionary Cash Flow

	Monthly	Annual
Part I: Income		
Salary/wage income (gross)	$_____	$_____
Bonuses	_____	_____
Interest/dividend income	_____	_____
Alimony and child support	_____	_____
Other income (self-employment)	_____	_____
Rental income (after expenses)	_____	_____
Capital gains	_____	_____
Pension income	_____	_____
Social Security income	_____	_____
Other income	_____	_____
Total income	$_____	$_____
Part II: Expenses Before Savings		
Home expenses		
Mortgage payment (incl. principal, interest, taxes, insurance)	$_____	$_____
Rent	_____	_____
House repairs/expenses	_____	_____
Property taxes	_____	_____
Utilities		
Heating	_____	_____
Electric	_____	_____
Water and sewer	_____	_____
Cable/phone	_____	_____
Groceries	_____	_____
Car loan payments	_____	_____
Car expenses	_____	_____
Credit card payments	_____	_____
Other loan payments	_____	_____
Federal income taxes	_____	_____
State income taxes	_____	_____
Social Security taxes	_____	_____
Other taxes	_____	_____
Insurance		
Life	_____	_____
Health	_____	_____
Auto	_____	_____
Disability	_____	_____
Other insurance	_____	_____

Clothing	_____	_____
Gifts	_____	_____
Other consumables (TVs etc.)	_____	_____
Child care expenses	_____	_____
Sports-related expenses	_____	_____
Health club dues	_____	_____
Uninsured medical expenses	_____	_____
Education	_____	_____
Vacations	_____	_____
Entertainment	_____	_____
Alimony/child support	_____	_____
Charitable contributions	_____	_____
Required pension contributions	_____	_____
Magazine subscriptions/books	_____	_____
Other payments/expenses	_____	_____
Total Expenses	$_____	$_____

Net Monthly Cash Flow = Total Income − Total Expenses = $_____

basis only, you must take into account the monthly portion of any nonmonthly expenses.

Although filling out this worksheet looks like a big job, it is an essential component of your financial-planning process. If you do a careful job now, you may be able to use this information for other purposes at a later date. Mortgage and other loan applications often require much the same information. Also, in several later chapters, I will ask you to refer to this worksheet to estimate your ability to pay car loans, make mortgage payments, and make contributions to college and retirement savings plans.

The Moment of Reckoning

Now you can calculate your net cash flow by taking the total from the income worksheet and subtracting the total from the expenses worksheet:

My Net Monthly Cash Flow = _____

Since we have included only *mandatory* savings (like required pension contributions) in your expenses, the net cash flow amount represents the amount left over that you have available for discretionary purchases and for saving.

Does your net cash flow surprise you? If so, you are not alone. Many people (men and women alike) do not have a good intuitive feel for their net cash flow. If your net cash flow is negative, then either you have omitted some of your income or you are financing some of your current expenses with borrowing (e.g., credit card debt, home equity loans). This kind of spending behavior cannot be sustained for very long and is a warning sign of future financial problems.

How Do You Stack Up?

There are a lot of studies that show that baby boomers have quite different spending habits from members of previous generations. The primary differences are that prior generations had less consumer debt, generally spent less on discretionary items, and were better savers. Government and private studies indicate that only one-third of all baby-boomer households are saving enough to support their retirement in the future.

For female-headed households, the statistics are even worse, which is particularly disturbing but not surprising. There are many factors contributing to women's lower wealth and savings levels. These include:

- Lower income

- High prevalence of nonpayment of child support

- Fewer jobs with pension plans

- More conservative investment choices

- Increasing cost of child care

Since women tend to live longer than men, their *smaller* average retirement wealth must support a *longer* period of retirement, often five to ten years longer than men's. In later chapters, I suggest some strategies to improve your saving and investment choices.

Summary

If you have read this chapter and followed the worksheets, you now should have:

- A comprehensive system of organization for your household and personal financial information

- An estimate of your assets, debts, and net worth

- An estimate of your monthly net cash flow and potential savings

- An understanding of your household's overall financial condition

Organizing your records and developing a basic understanding of your household's cash flow and net worth are the first and biggest steps toward financial success. The time you spend on this effort will pay off many times over. Contrary to what some would have you believe, control of your finances does not require that you have a complex computer program and update your information on a daily basis. You simply need to know what you have, what you owe, what you make, and what you spend. Armed with this information, you can easily determine the areas that need work. Now it's time to think about the future: to plan, to dream, and to take action to achieve those dreams.

CHAPTER 3

Setting Short-Term and Long-Term Goals for Financial Success

You need to read this chapter if:

- ✔ You do not currently have a list of short-term financial goals.
- ✔ You do not currently have a list of long-term financial goals.
- ✔ You aren't sure how to achieve the goals you have set.

Why Is Planning Important?

The age-old story of the grasshopper and the ant provides a lesson that is timeless. While the grasshopper was spending his summer lazing in the sun, the ants were busy preparing their nest and collecting food supplies for the winter. I don't need to tell you which one survived. In real life, of course, "saving for a rainy day" is easier said than done. Unlike earlier, simpler times, the world today is full of opportunities for spending money. Many people have large accumulations of "stuff" that they don't really need. (Take a look in your attic or basement if you don't believe this applies to you.) The importance of planning is that it helps you to focus on what *is* important—and this makes it easier to avoid accumulating "stuff."

For those with ample means, achieving financial goals may be a little easier—at least insofar as they do not have to skip meals to put aside some money—but for those who are struggling to pay the electric bill or to get out from under a mountain of debt, saving for retirement or college is not easy, and vacations are just a dream. However, when people have more income and wealth, their goals grow at least proportionately. The camping trip in the mountains becomes a skiing vacation in Aspen or the Alps. A new Mercedes instead of a Subaru. Dinners out at five-star restaurants instead of the local bar and grill. Goal setting and planning are still necessary, but the goals will be different.

Regardless of their walk in life, everyone can use a lesson in short- and long-term planning. In this chapter, I help you develop some realistic financial goals and then work on a plan to achieve those goals. In Chapter 4, I provide strategies for managing your cash and credit so that you can more easily achieve your goals.

How to Set Goals

I am a "list person," and I find that this seems to be a female trait (or maybe it is a trait of busy people). Both at work and at home, I find that I am most productive when I begin with a list. That's not to say that *everything* on the list ever gets crossed off, because lists have a way of getting longer rather than shorter. Nevertheless, if you don't begin with a goal, you never can accomplish it.

I find that the process of creating a list helps me to organize my thoughts and prioritize my time. A further advantage of using a list is that you don't need to keep as much information in your active memory, and this frees you up to focus on the tasks at hand. Even if you are a terrific multitasker, it is a relief to set some of the tasks aside and give your full attention to the ones at hand.

You will find that, in much of this book, I impose my list system on you. My hope is that you will find it to be a life skill that will benefit you as much as it has me. In Table 3-1, I have outlined the process of setting short-term and long-term financial goals.

Make a Wish List

Start with a wish list. Short-term goals are those that you would like to achieve in two years or less. The very fact that you are reading this book tells me that you have some goals in mind. For many people, short-term goals include debt reduction and saving for extras like vacations and cars. Anything longer than two years, I call a long-term goal. Unless you have a particularly wonderful pension plan with your employer, you should include accumulating wealth for your retirement as a long-term goal. If you have children, it is likely that saving for their college education will be on your list of long-term goals as well. But go ahead and dream a little—a larger home, quitting work to be a stay-at-home mom, or going back to school for an advanced degree. This *is* a wish list, after all. Of course, it won't necessarily be possible to achieve all of your goals in a short time, but it's important to put them on paper to help in the process of prioritizing them.

In case you are having trouble putting your goals into words, in Table 3-2, I have provided some ideas to get you started. But don't feel bound by these choices—every household's situation is unique, and its goals should be as well.

Table 3-1 Steps to Developing Short-Term and Long-Term Financial Goals

1. Make a wish list.
2. Be realistic.
3. Prioritize.
4. Itemize the steps to each goal.
5. Reevaluate your list annually.

Table 3-2 also includes a space for an estimate of the cost of each of your goals. This is only for starters, so there is no need to be ultra-accurate—just a "ballpark" estimate will do. For some of the long-term goals (e.g., saving for retirement and for college), you will be able to estimate the cost more precisely after you have finished some of the exercises later in this book. If these are high-priority goals for you, you may need to revisit this chapter later.

Think About What Is Most Important

The first step in being realistic about setting goals is to recognize that you probably already have more than you need. Many people, myself included, have large accumulations of things that they really don't need. This was made clear to me recently when I faced the possibility of losing all my worldly possessions:

Example: In June 2000, the Bobcat Wildfire in Colorado came dangerously close to my home. The firefighters suggested that we prepare to evacuate in case the fire continued along the

Table 3-2 Your Financial Wish List

Short-Term Goals	Priority (1 = High)			Cost	Long-Term Goals	Priority (1 = High)			Cost
Vacation	1	2	3	$_____	Reduce credit	1	2	3	$_____
New car	1	2	3	_____	Change jobs	1	2	3	_____
House repair	1	2	3	_____	College fund	1	2	3	_____
Car repair	1	2	3	_____	Remodel house	1	2	3	_____
Eat out more often	1	2	3	_____	New house	1	2	3	_____
Hire a housecleaner	1	2	3	_____	Go back to school	1	2	3	_____
Catch up on bills	1	2	3	_____	Retire comfortably	1	2	3	_____
Start an IRA	1	2	3	_____	Die rich	1	2	3	_____
Buy life insurance	1	2	3	_____	Other _____	1	2	3	_____
Other _____	1	2	3	_____	Other _____	1	2	3	_____
Other _____	1	2	3	_____	Other _____	1	2	3	_____
TOTAL COST				$_____	Total				$_____

path that they were anticipating—which was directly toward our house in the Rocky Mountain foothills. We packed the cars with the things we thought we couldn't live without, which was surprisingly little—our kids, our pets, a few changes of clothes, and our important papers. I also packed up needle-work and quilts that I had made over the years, since those were irreplaceable. A call to my insurance agent assured me that our policy was current and that it covered smoke damage.

Thankfully, the wind shifted and we didn't even sustain any smoke damage. But the point of this story is that we all should take the time periodically to think about what is truly important to us. While my family didn't lose anything in the fire, we gained much in that we were forced to think about what was truly necessary in our lives and what was superfluous. It's not the house, clothes, furniture, or other trappings of modern life that are important. Although it's nice to have all the extras, all we really need are our health, food, clothing, and shelter.

Try to Limit "Thing Wishes" to Ones That Have Long-Term Benefits

A depreciating asset is one that loses value over time. Many people's goals involve the purchase of consumables like TVs, cars, and furniture. These are depreciating assets because the minute you buy them, they begin to lose value. Things like these may make your life more enjoyable, as will vacations and baby-sitters, but from a financial point of view, they are not investments. In contrast, real estate (whether a new home, a second home, or remodeling) is an example of an investment, or an expenditure that will continue to pay off over time. Similarly, investments in education provide long-term payoffs. In some cases, jewelry, artwork, and collectibles may serve this purpose as well (although there are certainly plenty of cases in which these "investments" have not even retained their original value). Since good financial planning maximizes investments in assets that will appreciate in value and ultimately add to your wealth, you should consider this factor in setting and prioritizing your goals.

Be Realistic

I know it seems unfair for me to first tell you to make a wish list and then tell you to be realistic. However, being unrealistic is the major reason that people get in over their heads. Many people are unrealistic about the lifestyle that they can afford and therefore spend beyond their means year after year. There is evidence that, on average, Americans are doing this on a regular basis: The savings rate in this country is lower than that in any other developed nation, and consumer debt is at an all-time high. Although part of the blame for this problem goes to the companies that provide credit to almost anyone who applies, it is the individuals themselves who choose to spend rather than save.

Examples of unrealistic goals are things like winning the lottery or being independently wealthy (unless you are already pretty close, in which case you don't need to read this book). On your list of possible long-term goals, you might include an overall goal of financial independence or financial freedom, which is not the same as being independently wealthy. Financial independence simply means that you are not relying on another person (such as your husband or your parents) for your financial well-being, whereas being independently wealthy means that you are able to live entirely off your savings (without working).

So how can you set realistic goals? As an example, let's talk about vacations. Everyone would like to take a vacation at least once a year. If you are a person of limited means, it is okay to have this as a goal. However, your goal is to take a vacation, not to take a $5,000 cruise to the Bahamas. For the woman who has control of her finances, the type and cost of the vacation she takes will be determined by her budget, not by her dreams. Similarly, if you currently are heavily in debt, it may be unrealistic to set a goal of paying off all your debts in one or two years. Debt reduction is a very important and realistic goal, but the timing will be determined by your willingness and ability to go on the necessary financial diet.

Prioritize

After you have made an initial list and estimated the cost of each wish, you need to put them in order of their importance to you. Since it is difficult to come up with an absolute order, Table 3-2 asks you to set a priority of 1, 2, or 3 for each wish, with 1 being the highest priority. Keep in mind that to achieve any of these goals, you will probably have to sacrifice something else. If you currently do not have the funds to fix the car or take a vacation, then the only way to do so will be to spend less on other things or to earn more.

If you are married, it is a good idea to ask your husband to make his own list of priorities. Household money troubles are often the result of spouses having different attitudes toward money and differing opinions on short-term and long-term financial goals. If your goals do not coincide, then you should sit down and seriously talk about how each of you can achieve your most important goals. Marriage is a compromise, after all.

Identify the Steps to Each Goal

The important rule about lists is that you should break down the big items (goals in this case) into smaller, more easily achievable items. Most people find that being able to cross off items as they are achieved is very satisfying. Depending on your choice of goals, you will probably be able to use some of the lists in later chapters to identify the steps to achieving each goal. Fill in Table 3-3 as you proceed through the book.

If you are the type of person who needs immediate gratification, I suggest that you break down your list into even shorter-term steps. The satisfaction of being able to cross off or check off each item will help you stick to the program. For example, you might make yourself a check sheet that lists particular goals for the month or week. If sticking to a budget is one of your goals, you might have a check

Table 3-3 Steps to My Financial Goals

Short-Term Goals

Goal 1 _____

a. _____

b. _____

c. _____

d. _____

Goal 2 _____

a. _____

b. _____

c. _____

d. _____

Goal 3 _____

a. _____

b. _____

c. _____

d. _____

Long-Term Goals

Goal 1 _____

a. _____

b. _____

c. _____

d. _____

Goal 2 _____

a. _____

b. _____

c. _____

d. _____

Goal 3 _____

a. _____

b. _____

c. _____

d. _____

sheet that allows you to check off each week that you have been successful at doing so.

Keep Your Goals in Mind at All Times and Reevaluate Them Regularly

As you work your way through this book and learn more about your finances, your opinions and priorities may change. Regularly reevaluating your goals will ensure that your financial plan is appropriate to your needs and that you are on track to achieving your goals. Taking control of your finances will have its own rewards as you gradually free yourself from dependence on others, but progress will be slow, and it will be very easy to fall back into old habits. I recommend that you make a larger version of your goal list and attach it to the refrigerator or someplace equally prominent so that it will be "in your face" on a regular basis.

Over time, your needs and wants will inevitably change. So too should your financial goals be adaptable to new circumstances. A single woman's priorities will change if she gets married. A new higher-paying job may open up opportunities to strive for more distant financial goals. Most financial planners suggest that their clients come in to see them at least once every six months, and often every quarter. Your process of reevaluation should have a preestablished pattern as well.

Summary

If you have read this chapter and followed the worksheets, you now should have:

- A prioritized list of short- and long-term goals

- A partial list of the steps that you need to take to achieve each goal, with the remainder to be filled in as you read the other chapters in this book

You now have a destination. Whether it's saving for retirement or reducing your debt, the important thing is that you have a goal ahead of you. The rest of the chapters in this book provide the road map for getting there, so you can pick and choose among the topics as necessary. Most of you will find Chapter 4, on cash and credit management, to be useful. Chapters 5 and 6 cover aspects of employee benefits and health and life insurance that will apply to most as well. If your understanding of investment alternatives needs work, Chapters 7 through 10 provide a foundation. Finally, you can work on planning for big expenditures like cars, houses, education, and retirement in Chapters 11 to 14. Although this may seem like a long road to achieving your goals, trust me to give you the shortest and safest route to get there.

CHAPTER 4

Sticking to Your Financial Diet
Cash and Credit Management

You need to read this chapter if:

- ✔ You do not have a household budget.

- ✔ You have more than $2,000 in outstanding credit card debt.

- ✔ You are currently spending more than you earn each year.

- ✔ You want to achieve the financial goals you set in Chapter 3.

This chapter is all about developing a plan for spending your money. You probably thought I was going to say it was about how *not* to spend your money, but it's actually about making choices. I will assume that you have already taken a stab at organizing and evaluating your finances, as discussed in Chapter 2, and that you have developed a set of reasonable financial goals, as in Chapter 3. Now it's time to figure out how to spend your money to achieve the financial goals that you have set, within the confines of your individual financial circumstances.

It's Just Like a Diet

The steps to making and achieving your financial goals are deceptively simple, but the process of achieving them is kind of like a diet—a financial diet. And just like a diet, slimming down your budget isn't always as easy as it looks on paper. Old habits die hard.

Most women have had a lot of experience at dieting. Even if you have not been totally successful at losing those few extra pounds, you can still put your dieting experience to work in your financial plan. The long-term fix is going to require careful (and critical) evaluation of your current cash and credit behavior, a plan for change, and consistent adherence to your plan.

After years of experience with dieting, I have learned a few rules that seem to hold true. Most of them have their foundation in age-old wisdom, which tells us that human nature probably hasn't changed much in the last two millennia.

- A little here, a little there adds up.

- Keeping it off requires a change in behavior.

- Starvation diets always fail in the long run.

- Eat before you are hungry.

- Treat yourself occasionally.

- Fads work only for the person selling them.

- Don't keep snacks within easy reach.

- No pain, no gain.

Some of these may ring true for you as well. For those lucky ones among you who have never had to diet, I am sure that you have friends who have experienced yo-yo dieting over the years and so can still relate to these rules. In this chapter, I show you how each of these can be applied to your cash and credit management.

A Little Here, a Little There Adds Up

I particularly like this pearl of wisdom because it has a double meaning. Most budget problems stem not from really large purchases but from lots and lots of small ones. Another way to interpret this is to think about the process of saving. It doesn't need to be in big chunks. Just a little here, a little there will result in measurable outcomes.

With that in mind, the first step in establishing your financial diet plan is to see where the money is going. You have already begun this by filling in the cash flow worksheet in Chapter 2. Was your net cash flow negative? Do you run out of money at the end of every month? Do you look in your wallet and wonder where your cash has gone?

Professional diet counselors usually suggest that individuals first take stock of their daily food intake by keeping a log for a week or more. Many people are amazed how "a little here, a little there" adds up. The same is true of your finances. Use Table 4-1 to keep track of your daily expenditures for one week. Write down every penny you spend, even if it's only for gum. Although you can figure some of this backward with your checkbook log, the problem is likely your cash and credit expenditures, not your regular bills. The point here is to track your *extra* spending, since you already have an accounting of your spending on necessaries. If you are married or share a household with another person, it is important that all members of the household keep track of expenses for that week.

Once you have completed the expenditure log, go back to Table 2-4 to see if you estimated your expenses correctly. Combine the information you collected in that table with your weekly log to summarize your cash outflows in the left-hand side of Table 4-2, using either monthly or annual values (or both). (You'll fill in the new spending plan later in the chapter.) Or you can make your own list with categories that fit your unique financial circumstances. If you are comfortable with computers, you can create an Excel spreadsheet for this task or use a commercially available budgeting software package

Table 4-1 Daily Expenditure Log

Sunday		Monday		Tuesday		Wednesday		Thursday		Friday		Saturday	
Item	$	Item	$	Item	$	Item	$	Item	$	Item	$	Item	$

Table 4-2 Summary of Current and Projected Spending
(Summarize from Tables 2-4 and 4-1.)

Fixed Expenditures	Current Actual Monthly $	Current Actual Annual $	Monthly Trimmable Amount	Your New Spending Plan
Home expenses (mortgage, taxes, etc.)	$_____	$_____	$_____	$_____
Utilities (gas, electric, telephone, sewer, water)	_____	_____	_____	_____
Insurance (life, auto, disability, etc.)	_____	_____	_____	_____
Minimum credit card and loan payments	_____	_____	_____	_____
Car expenses (gas, tolls)	_____	_____	_____	_____
Taxes (property, income, social security)	_____	_____	_____	_____
Necessary child expenses (day care, child support)	_____	_____	_____	_____
Required savings (pension, college plan)	_____	_____	_____	_____
Total Fixed Expenditures	$_____	$_____	$_____	$_____
Discretionary Expenses	**Monthly $**	**Annual $**	**Monthly $**	**Monthly $**
Cable or satellite	$_____	$_____	$_____	$_____
Clothing	_____	_____	_____	_____
Auto repairs	_____	_____	_____	_____
Self-maintenance (hair, nails, cosmetics, etc.)	_____	_____	_____	_____
Household help	_____	_____	_____	_____
Club memberships	_____	_____	_____	_____
Charitable donations	_____	_____	_____	_____
Groceries	_____	_____	_____	_____
Optional child expenses (camps, baby-sitting, allowance)	_____	_____	_____	_____
Household items (furniture, décor, etc.)	_____	_____	_____	_____
Vacations	_____	_____	_____	_____
Hobbies	_____	_____	_____	_____
Electronic equipment (computers, TVs, etc.)	_____	_____	_____	_____
Eating out	_____	_____	_____	_____

Entertainment (movies, videos, sports, etc.)				
Magazine subscriptions and books	___	___	___	___
Entertaining (parties, alcohol, food)	___	___	___	___
Prescription drugs	___	___	___	___
Unreimbursed medical expenses	___	___	___	___
Gifts	___	___	___	___
Professionals (attorney, accountant, financial planner)	___	___	___	___
Pets	___	___	___	___
Dry cleaning/laundry	___	___	___	___
Pocket money (cash for coffee, gum, etc.)	___	___	___	___
Additional payments to credit cards, loans	___	___	___	___
Additional contributions to savings and retirement plans	___	___	___	___
Other	___	___	___	___
Total Discretionary	$___	$___	$___	$___

such as Quicken. This table should be a work in progress. You will want to revisit your budget with every pay increase or any other change in your personal or financial situation. By keeping it in a spreadsheet, you can easily revise it as necessary.

The critical component of this exercise is to take a close look at where your money is going. Most people are surprised to find that they spend much more on miscellaneous stuff than they think they do. The afternoon latte, the beer after work with your colleagues, and the $3 you hand over to your kids at the mall arcade add up over the course of a month to a significant amount of money—money that could perhaps be better directed to investment and/or debt reduction.

Example: When I did this exercise myself, I was surprised by the results. I had originally assumed that it was my husband and kids who were doing most of the excess spending, but I found that I was at least as guilty as the rest. My cash flow "unnecessaries" were mainly books, snacks, and hobby-related expenditures. For our household, the biggest problem was that a Barnes & Noble had opened in our town and my husband and I found it to be a great place to spend time while the kids *were at lessons or Boy Scouts. While we were there, we usually bought lattes, and we couldn't resist interesting books and magazines. There were times that we found ourselves visiting B&N four or more times a week. At about $6 for two lattes, this amounted to about $100 for the month.*

As the norm for families with children has begun to include multiple sports teams and dancing, gymnastics, and music lessons, many parents find that they are away from home at mealtime or that they have small amounts of time to kill while they wait for their children to be done with their various activities. This commonly leads to excess spending: Mom goes to the drugstore or the bookstore for entertainment when she really doesn't need anything. Since I live about twenty minutes outside of town, I have always been envious of mothers who can run home and do an extra load of laundry during guitar lessons—but now I know that the cost of living farther away isn't limited to the cost of extra gas for the car.

Singles and older couples may find that their extra spending is more related to social activities or to gift purchases. Whatever your particular vice, the important thing is to recognize it. That's the first step on any diet.

Take a closer look at any of your discretionary expenditures that you consider trimmable and put a dollar amount in the third column to represent the amount you could save by being more careful in your spending. In the last part of this chapter, you will use this information to complete the last column of Table 4-2 and establish the spending plan that will lead you to achieving your financial goals.

Keeping It Off Requires a Change in Behavior

Just as with a diet, it's easy to have good intentions. But it's also easy to fall into old habits and lose sight of the goal, particularly when the going gets tough. At our health club, I always dread the first couple of weeks of January. All those New Year's resolutions make the place a zoo. But by February, it's back to normal.

Restraint is more difficult for some people than for others. My metabolism is such that I can maintain my current weight with very little effort, but to lose weight, I have to cut back in the extreme. Similarly, you may find that the sacrifices required if you are to meet your financial goals may be considerable, and you need to be ready to change. Although the focus of this book is not on the psychological aspects of your relationship with money, there are people who use money to deal with underlying psychological problems or whose spending patterns are related to how they feel. If you think you are one of them, there are several excellent books listed in the appendix that might help you resolve some of these issues and change your behavior. A few common behaviors are discussed here.

I Shop When I'm Unhappy. Jokingly, my friends and I refer to what we call "shopping therapy." When one of us is unhappy about something, we take her shopping, which we argue is cheaper than a shrink. While we don't take this to the extreme, there are people who do. I heard of one case where a woman who was experiencing severe depression bought so much stuff that there was no room left to walk around in her house—it was filled to the brim with bags and boxes of things she had purchased and not even taken out of the packages.

I Can't Seem to Stop Buying   (Insert Your Own Vice) . All of us have something that we can't resist. For some people, it's shoes; for others, it's sweaters. There are some women who can't resist a good sale, even if it's something they don't need. As an avid quilter, I have found that I simply need to avoid going into fabric stores. I cannot seem to resist buying just a little bit of that new fabric that catches my eye, since it might be perfect for my next quilting project. I once saw a T-shirt that said "The one who dies with the most fabric wins!" The very fact that this T-shirt is being sold tells me that I am not the only fabric-a-holic out there.

The only solution to compulsive spending is to avoid putting yourself into the situation when it is possible. In my case, this means avoiding fabric stores. For someone else, it may simply mean avoiding stores altogether. Keep in mind that the retail industry does not want us to stop spending, and it will not make it easy for you. The Internet is truly the worst thing that has happened to compulsive spenders, since they no longer have to physically leave their homes. (The depressed woman in my example had actually made a lot of her purchases over the Internet.)

Starvation Diets Always Fail in the Long Run

In this chapter, I recommend a way of changing your cash and credit behavior, but I do not suggest that you cut out all the fun things in life. While starvation diets may produce big results in a short time, the dieter inevitably ends up back where she or he started because that kind of behavior cannot be maintained over a lifetime. Instead, you need to prioritize your expenditures and get rid of the ones that you really don't care about. Generally, most people can find enough "extra" money for a reasonable savings plan simply by cutting out small expenditures that they didn't even think about. That type of budget trimming is much more likely to become a lifelong pattern than an extreme "cut out all the fun stuff" strategy.

Eat Before You Are Hungry

Related to the idea of not depriving yourself is the idea that the best diets are ones that provide an eating plan. Some recommend that you eat six small meals at prespecified times; some may lay out the menu for every day. In financial planning, a common rule of thumb is to "pay yourself first." This simply means that if you take the money that you have targeted for a particular purpose and put it aside at the beginning of the month, rather than waiting until the end of the month to see what's left, you will be more likely to stick to your plan, and you will be more likely to avoid wasting the money on unnecessaries.

Treat Yourself Occasionally

Part of your plan should be occasional treats to yourself. An occasional ice cream sundae, having a dinner out with your spouse once a month, or buying yourself a new dress isn't going to break you. The important thing is to budget for the treat rather than do it compulsively. You might even plan to cut back on other expenditures, such as taking a week without the housecleaner, to make up for the cost of the treat.

Fads Work Only for the Person Selling Them

Avoid fads. Fad diets are a dime a dozen, and so are the gimmicky plans that promise to make you a millionaire. I guarantee that the person selling you a quick fix for your financial problems is laughing all the way to the bank. Don't believe anyone who tells you that he or she can change your financial future without any work on your part or at zero cost.

Don't Keep Snacks Within Easy Reach

Before the college where I teach moved to a new building, there was a snack vending machine right outside my office door. You can imagine what happened every day about 2 P.M., when my willpower was at its lowest ebb. That afternoon candy bar no doubt contributed to the several pounds that have snuck on over the years. Thankfully, my new office is three floors up from the snack machine, and I can resist it (most of the time).

In your financial plan, you need to be aware of your weaknesses. Many people find that leaving their credit cards at home is a good way to avoid impulse purchases.

Example: My husband no longer carries an ATM card in his wallet. We have always had a joint checking account, but every time I balanced the checkbook, I would find that he had withdrawn money from the ATM several times a month and didn't really know where the cash had gone. Since I was the one paying the bills, I could never be sure what the balance in the account was, so we resolved that the best way to handle things was for me to make all the withdrawals and give him cash.

The solution for our household was to dole out the cash on Sundays. The kids get allowances and lunch money. Rich and I get our cash allowance for the week as well. By the end of the week, we are usually a little short, but sticking to cash helps us keep our budgetary goals in mind.

No Pain, No Gain

Last but not least, perhaps the most important rule of any diet is to remember that in order to make progress, you will have to pay the cost. If your finances are already in pretty good shape, then perhaps the pain will be minimal. If you need a bigger financial makeover, the changes in behavior that are required may impose more costs on your lifestyle choices. But the benefits will be worth it! Keep your short- and long-term goals in mind. Perhaps you will be able to take a nice vacation each year, or perhaps your kids will be able to go to a more prestigious university. Or maybe early retirement will be in your future. Whatever your goals, remember that cash and credit management is the first step. Then you will be ready to tackle the process of investing your money for appreciation.

Managing Credit

The Good, the Bad, and the Ugly

First, the bad. In the United States, we have a big debt problem. The easy availability of credit cards has led many Americans to borrow more than they can realistically expect to pay back. According to some of my own research, a large percentage of households, even those of people nearing retirement, have a negative net worth because of heavy debt loads. Home mortgages, second mortgages, large car loans, and credit card debt top the list.

One of the big financial concerns for women a decade ago was the difficulty that they had in establishing credit in their own names. Today that is no longer much of an issue. Just about anyone can get a credit card. College students with no visible means of support are regularly offered credit cards with small limits (usually $300 to start with). As soon as they have made a few minimum payments, they may have their limits increased. In talking to my students over the years, I have found that when they graduate, they often have significant balances owed on multiple credit cards in addition to the student loans they have accumulated in four or five years of college. What did the credit card debt pay for? Not tuition and books. These students aren't even sure exactly what they bought. A round of beers or pizza for their friends. Maybe a new pair of jeans. But they didn't make enough money to pay off the balance each month—they barely scraped together enough to make the minimum payments.

Credit problems are not just an issue for the young. Even those who should know better can get in over their heads, as in the following example:

> *Example: Several years ago, I met a couple named Kurt and Beth who seemed to have it all. Kurt had a well-paid job as an engineer; they lived in a large, well-decorated home, and they went on expensive vacations several times a year. I was extremely envious of Beth, who was able to stay at home with her kids. Then, one day, Kurt's job was downsized. It turned out that they had been living beyond their means for many years, using credit cards and a second mortgage to maintain their lifestyle. In the end, they moved in with Beth's parents and declared bankruptcy. More than ten years later, they are still struggling to get back on their feet.*

Does that mean that I think credit is inherently bad? "Never a borrower or lender be"? Of course not. In fact, the availability of borrowing for home mortgages has spurred our economy and made it possible for Americans to live better than their parents and grandparents and to benefit from appreciation of their homes. But credit is something that is easily abused. And unfortunately, the companies that are peddling the credit cards benefit from this abuse. Every time you fail to pay off your balance, or you make a late payment, or you go over your credit limit, these companies get a significant benefit. You might have thought that they would prefer the good risks, but in fact the opposite is true. It's the bad risks that they make the most money on.

The features of other types of borrowing, such as car loans, student loans, and home mortgages, are discussed in chapters dealing with those specific assets. See Chapter 11 for student loans, Chapter 12 for mortgage information, and Chapter 13 for car loan information. In the remainder of this section, I review some of the features of credit cards, getting and maintaining good credit, and how you can go about reducing your debt load, if that is one of your financial goals.

Features of Credit Cards That You Should Understand

Annual Fees

Some credit cards charge an annual fee just for the privilege of having the card. These fees can range from $15 per year to as much as $75. As credit cards have become more competitive, many issuers have dropped their fees or reduced them. Here's the way to think about the fees: The company is effectively charging you extra interest at exorbitant rates. For example, suppose you have an outstanding balance of $1,000 on your MasterCard and the bank charges you its regular interest rate plus a $25 fee per year. The fee adds $25/$1,000, or $2^{1}/_{2}$ percent interest, to the rate you already pay. Some of the lower-interest-rate cards charge fees that make up for their reduced rates. Now suppose that you carry an average balance of $100. The fee is the equivalent of an extra 25 percent in interest per year. If you always pay off your credit card every month, the $25 fee on a zero balance is equivalent to paying infinite interest.

Credit Line

Credit lines can range from a low of a few hundred dollars to tens of thousands of dollars. It is not a bad idea to keep some amount of credit available for emergencies, but you should keep in mind that your credit limit may create restrictions on other borrowing, since your credit report will show potential creditors the amount of credit you have available, and they may be worried about your ability to pay should you decide to use all your available credit. If you have a low credit limit and would like to increase it, you can often call the issuer and request an increase if you have been a good customer in the past (paying bills on time, staying within your limit, etc.). Generally, if you attempt to charge a purchase that would take you over your credit limit, the charge will be rejected, subjecting you to potential embarrassment at the retail establishment. If you accidentally exceed your credit limit (e.g., when finance charges are added to your outstanding balance), the issuer is generally entitled to charge you a fee. This fee can range from $15 up. Many issuers are now charging a $30 penalty for exceeding your limit. (Think about the effective interest that this represents.)

Rate of Interest

Annual Rate. Credit card accounts are usually revolving credit accounts. This simply means that your payment obligation is continually updated, based on the latest balance, and that payments are applied to the oldest amounts due first. Interest is usually calculated on the average daily balance over the month in question. Therefore, if you make a large charge at the end of the month, your interest for the month will be less than if you had made that charge at the beginning of the month.

Teaser Rates. Many companies are advertising low-rate cards these days. Hardly a day goes by that we don't receive a credit card solicitation in the mail. If you wonder how these companies can offer you such enticing rates, you should carefully read the fine print. Most of these rates are good for six months only, after which they revert to a market rate of interest. Even when the offered market rate seems lower than average, there are other clauses that make up for it.

Example: One recent offer I received went something like this: An initial rate of 6.9 percent for six months, after which the rate would be 14.9 percent. The rate for balance transfers and *cash withdrawals was 18.9 percent. (Although the offer letter strongly encouraged using the new card to consolidate debt, the fact that the balance transfers would not qualify for the 6.9 percent rate was in very small print.) If you made one late payment, even during the six-month initial period, the penalty was $30 and the interest rate would adjust to 19.9 percent. If you made a second late payment at any time in the future, the penalty was the same and the interest rate would adjust to its maximum, which was, at that time, 22.9 percent.*

The moral of this story is, you need to read the fine print. You never get something for nothing. Credit cards are a risky business for lenders, and they would not offer them if there weren't a lot of profit potential.

Cash Advance Terms

Many credit cards apply different rates of interest to cash advances and to purchases, with the rate on cash advances often being a point or two higher. Why? When you take a cash advance, the credit card company loses two other potential sources of income. First, it does not receive its usual payment from the retailer, which ranges from $1/2$ to 3 percent of the purchase amount. Second, it loses the "float," which is the difference between the date on which the card issuer can charge you interest and the date on which it actually lets go of the funds. This amounts to a couple of days, at least, of lost interest. Another source of replacement income for cash advances is the fees that you are charged for use of an ATM if you use the machine to access the cash. These fees have increased recently to the point where you may now be charged $1.50 or more at the ATM, and the card issuer will charge you an additional $1 to $2. (If you have taken out only $100, think about the effective interest on that loan!)

Grace Period

One of the good things about credit cards is that you can get some free float yourself if you use your cards wisely. Most credit cards allow a twenty-five-day grace period from billing date to the date of payment. This means that you can effectively borrow the money for free from the date of purchase to the due date (assuming that you do not have an annual fee, of course). Keep in mind, however, that there is no grace period on cash advances.

Rebates

There are several types of credit cards that promise to give you a rebate toward something else. This includes cards that provide frequent flier miles for usage (sponsored by most of the major airlines) as well as those that give you "cash back" in the form of a reduction in your outstanding balance on purchases (such as the Discover card). In assessing the value of these "deals," you need to look at what your true savings are. Often these cards carry slightly higher rates of interest or have other restrictions that make them less attractive. However, you may still be able to take advantage of the deals if you use the card for the purchases and then transfer the balance to a lower-interest card each month or, better yet, pay off the balance.

Example: My friend Mary is a particularly savvy consumer. She knows how to take advantage of every deal or coupon that was ever invented. Her credit card strategy is aimed at maximizing her airline frequent flier miles. She applied for and received a no-annual-fee United Airlines VISA card, which promised to give her a frequent flier mile for each dollar of purchases (after her initial bonus of 5,000 miles). She also applied for a separate card for her husband and cancelled it after she received the free 5,000 miles. She uses her original credit card for all of the household expenses, including groceries, and pays off her balance every month. As her credit limit increased, so did the size of her purchases on the card (although she always pays it in full), so that within a few years of receiving the card, she and her family were able to use the miles for four round-trip tickets to Australia. Since Mary is not buying anything other than what she normally would have paid for anyway, these tickets were truly free.

Late Payment Penalties

All credit cards charge a fee for late payments. Like the overlimit charges mentioned previously, these can range from a low of perhaps $10 to as much as $30 for each month in which you are late. Most cards will also report late payments to credit-rating agencies, so this information will affect your ability to get other credit in the future, such as car loans and mortgages, and also the rates that you will have to pay.

Minimum Payments

On most credit cards, the minimum monthly payment is only a little bit more than the finance charge for the month. So if you don't pay off your balance each month and you don't make more than the minimum payment, you will never make much headway in paying back the loan. Compare this to car loans and mortgages, which include a predetermined amount of principal repayment that will enable you to pay off the entire balance within a predetermined period.

How long will it take you to repay the amount you have borrowed if you make only the minimum payment?

> *Example: Suppose you have a balance of $1,000, you don't make any more charges, and the annual rate of interest on the card is 16 percent. The minimum payment is $15, and you pay that amount every month. The monthly interest on $1,000 is 16/12 = 1.33 percent or $13.30, so your first payment will pay off only $1.70 of the outstanding balance. Now here's the really scary part: After three years of making payments of $15 per month, you will still owe $923. You will finally pay off the original $1,000 in 166 months (that's almost 14 years), and the interest you will have paid over that time will be more than $1,400.*

If you are thinking about switching credit cards or consolidating your debt in order to reduce your overall payments, you can compare card offerings at *http://www.financenter.com/compare/cards? compare.fcs.*

It's Easy to Ruin Your Credit Rating but Not So Easy to Fix It

What Makes Your Credit Rating Good

You might at first think that having no credit outstanding would give you the best credit rating, but in fact, you need to have had some credit in the past to show that you are capable of managing it. The best credit rating will go to a person who has borrowed and repaid on time. Most lenders report loans to credit-rating agencies and rate you on your bill paying. If you have been thirty or sixty days late on any bills, this will be noted.

If you are a woman who has not had credit in her own name before (for example, if you are newly widowed or divorced), it is important that you establish your own (as opposed to your husband's) creditworthiness. You should take a small loan from the bank or open a credit card in your name, make small purchases, and pay for them in a timely manner.

What Will Make Your Credit Rating Fall

Lenders are interested in assessing your willingness and ability to pay your debts. This will be evidenced by your amount of outstanding credit and your payment habits. Your credit rating is obviously going to be negatively affected by late payments and defaults on debts. But it will also go down if you have too much credit or if there are too many inquiries about your credit status. The implication of the latter is that you may be simultaneously applying for multiple credit cards or loans. Keep this in mind before you shop for mortgages over the Internet. Any application that you make will result in a credit inquiry and may reduce your credit rating. Declaring bankruptcy is perhaps the most serious negative event, but potential creditors may be more concerned about a current history of bad credit habits than they are about an older bankruptcy.

Although the conventional wisdom is that your credit report will include only more recent information, this is not true. Unless you specifically request to have information removed (which is particularly important when it is false) and the agency agrees to do so (which it doesn't have to if the information is true), you may find ages-old information still being reported. On my own credit record, for example, credit cards that I cancelled more than ten years ago are still listed, although the outstanding balance is shown as zero. The problem is that the agency does not say specifically that the balance is zero because I cancelled the card. Some examples of items that will generally not appear on your credit rating are gas, electric, and telephone bills. Judgments against you may be reported, as may outstanding child support and alimony.

How to Fix It

The bad news is that even though it doesn't take long to mess up your credit, the road to improving it is very difficult. The items that were reported to the rating agencies may never go away, so the best thing you can do is establish a pattern of good credit management so that you can convince potential lenders that you have changed and are now a better risk. Clearing up incorrect information in your credit report, reducing your debt load, and making payments on time are the best strategies.

Removing Incorrect Information

Example: Veronica applied for a mortgage and was told that her credit report included an outstanding student loan that had been in collection status. She knew that she had paid the loan in full approximately eighteen months previously, but it was reported as unpaid. She contacted her original lender and found that it had received payment from the collection company assigned to her case, but it had neglected to notify the credit agency.

If you are ever denied credit by a lender, you are entitled by law to receive a copy of your credit report for free and an explanation for the reason for denial. In addition, you can always request a copy of your report for a fee. Unfortunately, there is no guarantee that all the agencies will have the same information. If you check your credit report and correct the information in that report with one agency, the others may still have the incorrect information. Three of the largest credit-reporting agencies are TransUnion (1-800-916-880), Experian (1-800-682-7654), and Equifax (1-800-685-1111). An Equifax report can be purchased online at *http://moneycentral.msn.com/investor/creditreport/main.asp.*

Reducing Your Outstanding Debt Load

Do You Have a Credit Management Problem That Needs Addressing?

How much debt is too much? While this will depend on your individual circumstances, answering yes to any of the following questions probably means that you have too much debt:

- Are your total payments on loans and credit cards more than 35 percent of your total gross monthly income?
- Is your outstanding consumer debt more than 10 percent of your annual income?
- Do you have trouble paying your bills each month?
- Do you worry about your debt?
- If you were to become unemployed, would you be in danger of defaulting on your loans or credit cards?
- Are your credit card balances at their limits?
- Have you been unable to reduce your credit card balances over time?
- Have you ever made a credit card payment by using a cash advance from another credit card?
- Do you consistently make late payments?
- Do you not know how much you owe?
- Are you spending more each month than you earn?

There are two ways to fix this problem. One is to pay off the debt, and the other is to declare personal bankruptcy. In either case, you need to eliminate credit card usage from your normal spending patterns.

Debt Reduction

The purpose of the cash flow exercise in the first part of this chapter was to see where you could come up with some extra money for debt reduction and/or investment. Since the rate of interest on most debt is higher than the rate you can earn on average-risk investments, your first step must be to reduce your outstanding high-interest debt. If you have a choice of which debt to pay off first, you should opt for the accounts that have the highest interest and fees.

> *Example: Annette, a single thirty-something, earns $40,000 as a high school teacher. She has accumulated $10,000 in debt on three credit cards, in addition to having a car loan and a mortgage on her condo. Her monthly credit card minimum payments are about $150. Based on Table 4-2, Annette estimates that she can trim about $100 per month from her budget by bringing her lunch to school and cutting down on eating out. Her financial planner estimates that she will be able to pay off her debt in about five years if she continues to make monthly payments of $250. However, the planner also notes that her car loan will be paid off in two years. If she then puts the $250 payment toward her debt reduction, for a total payment of $500, she will be able to zero out her credit card balances in less than three years. At that time, she can direct the $500 per month toward an investment account or other earning asset.*

Table 4-3 will help you to estimate how long it will take you to pay off the balances on your credit cards under various assumptions about the interest rate on the card. Pick the rate that is closest to the average rate on all your cards and pick the dollar amount that is closest to your total indebtedness. The amount shown in the table is the payment that will be necessary in order to completely pay off the indebtedness in a specified number of months. An online calculator

Table 4-3 Payments Necessary to Achieve Debt Reduction Goals

Months to Pay	Interest Rate	Amount of Total Indebtedness					
		$1,000	$2,500	$5,000	$7,500	$10,000	$15,000
12	15%	$90.26	$225.65	$451.29	$676.94	$902.58	$1,353.87
	18%	$91.68	$229.20	$458.40	$687.60	$916.80	$1,375.20
	21%	$93.11	$232.78	$465.57	$698.35	$931.14	$1,396.71
24	15%	$48.49	$121.22	$242.43	$363.65	$484.87	$727.30
	18%	$49.92	$124.81	$249.62	$374.43	$499.24	$748.86
	21%	$51.39	$128.46	$256.93	$385.39	$513.86	$770.78
36	15%	$34.67	$86.66	$173.33	$259.99	$346.65	$519.98
	18%	$36.15	$90.38	$180.76	$271.14	$361.52	$542.29
	21%	$37.68	$94.19	$188.38	$282.56	$376.75	$565.13
48	15%	$27.83	$69.58	$139.15	$208.73	$278.31	$417.46
	18%	$29.37	$73.44	$146.87	$220.31	$293.75	$440.62
	21%	$30.97	$77.41	$154.83	$232.24	$309.66	$464.49
60	15%	$23.79	$59.47	$118.95	$178.42	$237.90	$356.85
	18%	$25.39	$63.48	$126.97	$190.45	$253.93	$380.90
	21%	$27.05	$67.63	$135.27	$202.90	$270.53	$405.80
72	15%	$21.15	$52.86	$105.73	$158.59	$211.45	$317.18
	18%	$22.81	$57.02	$114.04	$171.06	$228.08	$342.12
	21%	$24.54	$61.34	$122.68	$184.02	$245.36	$368.04

that can be tailored to your individual circumstances is available at *http://www.debtfreeforme.com/calcs/index.htm.*

> *Example: In Annette's case, since she knows how much she can afford to pay, she can look down the $10,000 column to see what $250 per month will do for her. She sees that, at 18 percent average interest, she can pay off that amount in sixty months if she makes monthly payments of $253.93.*

Debt Consolidation

If your monthly payments are more than you can handle, one possible option is debt consolidation. In this type of arrangement, you borrow from a single lender an amount sufficient to cover all of your credit card debt and use it to pay off the credit cards. The key factors in the success of this strategy are (1) the debt consolidation loan must have a lower rate of interest than the credit cards, and the lower the better, and (2) you *must* cut up the credit cards so that you don't run up your bills again. A good online source of information about credit management and debt consolidation is the web site operated by American Consumer Credit Counseling, a nationally recognized nonprofit organization that is organized to help people resolve their credit problems: *http://www.consumercredit.com/*.

> *Example: In Annette's case, suppose that she could use her home equity as collateral for a second mortgage. If the mortgage rate were 10 percent, her payments on a sixty-month loan would be $213 per month. If she were to pay the full $250 per month on that loan, paying extra principal each month, she could pay off the entire $10,000 in forty-eight months.*

Bankruptcy

Although I am by no means recommending bankruptcy as a cure for your financial problems, it may be the answer for people who are in *dire* circumstances. Sometimes these are brought on by loss of a job or an extended period of disability. The nice thing about bankruptcy law in the United States is that it can allow a person to have a fresh start financially. The downside is that this will be *truly* a fresh start, in that it will be seven years before you can buy a home or a car, unless you have cash. There are also some types of debts that are "bankruptcy-proof," which just means that you can't get rid of them in bankruptcy. These include government-guaranteed student loans and child support obligations, among other things. In the process of bankruptcy, you will lose most of your possessions, because they will be liquidated to pay your creditors what they are owed. The law allows you to keep only small dollar amounts of home equity and automobile value, home furnishings, clothing, tools of the trade, and other categories. But all your credit card debt *will* be wiped out. At the time of this writing, Congress is in the process of passing bankruptcy reform legislation that will make it more difficult to declare personal bankruptcy and will impose a greater cost on those who do.

Before you take such a drastic step, you should consult a credit counselor first to see if there are intermediate steps that might be possible. The Consumer Credit Counseling Service will probably have a local office in your area. It also provides online consumer credit counseling on its web site at *http://www.cccsintl.org*. Arrangements for reduced payments to creditors can sometimes be worked out (since creditors would rather get something than nothing). In addition, this nonprofit organization will be able to provide additional resources for you to use in investigating your options.

Your New Spending Plan

Now you are finally ready for the last step in cash and credit management—establishing a spending plan, a.k.a. a budget. In Table 4-2, you looked at your past spending behavior and noted the items that you thought you could trim. You have also calculated the amount that you will need to pay each month in order to reduce your credit card debt. While your plan may change as you work your way through this book, at this point, you are ready to make some changes that will lead you toward achieving your goals. Follow these steps to create your new spending plan:

1. Calculate the additional funds that you will have available from trimming your cash expenditures.

2. Fill in the lines on the spending plan for your fixed expenses and the new values of the expenses that you have trimmed.

3. Using your prioritized goal list (Table 3-2), allocate your extra funds to the most important goals on your list.

4. Refer to the relevant later chapters in this book to determine the amounts to allocate to retirement and college savings.

What If Trimming Isn't Enough

Ideally, a little trimming will allow you to have something left to allocate toward your goals. But yours may be an extreme case. Maybe you have a low-paying job or you have extraordinarily large debts to repay. Or perhaps you are approaching retirement and you haven't started saving yet. If you find that there simply isn't enough to go around, more extreme measures may be required. Although some of these are discussed in more detail in later chapters, here are a few possible solutions to your financial woes:

- Create a zero-based budget. This simply means that you start, not with what you are already spending, but with the absolute necessities and build your budget from there until you run out of money. Since retirement savings should be considered a necessity, something else will have to go.

- Take a second job. Although you are already a busy person and may feel stretched at the seams, most credit counselors will recommend that the best way to get out of debt is to take a second job and use *all* of your income from that job to reduce outstanding debt until it's paid off. Then you can quit.

- Sell your home and buy a smaller one. Use the money you save on mortgage payments to reduce debt and increase savings.

- Consider a side business. Many women earn extra dollars by marketing their hobbies, giving music lessons, or providing child care. The wife of a friend of mine has a side business in which she buys "junk" at yard sales and sells it for a profit on the Internet and through flea markets. A warning about self-employment income: as much as half of your net income will go for taxes.

Summary

If you have read this chapter and completed the worksheets, you should have:

- Evaluated your current spending behavior

- Evaluated your current credit card usage and indebtedness

- Determined which of your current monthly expenditures are trimmable

- Established a new spending plan that will lead toward achieving your financial goals

For busy women, cash and credit management are perhaps the most difficult components of their financial plan because these areas require an attention to detail and a level of consistency in behavior that is difficult to manage in a time of stress (which is *all* the time for many). The key success factors, as with any successful diet, are to recognize your problems and to make permanent modifications in your behavior. Unfortunately, we all know how easy it is to fall into spending habits that cost money but don't provide significant benefit. Fortunately, when the benefit is small, the cost of changing one's behavior is small as well. For more serious credit usage problems, facing the problem is the first step to solving it, and there are many sources of help available.

CHAPTER 5

Making the Most of Employee Benefits

You need to read this chapter if:

- ✔ You don't understand all of your benefit options.

- ✔ You want to know more about different types of health plans and their advantages and disadvantages.

- ✔ You want to know more about different types of employer retirement plans and supplemental tax-qualified retirement savings programs.

- ✔ You don't know what a flexible spending plan is.

- ✔ You want to know what your disability insurance options are.

- ✔ You want to know how to keep your health insurance in force if you lose your job.

As a college professor, I often find myself in the position of helping students make decisions between alternative job opportunities. A couple of questions I commonly ask them are:

"What does the benefits package look like?"

"What type of pension does the company provide, and how much does it contribute toward the plan?"

Inevitably, the students don't really know and had not thought that this information was important. In one of the courses that I teach at Colorado State, a survey of risk management and insurance, I cover employee benefits. There are always students who thank me afterward and ask why the material isn't required for everyone in the business college, or even for all college students. As students begin looking toward their future employment, starting families, and investing for the future, even a cursory understanding of employee benefits is of obvious value, since it is a subject that most people have to learn about on their own.

If you are like most people, you probably made your employment decision with very little consideration of the "extras" that came with the job, unless they were immediately tangible, like a car or housing. In fact, the benefits package can, in some cases, represent as much as a third more in equivalent income if you consider the amount you would have to pay to buy the benefits on your own. Since employers are essentially buying in bulk, they can get terrific rates on various types of insurance and services and pass that savings on to you.

So why do so many people pay so little attention to employee benefits? Do any of the excuses in Table 5-1 sound familiar? Check all of them that apply to you.

What Do I Do If My Employer Doesn't Provide Benefits?

Employers can offer almost any type of benefit to their employees, or they can offer no benefits. On average, women in the United States have fewer benefit options and less generous plans, primarily because of occupational and industrial segregation. This is not the result of discrimination per se; it is just that women have traditionally gravitated to occupations and industries that pay lower benefits to

Table 5-1 Excuses for Ignorance of Employee Benefits

	That's Me
1. I don't have time to read the materials my employer gave me.	_____
2. I was desperate for a job, so the benefits didn't really matter.	_____
3. It's so boring, I can't stand to read all that junk.	_____
4. Don't all employers offer the same deal?	_____
5. I don't need health insurance (life insurance, pension, disability insurance).	_____
6. That tax stuff is too complicated.	_____
7. I just asked the human resources person what to do.	_____

both male and female workers, in some cases because they are less likely to be unionized. Examples include secretarial and retail employment. As more women move into managerial positions, this is gradually changing. Even better news is the currently low rate of unemployment in most of the United States. When it's hard to find employees, companies are more likely to use perks as a means of attracting and retaining qualified people.

If your employer doesn't offer benefits (or if the benefits are not very generous), it wouldn't hurt to ask why. In some cases, it is because the management doesn't think that employees would value the benefits. This may not be an incorrect assumption. There were some academic studies in the 1980s and 1990s which suggested employees valued benefits at a fraction of their true cost and that many did not even know what type of pension they had or how much it was worth. This would imply that workers would prefer to have the cash rather than the benefits, even if the benefits were worth more than the extra dollar or two per hour that they might get instead. Nevertheless, employers can often be convinced to set up mechanisms that will enable employees to buy particular benefits on their own but at the lower group rates. The only cost to the firm is the administrative expense and hassle of getting the plan going, and there are companies that will do all the legwork. The bottom line is, it never hurts to ask.

Benefit Options

In Table 5-2, I provide a laundry list of benefit options that might be provided by an employer. In some cases, employers pay the entire cost of the benefit; in other cases, they may just arrange for employees to purchase these benefits on their own. You should not expect to receive all or even a large proportion of these benefits from any

Table 5-2 Types of Employee Benefits

Category	Choices	I HAVE	I WANT
Health	Health maintenance organization (HMO)		
	Fee-for-service plan (e.g., BC/BS)		
	Hybrid plans		
	Catastrophic insurance		
	Medigap insurance		
	Dental insurance		
	Long-term care insurance		
Disability	Short-term		
	Long-term		
Retirement	Defined-contribution		
	Defined-benefit		
	Cash balance		
	Employee stock ownership		
Bonuses	Cash bonuses		
	Stock bonuses		
	Stock options		
Flexible spending	Child care		
	Medical expenses		
Maternity	Without pay		
	With pay		
Life insurance	Term insurance		
	Permanent insurance		
Other	Prepaid legal services		
	Tuition reimbursement		
	Counseling/substance abuse help		
	Adoption subsidies		
	On-site child care		
	On-site health club		

given employer, but at a minimum, you should look for at least a decent health plan and a retirement plan. Even a "Scrooge" employer can set up plans at group rates and require that you pay for them out of pocket. The tax advantages to you and the savings through the group contract are still benefits, even if your employer doesn't want to contribute to the cost.

Cafeteria Plans

Many employers, in the interest of best serving the needs of their employees, have begun offering benefit packages that provide employees with a certain amount of money that they can apply toward a variety of benefit choices. Because choosing between the different options is sort of like picking items on a menu, these plans are known as cafeteria plans.

The advantage of a cafeteria plan is that it avoids the wasteful use of benefit dollars for benefits that the employee does not need (e.g., the employee's spouse may already have family health coverage) or does not want (e.g., life insurance for a person with no dependents and a large bank account).

Example: The two major employers in Fort Collins, Colorado, are Colorado State University (CSU) and Hewlett-Packard (HP). Although CSU offers reasonably comprehensive health insurance, the university contribution is insufficient to cover the full cost of the most comprehensive family coverage, so part of it must be paid by the employee. By contrast, HP provides complete coverage for its employees' families. Therefore, CSU employees with spouses who work at HP generally choose to get their health insurance from HP and to use their CSU benefit dollars for other purposes. If CSU required everyone to participate in its health insurance plan, families might end up with double coverage (but not double benefits, since you can collect for the same expense only once).

The organization of the rest of this chapter follows the categories in Table 5-2. For each category of benefit, I provide you with the basics of what the benefit is; the terminology necessary to understand the differences among plans; and, where applicable, recommendations for optimizing your use of the benefit option. In all cases, you should consult the specific plan documents for details of your own coverage.

Health Insurance

Access to Health Insurance

Nearly a decade ago, Hillary Clinton made headlines with her focus on national health care. Since then, politicians have avoided opening that Pandora's box again, but the issues identified at that time are no less true today. Health costs are still increasing at an alarming rate, health insurance rates are extremely high, and certain groups (children and older women) are particularly at risk of being uninsured. According to a recent report from the U.S. Census Bureau (*http://www.census.gov/hhes/*), more than 16 percent of the population has no health insurance coverage (that's 44 million people!).

Employment patterns play a big role in the differences in coverage for men and women. Two-thirds of workers at large companies (those with more than 100 employees) are covered by their employer's plan, whereas less than a third of those at small companies have employer health plans. Since women are more likely to be low-wage workers and to work for companies that do not provide benefits, employment coverage rates tend to be lower for women. However, women's overall coverage rates are slightly higher, since many women are covered under their husbands' plans. With the high cost of individual insurance, many women cannot afford to buy insurance on their own. About one-quarter of the uninsured have income of less than $25,000 per year. For the lowest-income families, Medicaid may provide some relief. Unfortunately, recent changes in that program have actually increased the number of uninsured working women.

Given the difficulty and expense associated with buying health insurance on your own, it pays to seek out employers who offer health coverage and to be well informed about your health insurance options.

Fee-for-Service Versus Managed Care

Although there are literally hundreds of different variations on health plans, they fall into two general categories that are worth thinking about. Many employers will allow you to choose from a menu that includes both types. In this section, I explain the main characteristics of each type of plan, but there are many variations. I have included several additional resources and web sites in the appendix.

The traditional type of health-care plan, originating with Blue Cross/Blue Shield many years ago, makes payments based on the services that you receive, which is why it is termed *fee for service.* Since *you* are the one who decides which services to seek out, you have little incentive to be conservative in your health-care expenditures once you have reached your deductible limit for the year. In most plans of this type, your copayment once you have met your deductible is no more than 25 percent of the cost of the service received and often lower than that as long as you are using a participating physician. If consumers are not worried about the cost, then the providers of medical services (doctors and hospitals) can recommend additional tests and interventions even if not medically necessary. The result over the years has been skyrocketing medical costs; in some years they have increased at two to three times the rate of inflation.

In the mid-1980s, when the rising cost of medical care was first identified as a serious economic problem, a type of health insurance arrangement, termed *managed care,* which had been in existence previously but was not a significant component of the market, was touted as the panacea for all the problems of the health-care system. Managed-care plans (the best known being health maintenance organizations, or HMOs) attempt to control overall health-care costs by working with physicians and hospitals to contain costs. In most cases this is accomplished by contracting in advance for services and by giving the medical care providers incentives to control costs. If you opt for an HMO, you may find that there are only a few doctors in your area who participate in the plan. Although specialists are not usually members of HMOs, participating physicians can refer their patients to a specialist when they feel this is warranted, in which case the cost of the specialist's treatment will also be covered by the plan.

Example: In 1985, my younger son, Kristopher, who was less than a year old at the time, had a serious asthma attack that resulted in a short hospitalization. We were participating in an HMO, and we had identified our family pediatrician as the primary care physician for our son. After Kris had returned home, we wanted to see a pediatric allergist for consultation regarding long-term treatment. The pediatrician said that his office could provide the same service as the allergist, and therefore he was unwilling to give us the referral. Without a referral, the cost of the appointment and later treatment would not be covered by the HMO plan. Upon further investigation, we found that our health plan, like many HMOs, paid our pediatrician a flat fee per year per patient. If he referred us to the allergist, the allergist's fee would be deducted from his total for the year.

The goal of managed care is to reduce the likelihood and necessity of more expensive interventions by encouraging regular visits to the doctor (preventive medicine). In addition, such plans are structured so that the participating physicians are less likely to refer patients to expensive specialists unless they deem such care to be necessary.

The benefits under HMOs are very comprehensive, if you don't mind losing the choice of physician and having to get referrals in order to see specialists. Although you will usually have to make a small copayment per visit (usually $5 to $15), *all* your other costs are covered. In considering the pros and cons of managed care, the jury is still out on whether they have helped contain health-care costs, but they do tend to work out as the best option for people with consistent medical needs (as opposed to those who barely need their annual physical). Young families with small children find them particularly beneficial, since they never have to think twice about whether they can afford to take the baby to the doctor for the latest case of sniffles—it's worth the extra $5 for the peace of mind.

When HMOs were first invented, their premium rates tended to be comparable to or lower than those of Blue Cross/Blue Shield plans. Today, this is no longer true. Because of their fairly comprehensive coverage and the tendency for people with unlimited coverage to take advantage of it, HMO plans are now often the most expensive health plan alternatives. It would be rare for you to find comprehensive HMO family coverage for less than $5,000 per year.

In order to better understand the distinctions among your plan options, you will first need to familiarize yourself with some of the terminology in Table 5-3.

Weighing the Differences

The best way to illustrate the differences among plans is to use an example that includes some common features. The facts in this case are drawn from the choices that a particular employer offered its employees for health coverage beginning in January 2001. (I have simplified the actual choices offered to make the analysis more generally applicable.) Since health plans may differ on a lot of little details, you should read the plan offerings carefully, paying particular attention to features that are important to your own situation. In this case, as with many employers, the true cost to the employees is not the full premium amount, since the employer provides a certain amount of dollars to be used for benefits at the employees' choice (a cafeteria plan, as discussed previously). The benefits pay was approximately $5,000 for the year 2001 for average-salary employees. However, since benefits pay can often be received as cash when the benefits are not necessary, this example looks at the decision as if employees were subject to the true cost:

> *Example: For the year 2001, this employer offered three health insurance plan choices. Two were fee-for-service plans that*

Table 5-3 Health Insurance Terminology

Term	Definition
Insured	The person(s) covered under the policy.
Deductible	An amount of money that must be paid for by the insured out of pocket before the insurer will cover any costs. Many policies have per-person and per-family deductibles.
Coinsurance	After the deductible has been paid, the percentage of covered expenses that must be paid by the insured, usually 10 to 30 percent. The remainder is covered by the insurer.
Cap	The maximum amount that the insurer will pay out on a policy. Often this is a lifetime cap.
Preexisting condition	A condition that you had at the outset of the policy; most health insurance plans will not cover such a condition until a specified period of time (usually 6 to 12 months) is up.
Stop loss	After this limit is reached, the insurer will pay 100 percent of all covered expenses.
Copay	Like coinsurance in that you are sharing the cost with the insurer, but in this case, you pay a flat fee for particular services, such as doctors' visits.
Primary care physician	A physician, chosen from a limited list in a managed-care plan, who must preapprove all care for the patient.

differed in their deductibles and limits, and the third was an HMO.

- Fee-for-service plan 1 (FFS1): *Premium $486 per month for family coverage. Deductible $400 per person/$800 per family; 80 percent/20 percent coinsurance to $10,000 per person/$20,000 per family of covered expenses. Well-care visits (regular physicals, mammograms, and prostate screening) covered under the plan at 100 percent without being subject to the deductible. Prescription drugs $10 per prescription.*

- Fee-for-service plan 2 (FFS2): *Premium $379 per month for family coverage. Deductible $800 per person/$1,600 per family;*

80 percent/20 percent coinsurance to $20,000 per person/$40,000 per family of covered expenses. Well care (regular physicals) not covered under the plan. Prescription drugs $10 per month supply.

- Managed-care plan 3 (HMO): *Premium $625 per month for family coverage. Copays of $10 per office visit, $200 for hospital admission. Well care and all other care in excess of the copay covered at 100 percent subject to referral by primary care physician and $10 copay. Prescription drugs $5 per prescription.*

How should you decide among these plans? The steps to follow aren't extremely difficult, but the ultimate decision is going to require a judgment call on your part as to the relative healthiness of your family. Table 5-4 provides a sample of the type of analysis you might undertake if you were offered the three choices in this example. The estimates in the table are based on my own family's health. In general, we are above average health and usually never meet our deductible. The worst-case scenario used here is not really the worst possible scenario (such as a serious cancer diagnosis involving a bone marrow transplant, chemotherapy, or some such procedure), but rather is a worst case considering our risk factors. Since we are a relatively young family, the odds are that our most serious year would be one with a broken bone or a torn knee ligament. My husband has had some knee trouble, so we are anticipating the possibility of future knee surgery.

Step 1: Summarize the important features of the plans you are choosing from. In Table 5-4, I have listed the major features side by side for comparison. Pay particular attention to the areas in which the plans differ, as opposed to the things that are similar. For example, in my real-life decision, I would immediately eliminate the HMO if our pediatrician was not one of the allowed primary care physicians (PCPs). In addition to choice of physician, an important issue for women is whether an HMO allows them to name both a general practitioner primary care physician and a gynecologist/obstetrician,

Table 5-4 Example Problem: Comparison of Health Policies

Step 1: Summarize plan features and costs

	FFS1	FFS2	HMO
Premium per month	$486	$379	$625
Deductible	$400/$800	$800/$1,600	N/A
Copay	N/A	N/A	$10/visit
Hospitalization	80% after deductible	80% after deductible	$200 copay
Coinsurance	80%/20%	80%/20%	N/A
Stop loss	$10,000/$20,000	$20,000/$40,000	None
Lifetime maximum	No limit	No limit	No limit
Physician choice	Yes	Yes	No
Specialists	No restriction	No restriction	PCP approval
Prescriptions	$10 copay	$10 copay	$5 copay
Well-care coverage	Yes, 100%	No	Yes, $10 copay

Step 2: Estimate most likely and worst-case health expenditures

	Most Likely		Worst-Case	
1. Checkups/shots	four @ $80	$320	four @ $80	$320
2. Mammogram	one @ $120	$120	one @ $120	$120
Total Well-Care		$440		$440
3. Office visits	six @ $50	$300	twelve @ $50	$600
4. Hospitalization	N/A	$0		$10,000
5. Surgery	N/A	$0		$5,000
6. Other	N/A	$0		$3,000
Total nonprescription		$740		$19,040
7. Prescriptions	six @ $30	$180	fifteen @ $100	$1,500
Estimated Medical Costs Total		$920		$20,540

Step 3: Estimate out-of-pocket costs under each scenario

Most Likely	BC/BS 1*		BC/BS 2*		HMO	
Premium	twelve @ $486	$5,832	twelve @ $379	$4,548	twelve @ $625	$7,500
Noncovered expenses		$0	well care	$440		$0
Deductible/copay	($740 − $440)	$300	($740 − $440)	$300	six @ $10	$60
Coinsurance		$0		$0		$0
Prescriptions	six @ $10	$60	six @ $10	$60	six @ $5	$30
Total		$6,192		$5,348		$7,590

Worst-Case	BC/BS 1		BC/BS 2		HMO	
Premium	twelve @ $486	$5,832	twelve @ $379	$4,548	twelve @ $625	$7,500
Noncovered expenses		$0	well care	$440		$0
Deductible/copay		$800		$1,600	eleven @ $10	$110
Coinsurance	0.2 × $10,000	$2,000	0.2 × $17,000	$3,400		$0
Prescriptions	fifteen @ $10	$150	fifteen @ $10	$150	fifteen @ $5	$75
Total		$8,782		$10,138		$7,685

*Blue Cross/Blue Shield.

who is then allowed to recommend treatment without prior approval of the general practitioner.

Other issues that might arise that do not differ among the plans in this example include preexisting condition limitations, coverage for chiropractic care, and coverage for counseling or treatment of mental illness. Many plans will not cover any costs related to a preexisting condition until you have been with the plan for a specified waiting period, usually six months or one year. You may, however, be eligible for continuous coverage under federal legislation called the Health Insurance Portability and Accountability Act of 1996 (HIPAA) if you had group health insurance with a previous employer. Because of the ongoing nature of chiropractic and mental health care, plans may entirely exclude them or they may be subject to limitation on the number of visits or total dollar coverage.

Note that if you are choosing between potential employers with different benefit options, you can do a similar comparison and consider the additional benefits under the better plan as adding to your bottom-line income. This is particularly important in comparing jobs with disparate salaries.

Step 2: Estimate your most likely health-care costs and the worst-case costs. When insurers evaluate their expected claims on policies, they must do exactly this. By using past experience on your employer's plan and other plans, they estimate what their claims will be under the policy. Since your employer's plan is a group plan, the insurance company must charge everyone the same premium, regardless of their particular risk factors, and, more important, they cannot exclude people from the plan, even if they are high risk. This implies that if you have higher-than-average risk, you should be getting a pretty good deal, whereas low-risk individuals are usually paying more than their fair share.

Most people should expect to at least have an annual physical examination and one to two office visits for other problems such as colds and minor injuries. If you or anyone in your family has a chronic condition that requires regular physician visits or drugs, such as asthma, diabetes, or ADD/ADHD (attention deficit disorder/

attention deficit hypersensitivity disorder), you should include these costs in your most likely scenario. The worst-case scenario is much more difficult to estimate, and I usually recommend that people assume that it will exceed the deductible and approach or exceed the stop loss. This will allow you to estimate the worst case for out-of-pocket expenditures. In this case, I assumed that the large expenditures for the worst case were incurred by a single family member, and therefore were subject to the smaller stop loss limit.

Step 3: Estimate the out-of-pocket costs for each scenario. In all three cases, your most significant cost will be your premiums. Many of you may be surprised by the annual cost of comprehensive coverage such as that offered by this employer. Many employers do not tell their employees what the total cost of their benefits amounts to; instead, they simply list the amount that the employee must contribute toward the plan, which is likely to be much less than the full cost. Although this avoids some sticker shock, it also tends to make employees undervalue their benefits. Although the HMO option in this example is very expensive, it also has very comprehensive coverage and very little out-of-pocket costs beyond the premiums. Note that if you do not have a flexible spending plan arrangement with your employer, this enables you to pay for most of your health costs with pretax dollars, if it is a tax qualified plan.

For the HMO, out-of-pocket costs are usually fairly easy to estimate, since your only costs will usually be the copays for office visits and hospitalizations. In the case of fee-for-service plans, since deductibles are usually separately given per person and per family, you may want to conservatively assume that the health costs are spread evenly across family members. Keep in mind that expenses that are not a benefit of the plan, such as well care in the case of plan FFS2, cannot be used to meet the deductible or stop loss limits. In the first plan, after the deductible of $800 is met for the family, you will be responsible for 20 percent of all charges up to the stop loss limit, after which the insurer will pay 100 percent of the charges. Thus, where I have estimated a worst-case scenario in excess of $10,000 (for one person), the maximum coinsurance will be 20 percent, or

$2,000. With a stop loss of $20,000, you would be responsible for approximately double that amount.

Now comes the judgmental part. If I have a good year with fairly normal (low) health costs, then I would rank the high-deductible FFS2 plan first (with out-of-pocket costs of $5,348) and the HMO last (with out-of-pocket costs of $7,590). But if I should have a bad year, the out-of-pocket costs for the HMO will not be much higher, whereas both FFS plans will result in higher expenditures.

If I have eliminated the HMO from consideration because of restrictions on physician choice, my decision (and yours in most cases) will come down to my expectations for my health-care needs for the coming year. Facing this decision for the year 2000, I would have taken the high-deductible/low-premium FFS2 plan and never met half the deductible for the year (as I had estimated). For 2001, I would choose to take the low-deductible FFS1 plan in anticipation of possible knee surgery for my husband. If it turns out that he doesn't have the surgery, I will end up paying a few hundred dollars more for my health coverage. If I anticipated larger medical expenditures in that year, I could increase my flexible spending plan contribution (which is discussed later in the chapter) so that my out-of-pocket expenditures could be made pretax, thus saving 28 percent or more of my estimated cost.

Disability Insurance

One of the most overlooked benefits is disability insurance. No one ever thinks about it until she or he needs it! The surprising truth is that one out of three people will be disabled for at least three months at some point in their life. If you have a reasonable amount of savings or if you can rely on other family members, a short period of disability may not be a problem for you financially. But many people who find themselves unable to work use up their financial resources quickly (which may have previously been earmarked for retirement or their children's education).

What Is a Disability?

One of the most important questions to ask when looking at various types of disability coverage is the definition of disability. There are extreme variations that will affect your ability to be compensated under the plan. Compare the following definitions:

- Unable to perform the primary functions of your own occupation

- Unable to perform the primary functions of any occupation to which you are reasonably suited by experience and education

- Unable to perform the primary functions of any occupation

- Unable to do any kind of substantial gainful activity (Social Security definition)

- Unable to perform the primary functions of daily living (feeding oneself, dressing)

It should be obvious to you from looking at these definitions that you could be disabled under one definition but not under another. The most liberal definitions are often referred to as "own occupation" policies, and these tend to be more expensive than less extensive coverage, for obvious reasons. Many insurers have dropped this type of policy and/or have limited coverage as a result of higher than expected claims in recent years.

The Social Security definition is very strict, since this is intended to be the last resort. If you are capable of working at McDonald's, even if you were previously a high-level executive at a major corporation, then you will not be eligible for these benefits. The last definition on the list is usually applied only to continuation of long-term benefits beyond a specified policy period.

Example: Julie, a hand surgeon, has her own occupation disability insurance that promises a benefit of $10,000 per month for ten years if she becomes disabled to the point where she cannot work as a hand surgeon, after which it will continue to pay only if Julie cannot perform the functions of daily living. After seeking treatment for tremors in her hand, Julie is diagnosed with multiple sclerosis and is unable to continue *working as a hand surgeon, although she can still practice medicine. She collects $10,000 per month under the policy for ten years, as specified in the policy. At the end of ten years, she will no longer receive a benefit.*

Short–Term Disability

Most employers provide coverage for short-term disability of their salaried workers in the form of sick days. Hourly workers are not usually as fortunate, since, even if they have the right to take a sick day, they do not get paid when they do not work.

Employers may have specific short-term disability insurance that will pay workers' salaries when the disability is temporary. For disabilities caused by on-the-job injuries, short-term coverage may be provided through a workers' compensation plan, but non-work-related disabilities require a separate plan. Common features of these plans are that they require a waiting period (one to four weeks) before the worker can receive the benefit and they allow the worker to collect for only a short period of time (rarely more than two years). Many employers self-insure for short-term disability, which really just means that they *don't* insure; they cover the costs out of current cash flows. Coworkers may pick up the tasks of their temporarily disabled colleagues.

> *Example: Diane, a cashier for a large retailer, was in a car accident in June. As a result of her injuries, she cannot stand for long periods of time and is therefore unable to return to work right away. Since this was not an on-the-job injury, workers' compensation will not cover her. Her employer has a short-term disability plan that provides 60 percent income replacement for one year after a waiting period of thirty days. After the thirty days have passed, Diane can make a claim and will eventually receive a monthly check for 60 percent of her preaccident earnings, not including the waiting period.*

Is Pregnancy a Disability?

A common question that women ask is whether they can access short-term disability benefits for maternity, either prebirth or post-birth. The answer depends on the definition in your policy and the attitude of your employer. If your pregnancy has no complications, you are unlikely to meet any definition of disability prior to the birth of your child unless your job is extremely physical (e.g., you are a police officer). After the birth of your child, particularly if you have a Caesarian section delivery, several weeks of recuperation may be necessary. If the waiting period is short enough, you may qualify for a couple of weeks of coverage. In cases where the woman is extremely ill, either before or after the birth, disability policies may provide coverage.

> *Example: When Linda was four months pregnant, her physician put her on complete bed rest for the duration of her pregnancy because she had a history of miscarriages. She eventually reached full term successfully, but she missed five months of work. She maintained her income throughout the pregnancy by initially using sick days and then making a disability claim under her employer's policy.*

Long-Term Disability

While most people are able to financially manage a short period of disability, it becomes much more difficult when the disability extends to six months or more. Long-term disability policies may be available for purchase through your employer, and they are also available for individuals to buy on their own. In addition, if you are eligible for Social Security, you may qualify for benefits from that program as well (subject to a five-month waiting period). However, most plans limit your ability to recover more than a specified percentage of your predisability earnings, so duplication of coverage does not make sense.

Waiting periods for long-term disability are usually three to six months, but they can be as long as one year. In most cases, you cannot collect any back pay for the waiting period, although you may have been covered by a short-term disability plan during this period.

Pre- or Posttax. If you buy long-term disability insurance through your employer, you may have the option of paying for it with pretax dollars. Although the current tax savings may seem to be a good deal, keep in mind that you will have to pay tax on the benefits you receive should you become disabled. If you are currently making $4,000 per month before taxes and your plan will pay a 60 percent benefit, you are eligible to receive $2,400 per month. If you must pay tax on this, your net disability pay may not be sufficient to meet your income needs. For example, if you are in the 28 percent tax bracket and are subject to a 5 percent state tax, the net amount you will receive is 67 percent of $2,400, or $1,608, only 40 percent of your predisability pay. In general, it is better to pay for the insurance with after-tax dollars so that your benefits, if received, will be tax free.

Retirement

In Chapter 14, I provide a lot more information about making retirement saving decisions. In this chapter, the focus is primarily on educating you about the options available through employer-provided retirement plans. Since retirement plans are one of the most important employee benefits, this section outlines the possible choices that you might encounter.

Defined Benefit Versus Defined Contribution

The most important distinction in employer plans is the type of promise that is being provided by your employer. Employer plans can either promise you a particular retirement benefit in the future ("defined benefit") or promise you a particular level of current contribution to your plan ("defined contribution"). Many employers offer supplemental 401(k) or 403(b) plans that allow employees to contribute to their plans and, in many cases, allow employees a wide range of investment options. The names of these plans are derived from the section number of the statute that defines the parameters under which the plans can be offered and their tax status.

How common are the different types of plans? The Department of Labor reports that in 1996, 22 percent of all wage and salary workers in the United States had a defined-benefit pension plan (down from 38 percent in 1977), 23 percent had a defined-contribution plan (up from 7 percent in 1977), and 16 percent had a supplemental plan (up from 10 percent in 1977). From these statistics, you can see the general trend: more defined-contribution plans and fewer defined-benefit plans. Within these general categories, there are many variations, but as a starting point, I want you to consider the differences in your risk exposure under the two types.

If an employer promises that it will pay you a benefit equal to 60 percent of your final pay at the retirement date, then the risk of not having enough saved to make good on this promise is borne by the employer. If, on the other hand, the employer promises to make a current contribution equal to 3 percent of your current pay, then your final benefit will be determined by the accumulation in that account on the date of retirement, which may be insufficient to give you the necessary level of retirement income. The risk is therefore borne by the employee. It may come as no surprise to you that fewer employers are providing defined-benefit plans and that many that do provide them have rewritten benefit formulas to be less generous to employees.

Advantages and Disadvantages of Defined-Benefit Plans for Women

Job Tenure and Switching. Defined-benefit plans usually use formulas that give greater benefit accruals to people who have been at the company longer. Since women, on average, are more likely to change jobs over their working career and are more likely to have breaks in their working career (for example, if they stay home while their children are young), they will not receive as much from defined-benefit plans as their male counterparts will.

> *Example: Robert and Jessica begin work with the same employer at age twenty-five and receive the same $25,000 salary. Their pension is a defined-benefit plan that promises them a benefit equal to 2 percent of their final average salary for every year of service. Robert stays at this job for forty years, and Jessica switches jobs every ten years. At retirement, Jessica is entitled to collect from all four employers' plans, but each will*

*calculate her benefit entitlement based on the last salary that
company paid her. Table 5-5 shows the benefits that each will
receive.*

The defined-benefit plan implicit penalty for job switching can
be very high. In this example, Jessica's total benefit from her four
employers' plans ends up being a little more than half of Robert's
benefit, despite their identical earnings history. Employers who use
this type of plan are trying to reduce employee turnover, which is an
understandable objective, but this ends up unintentionally penaliz-
ing employees (regardless of gender) who must leave jobs for family
reasons.

Given the penalties for job switching, it should come as no surprise that breaks in a woman's working career can have even more
serious consequences (although this is not a problem that applies
solely to defined-benefit plans). Historically, women have had
shorter working careers than men and have been more likely to take
time off for family reasons (both for raising children and for caring
for failing parents). Formulas based on job tenure and salary are thus
less beneficial to women on average.

Vesting Rules. *Vesting* refers to the amount of time you must work
for an employer in order to be eligible to receive benefits under the

Table 5-5 Example of Defined-Benefit Job-Switching Cost

Jessica and Robert's Salary History		Jessica's Pensions	Robert's Pension
4% raise per year		20% of final salary at each employer	80% of final salary
Age	Salary		
25	$25,000		
35	$37,006	$7,401	
45	$54,778	$10,956	
55	$81,085	$16,217	
65	$120,026	$24,005	$96,020
Total Pension Benefit		$58,579	$96,020

pension plan. Vesting schedules may be designed to give you complete rights to benefits at a certain date, or they can vest you on a schedule, such as 20 percent vesting after one year, 50 percent after two years, and 100 percent after three years. If your employer is making contributions toward your plan and you leave the company before the required vesting date, you do not get to keep the employer's contributions and, with a defined-benefit plan, you will not have any claim on benefits from those contributions at retirement. Any contributions of your own money that are made to the plan are still yours, however. Changes in federal law have shortened vesting schedules so that they do not take advantage of shorter-tenure workers to such a great degree. Many companies offer immediate vesting or very short vesting schedules.

Government Insurance. The Pension Benefit Guarantee Corporation provides defined-benefit plan participants with insurance against the possibility that their employer or their employer's plan goes bankrupt prior to the time that they need to receive benefits. Unfortunately, if your employer's plan is terminated early in your working career, the effect is similar to the effect of job-switching, since the maximum insured amount is the benefit you *would have* received if you had quit work on the date the plan terminates. In other words, your final salary at the date of bankruptcy is deemed to be your final salary under the plan.

Predictability of Future Benefits. Although nothing is absolutely certain, an advantage of defined-benefit plans is that it is easier to forecast your future retirement income when you have such a plan. Employers are now required to provide their employees with estimates based on specified income growth assumptions and a normal retirement date. This is very valuable for financial planning, because it makes it easier to determine the additional savings required if you are to meet your retirement income goals. By contrast, the income that will be generated from defined-contribution plans is much less certain, since it depends not only on income and retirement date, but also on investment returns over many years.

Advantages and Disadvantages of Defined-Contribution Plans

There are many variations on defined-contribution plans. Employers are free to determine the amount that they contribute, as long as they don't unfairly discriminate in favor of the highly paid employees at the company—by giving higher contributions levels to the management of the company, for example. Discrimination of this sort can result in the loss of tax deductibility for contributions made by the employer and loss of tax deferral of plan earnings to the participants. Some companies offer very generous benefits and/or match employee contributions to the plan, and others offer plans that are funded solely by employee contributions.

Some Employer Pension Rules You Should Follow

Although you generally do not have control over what type of pension plan is offered by your employer (unless you have several choices of employment), you do have the power to make wise decisions within the confines of your plan. Some important rules that will help you to maximize the retirement income you receive down the road are outlined in Table 5-6 and discussed more fully in this section.

Know Your Plan. You should not be one of those people who says "Who cares?" when asked about the details of your pension plan. As a woman, you need to finance a longer period of retirement than a

---

Table 5-6 Rules That Will Help Maximize Your Pension

1. Know your plan.
2. Take advantage of employer matches.
3. Maximize your tax deferral.
4. Don't be too conservative in your investment choices.
5. Understand your investment options.
6. Don't spend your lump-sum distributions.
7. Don't invest too much in your employer's stock.

typical man does, and therefore you need to be even more aware of how your employer's plan will help you to achieve your retirement goals. When you are offered the opportunity to participate in a pension plan, by all means do so. When you are comparing job offers from different employers, make sure you consider their retirement plan options as important elements of the overall package. Some of the things you should take into consideration are listed in Table 5-7.

Take Advantage of Employer Matches. Employer matches are the best deal around. If your employer offers to match the first 5 percent of salary that you contribute, you have immediately made a 100 percent return on that contribution. Although you might think that you cannot afford to make those extra contributions, actually you cannot afford *not to.*

Maximize Your Tax Deferral. The government places limits on how much an individual can contribute to a tax-deferred account in a given year. Very few lower- and middle-class families come close to these limits, since they often find it difficult to make ends meet. If at

---

Table 5-7 Things to Know About Your Pension

1. How much does your employer contribute?
2. Are you required to contribute?
3. Does your employer match any or all of your contributions?
4. If you leave, what are your options for receiving the pension?
   - a. Keep it in the current plan.
   - b. Roll it over into a new plan or an IRA.
   - c. Receive a lump-sum distribution.
5. What benefits can you expect at retirement?
6. What are your investment options, if any?
7. How often can you change your investment allocations?
8. Can you make cash withdrawals from your plan?
9. Can you borrow from your plan, and at what terms?
10. When you retire, what are your payout options?

all possible, you should try to save the maximum allowed, which is $10,500 in 2001. Not only will you reduce your current state and federal income taxes, but you will also maximize the power of compounding to increase the amount you have accumulated when you retire.

Don't Be Too Conservative in Your Investment Choices. Pension and retirement plans are long-term investments. In later chapters, we explore the concepts of risk and return, but for now, suffice it to say that your pension should be invested in stocks when you are in the early part of your working career.

Understand Your Investment Options. Many employers now offer a variety of investment choices for pension plans. Even more traditional defined-contribution plans that were previously run by professional managers now offer participants the right to choose their allocations. The reason for this is that it reduces the likelihood that the plan sponsors will later be sued for failure to manage the plan assets appropriately. Under current law, if the sponsor allows you to allocate between at least three alternatives that differ in risk and return characteristics, it cannot be held responsible for pension shortfalls due to unexpected market conditions.

Since you are being required to take some responsibility for your choices, you must be sure to be an informed consumer. The investment chapters in this book provide you with enough information to help you with this decision.

Don't Spend Your Lump-Sum Distributions. When you leave an employer, your pension accumulation (including your employer's contributions if you are vested) may be distributed to you in the form of a lump sum of money. If you do not roll over the money into another tax-deferred plan, you must pay taxes on it as a preretirement withdrawal. You must also pay a 10 percent penalty if you are not yet $59^1/_2$ years old. And you will lose the tax deferral of any earnings you would have made on that money up to the time you withdraw it at retirement.

Studies show that more than half of those who receive a lump-sum distribution spend it all rather than rolling it over into an IRA or other tax-deferred plan. Unfortunately, women are more likely than men to cash out. Some explanations that have been offered for this are that women's distributions are relatively small and that women are more likely to be cash-constrained and thus need the money for other purposes.

While it used to be difficult to implement a rollover, today it is very easy. Most financial institutions offer the opportunity to open individual retirement accounts (IRAs), and the law does not limit the amount that can be contributed to one of these plans through a rollover (in contrast to the annual limit on tax-deductible contributions). If you choose to spend part or all of your rollover, this is part of your retirement nest egg that can never be recovered. Here's an example that shows the potential impact on retirement wealth:

Example: Melanie has been working for the same employer for five years and has accumulated $25,000 in her 401(k). She quits her job and takes a new job at another employer that also has a 401(k). She uses the lump-sum distribution from her plan (less taxes and a 10 percent penalty from the IRS) to buy a car. After federal tax, state tax, and the penalty, her $25,000 was worth $14,250. If she had left it in her retirement account for thirty years earning a conservative 8 percent interest per year, this $25,000 would have grown to $251,566 before taxes!

Don't Invest Too Much in Your Employer's Stock. Although we will revisit this issue in a later chapter, it is worth mentioning here. Many employers allow employees to invest part of their pension in the employer's stock. The idea is that it will build company loyalty and increase the productivity of the company. Unfortunately, it is a bad idea for the employee. If your company goes out of business, you stand to lose both your job and your pension. My own research has shown that women are less likely to invest in their employer's stock than men are, but they still do so, particularly at companies that automatically put part of their pension there and require a specific action to move it. My own recommendation is to avoid your employer's stock altogether, but if you feel compelled (or are required) to keep some of your pension there, keep it to the minimum.

Flexible Spending

Most larger employers allow employees to participate in a flexible spending plan. This is a plan that allows you to make certain expenditures for health care and dependent child care on a pretax basis. While this can be a terrific benefit, effectively allowing you to cut your out-of-pocket costs by 28 percent if you are in that marginal tax bracket, the design of these plans leaves something to be desired.

Here's how these plans work: You decide prior to the beginning of the tax year how much you would like your employer to set aside in the flexible spending account to cover allowable expenses. This money is taken out of your check each month on a pretax basis. As you make allowable expenditures, you send in the receipts to the plan and it reimburses you. If you fail to use all the amount in the account in a given year, the remainder is lost.

> *Example: Elaine has a son in day care at a cost of $150 per week. She allocates the maximum amount to her flexible spending plan ($5,000) and has the money taken out of her paycheck each month ($417). The plan also charges her a service charge of $8 per month, so the net amount that she can claim is $4,904. Each month, Elaine submits a form to the plan with receipts for the $600 she has paid and then gets a check in the mail to reimburse her from the account until the $4,904 is used up. Note that Elaine would have to earn $833 per month to pay $600 in child care with after-tax dollars.*

It may come as no surprise to you that many people opt not to participate in flexible spending plans even when they may result in lower expenses. The main reasons are:

- *The paperwork.* You need to keep receipts for all covered expenses and submit them for reimbursement. This is more complicated for health expenses since the reimbursing service often requires insurance company statements as well as provider billings.

- *The out-of-pocket costs.* You must put money in the plan at the same time as you are incurring the costs. Even though you eventually get the money back, some people cannot afford the double payment.

- *The risk of losing the money.* Since you must forecast these expenses at the beginning of the year, there is a risk that you will overestimate your needs and lose the money.

Example: Since my family is relatively healthy, I usually opt for a small flexible spending amount to cover my deductibles and coinsurance. For 2000, I had $1,000 put into my flexible spending plan. I submitted receipts about every two months. In November, I looked at my plan and discovered that I had $350 left and no receipts left to claim. Rather than lose the money, I made an appointment with my eye doctor and got a new pair of glasses. I ended up about $50 short for the year. Even with this shortfall, however, I estimate that my out-of-pocket medical expenses were about $200 less than they would have been without the plan.

Flexible spending plans are an example of a law that has a regressive impact. While on its face it appears to be available to everyone, in practice, only large companies offer this arrangement because of the administrative headaches. So households that do not have access to this type of arrangement end up paying the full amount of their health- and child-care costs, whereas those with better jobs (who can also better afford to make the double payments) are able to save at least 28 percent of the cost, up to the maximum. I'm glad to be one of the lucky ones, but I can't help but think that it isn't very fair. A more equitable rule would apply to everyone or no one.

Life Insurance

Many employers, particularly those with more extensive benefits packages, offer some sort of life insurance to their employees. Since this life insurance is part of a group plan, the insurer has little ability to distinguish the risks of the people who opt into the plan, and the insurance will therefore be more expensive than individual policies for those with good life expectancies. If you are above average risk, this may be an opportunity for you to purchase some life insurance at more favorable rates. Usually these policies have fairly low limits, such as $50,000, and require some proof of insurability for higher limits.

You should read Chapter 6 before making a decision about life insurance. If your employer requires that you have some level of insurance, it will usually exempt you from purchasing the benefit if you can show that you are otherwise insured.

Prepaid Legal Services

In an effort to attract and retain workers, employers have been experimenting with various unusual benefit options. With prepaid legal services, the employer has contracted with one or more law firms for group rates for standard types of legal needs, such as review of loan documents for home purchases, writing a will, or divorce and child support. The contract may allow for free consultations, preset rates for certain services, and reduced hourly charges for additional services needed.

Tuition Reimbursement

Larger employers often provide reimbursement for tuition as long as the program of study is related in some way to the requirements of the job. The reimbursement usually will depend on the employee's receiving a minimum grade in the course as well, often a B or better.

Flextime, On-Site Child Care, and On-Site Health Facilities

These three types of employee benefits are linked together in this section because they have been developed to meet similar employer goals. As more women have entered the workforce, employers have found that the number of days their employees have missed in order to care for sick children has increased. In addition, women are more inclined to cut back on work hours to spend more time with their children. Many employers have noted increased job satisfaction on the part of both male and female workers when they have made work hours more flexible. This may take the form of flexible start times, allowing parents to be home for children before or after school, or shorter workweeks, such as four ten-hour days instead of five eight-hour days.

If your employer does not currently provide these types of options, it never hurts to ask. Many employers are willing to consider alternative arrangements as long as they do not interfere with the operation of the business. The downside of making such an arrangement is that it may not be well received by fellow employees.

Example: Susanne is an administrative assistant for a company manager. A single parent of her son, Sean, she requests permission to work from 9:00 to 5:00 instead of her employer's standard 8:00 to 4:00 shift. She is given permission, but she finds that her "late" arrival is continually being criticized by her coworkers, particularly those with lower-level positions. Since everyone else leaves at 4:00, they do not see that she is working long after they are gone.

On-site child care, either for regular needs or for sick children only, is also a way that employers can better meet the needs of working parents. With the high cost of child care, employers may be able to attract better employees by subsidizing this cost and providing a convenient location where new mothers can leave work to nurse their baby or can visit their children during their lunch hour. Most regular child-care facilities will not take children who are obviously sick (fever, vomiting, coughing), so larger companies can reduce the number of "personal days" that their employees must take by setting up a sick room, staffed with a health-care worker.

In addition to meeting the needs of working parents, on-site health-care facilities can reduce the number of hours that are lost because of doctor and dentist visits and can also reduce out-of-pocket health costs if the employer can make a favorable deal with the health-care provider. By providing convenient and cheap access to preventive care, days lost from work for more serious illnesses may also be reduced. Some employers have incorporated fitness centers for this reason as well. Keeping employees physically fit tends to reduce stress and minimize illnesses.

What Happens to Your Benefits If You Lose Your Job?

If you are laid off or fired from your job and you don't immediately begin working elsewhere (or if the new company has inadequate benefits), you may be entitled to keep your old health insurance at your own expense. The law that applies to this type of situation is called COBRA and applies to companies with more than twenty employees (although many states have similar laws that apply to smaller companies). Your employer is required to notify you that you can pay for your own benefits at 102 percent of the group rate for eighteen months after you leave the job. This will almost always be less expensive than purchasing the benefits on your own (average $400 per month), and if you are in poor health, an individual health insurance plan could subject you to a waiting period before covering your preexisting condition. When I left my first teaching job to begin my Ph.D. program, I opted to extend my coverage for the eighteen months allowed and pay for it myself.

Summary

If you have read this chapter, you should know:

- What your employee benefit options are

- The difference between defined-benefit and defined-contribution retirement plans and the pros and cons of each

- The rules you should follow to maximize your retirement plan benefit

- The difference between fee-for-service health plans like Blue Cross/Blue Shield and managed-care plans like HMOs

- How to choose among your health plan options

- How to make use of a flexible spending plan

- How to keep your health benefits in force if you lose your job

Employee benefits are an important component of your compensation plan, and you should evaluate them carefully in making decisions between different jobs. A good benefits package may be worth one-third or more of your salary in comparable cash compensation! Unfortunately, women have historically been employed in professions and industries with poor benefits coverage or none at all, and today we are still working to improve this situation. The key factor is that we must ask for what we want, since few employers will be willing to pay the cost if they think that their workers don't value what they are giving them. And when you are offered a choice, make your decisions between options wisely, with full consideration of the risks and rewards.

CHAPTER 6

Protecting Your Loved Ones With Life Insurance

You need to read this chapter if:

- ✔ You currently have little or no life insurance.

- ✔ You have dependents.

- ✔ You are a principal in a family business that has assets but little cash.

- ✔ You don't understand the differences between types of life insurance.

- ✔ You don't know how to evaluate your life insurance options.

If you are one of those people who have not taken the time to think about their life insurance needs, you are not alone. Although most families have some life insurance protection (85 percent in

1992), most have too little. The average face value of life insurance per insured household in the United States in 1998 was $178,600, according to the American Council of Life Insurers, and the total amount of life insurance in force in the United States is a whopping $14.47 trillion. But only 38 percent of adult women have any life insurance at all, and men have traditionally purchased higher face amounts. The average size of women's policies in 1997 was only $92,850, whereas men on average had $175,280 in face value.

Another issue that affects the insured status of individuals is whether they stick with their decisions to buy life insurance. The lapse rates on new policies are relatively high—about 15 percent of ordinary life insurance policies are dropped in the first two years, compared to a 6 percent overall lapse rate. This may be an example of people not sticking to their goals.

Financial planners will tell you that next to buying a home and saving for retirement, the purchase of life insurance is a person's most important financial decision. This is an aspect of your financial plan that you as a woman interested in improving your financial situation *must* become informed about.

Why are so many people uninsured or underinsured? The easy answer is that no one likes to think about dying. The other problem is that people are somewhat distrustful of the agents who are trying to sell them the insurance. Although these agents are holding themselves out as experts, their advice is somewhat suspect, since we know that they are trying to sell us a particular product.

In this chapter, I give you one major message: If you have dependents who rely on you for either income or services (yes, being a homemaker counts), you *should* have life insurance. There are lots of variations on this theme, a number of different insurance options, and some confusing terminology. But the essence of this type of insurance is pretty simple. You pay premiums while you are living, and, if you die during the policy period, the insurer will pay the face amount of the policy to your designated beneficiaries (usually your spouse or children).

The Short Version of How Insurance Works

Although I will talk later in the chapter about different types of life insurance and differences in how they are priced, a quick explanation of how insurance works is necessary at the outset if the rest of the chapter is to make sense.

For those who are most in need of life insurance—young people with dependents—life insurance is very cheap! By pooling together millions of policyholders who each have a relatively low risk of dying in the near future, insurers provide an incredibly valuable service to everyone: They spread the cost of dying.

As a simple example, suppose that you are one of 100,000 people who each has 1 chance in 1,000 of dying within the next twelve months. On average, 100 of the people in this group will die this year. So if each person in the group puts $100 in a pool, the pool will have collected $10,000,000 (100,000 times $100) and will therefore be able to pay $100,000 to the families of each of the 100 people who die during the year. Of course, we cannot guarantee that only 100 people will die, so perhaps we might ask everyone to contribute an extra $25 to cover the risk that the pool may be unlucky. And even then, we might have a bad year and not be able to pay out as promised.

Unlike the simple pool in my example, insurance company pools are so large that the companies are able to predict with a fair degree of accuracy (except in rare cases such as newly discovered diseases like AIDS) how many will die in a given period, so the "risk charge" is very low. But insurers are in business to make a profit, so they also charge something for their expenses (such as agent commissions) and their profit, and these charges differ across insurers. As you might expect, larger insurers can often provide better rates than small insurers, since they can spread these expense, profit, and risk charges across a larger group of policyholders.

Not Everyone Needs Life Insurance

Any time you consider buying insurance of any type, the first question you should ask is: What's the cost of *not* insuring? In this case, the answer will depend on who you are. Here are a few possible scenarios, one of which probably applies to you:

Head of Household, Married, No Children

Holly is a young professional who plans to have children eventually, but she and her husband are currently focusing on their careers. Although Holly earns more than her husband, they live on their combined income of about $90,000, and they have recently moved up to a larger home in a nice neighborhood.

If you are the primary source of income for your household, then your death would mean the end of this income for your husband. If you and your husband have been living on two incomes, you may have made financial commitments (such as a large home mortgage) that he will be unable to maintain without your income.

Head of Household With Children

Vickie is the primary source of income for her family; her husband's income is supplementary. This is the scenario closest to my own family situation. Since I have flexible work hours, I still do most of the grocery shopping, cooking, and transportation of kids to various extracurricular activities. We recently moved into a new home that my husband built, and the mortgage is too large for him to be able to pay without my income.

If you are married, the same issues that emerged from Holly's case will apply. If you have children, it is even more likely that the surviving spouse will want to remain in the family home for the sake of stability for the children. Whether or not you are married, the responsibility for children creates further concerns. Will your spouse or the children's designated guardians be able to earn enough to provide for their education without your help? Are there child-care or household maintenance costs that will now be incurred in your absence?

Homemaker

Jill is a stay-at-home mom. Her husband, a manager at a large corporation, works long hours and does not have time to do many of the household chores. Jill does all the cooking, cleaning, and child care.

Women who do not work outside the home usually provide valuable services to their family, including cooking, laundry, household financial management, transportation of children to activities, and household maintenance. A common misconception is that if you don't provide dollar income to the household, you do not need to have life insurance. Upon your death, some of these services may have to be performed by hired help, which will be significant additional cost to your survivors.

Single With Dependent Parents

Sue's children are grown, finished with college, and employed. Her parents are aging, and, although they have some savings, they may need to rely on help from her in the future should they have serious health problems. At present, Sue visits her parents, one of whom suffers from Alzheimer's, frequently.

Although single women may not have spouses or children who are dependent on them, they may be providing services or support to aging parents, who would therefore experience a financial loss upon their death. Even in cases where parents are not yet dependent, parents who have little or no financial resources may be expecting help from their children in the future.

Single With No Dependents

Joan is a single professional in her forties. Her parents are well off, and she has three siblings.

Joan does not appear to have anyone who is relying on her for support, financial or otherwise. Thus, in the event of her death, there is no one who will experience a hardship as a result.

* * *

With the exception of the last case, all the women in these examples should have some amount of life insurance, unless they have sufficient wealth to substitute for the value of what they provide to the household. The cost of not having insurance is the burden that your death will place on your loved ones. The amount of insurance necessary depends on the estimated costs to your survivors.

The rule of thumb often used by professionals is that you should carry life insurance (or have savings that will provide the equivalent protection) that has a face value of five to eight times your annual income. This is a pretty broad range, so the rule of thumb doesn't provide a great deal of guidance. If you make $50,000 per year, you should have a minimum of $250,000, but perhaps as much as $400,000. Since most young families do not have large amounts of savings, life insurance can be an inexpensive way to meet that goal. As savings rise and/or insurance needs decline (as in the case when dependent children leave the home or dependent parents pass away), insurance coverage can be reduced.

Table 6-1 is a worksheet that you can use to estimate your life insurance needs more exactly. This is a relatively complicated calculation, but as you become more familiar with your financial plan and household budget, it will not take that long to work through. When you are uncertain about some of the values, err on the side of overestimation. For example, consider Holly's case from the earlier example:

Example: Holly is married and has no children. Her household combined gross income is $90,000, with take-home pay of about $50,000. About 60 percent of the income comes from Holly's job. Their total estate is under the estate tax limitation, so Holly estimates that the expenses of her death will be no more than $15,000. Holly's household has total debt of $200,000 (student loans, mortgage, car loans, and credit card debt). They have no children, but Holly's husband is attending graduate school at night, so she estimates additional education expenses of $25,000. Since she does not have children or

Table 6-1 Estimating Your Life Insurance Needs

Expenses of Your Death
1. Uninsured medical expenses (deductible and copay) $_____
2. Funeral costs (average $10,000, but less for cremation) $_____
3. Estate taxes (estimate 55% of amount > $675,000) $_____
4. Probate costs (estimate 4% of assets) $_____
5. State inheritance taxes $_____
6. Legal fees, estate administration (estimate 1% of assets) $_____

Outstanding Debt (if you want to be able to pay it off at death)
7. Mortgage $_____
8. Car loan(s) $_____
9. Credit card balances/other loans $_____

Education Costs for Children or Spouse
10. Estimated cost of tuition (see Chapter 11)
    Cost of 4 years of education   _____
    Times number of people to educate
    (estimate $60,000 public/$120,000 private) _____ $_____

Cost of Lost Support Services
11. Annual child-care/elder-care costs
    (estimate min. $100–150 per week,
    $60–75 per week for after school only)   _____
12. Annual housekeeping costs
    (estimate min. $40–60 per week)   _____
13. Total cost of lost support services:
    Total of 11 + 12   _____
    Times number of years support needed   _____   = $_____

Effect on Household Income and Expenses
14. Counseling costs for adjustment to loss
    (estimate $50–75 per hour unless covered
    by insurance) $_____
15. Your contribution to household income   _____
16. Reduction in family expenses
    due to death (estimate 10–20%)   _____
17. Net effect on household income and expenses
    Line 15 minus Line 16   _____
18. Amount to replace lost income
    Multiply line 17 by number of years to replace $_____

Spouse Retirement Income Effects
19. Retirement savings needs
    (from Table 14-1)   _____

Calculation of Life Insurance Needed
20. Total of all amounts in right-hand column $_____
21. Subtract amount of current savings/investments $_____

Total Life Insurance Needs $_____

dependent parents, Holly is not concerned about lost support services.

If Holly were to die prematurely, the net effect on household income and expenses would be substantial. The household net income would go from $50,000 to $30,000. Holly estimates that household costs would only go down by $10,000, so the net effect of her death on household cash flow would be a reduction of $10,000 per year for an estimated three years while her husband completes his schooling. They currently have savings of $30,000.

So how much insurance does Holly need? Adding up her estimated costs of $15,000 for funeral expenses, $200,000 for outstanding debt, $25,000 for her husband's schooling, and $30,000 for lost income gives a total of $270,000. With $30,000 in savings, this leaves a recommended life insurance amount of $240,000. Note that a rule of thumb of five times earnings would have resulted in a similar answer ($250,000), eight times earnings would perhaps have been too much. In general, the lower multiplier will probably be a safe estimate for individuals without children or significantly dependent spouses.

What Are Your Choices?

Because life insurers are constantly trying to provide products that will meet the needs of a diverse consumer population, there are many different types of insurance available. They fall into two general categories: those that provide *death protection only* and those that provide *death protection plus savings*. As with investments discussed in other parts of this book, you should evaluate the benefits of this type of saving against the alternatives that are available to you. Insurance agents generally make much larger commissions for selling you the policies that include savings features, so they are likely to encourage you in that direction.

The basic features of the most common types of policies are described here and summarized in Table 6-2.

Table 6-2 Comparison of Types of Life Insurance

Type of Policy	Premium Level	Period of Policy	Death Benefit	Cash Buildup	Choice of Investments	Proof of Insurability
Term insurance						
Regular term	Increases w/age	Usually 1 year	Constant	N/A	N/A	Required
Increasing term	Increases w/age	1–10 years	Increases w/age	N/A	N/A	Required
Decreasing term	Increases w/age	1–10 years	Decreases w/age	N/A	N/A	Required
Level term	Constant	5–10 years	Constant	N/A	N/A	Rules differ
Renewable term	Increases w/age	5–20 years	Constant	N/A	N/A	Required at beginning only
Permanent insurance						
Whole life insurance	Constant	10+ years	Increases w/cash buildup	Yes	No	Required at beginning only
Universal life insurance	Flexible	10+ years	Increases w/cash buildup	Yes	Yes	Required at beginning only
Variable life insurance	Constant	10+ years	Increases w/cash buildup	Yes	Yes	Required at beginning only
Single-premium life	One-time payment	Whole life	Increases w/cash buildup	No	No	Required at beginning only

Term Insurance

Term insurance provides death protection for a specified period of
time, usually one year. The premium is based on the policyholder's
assessed risk of dying and is primarily a function of age, although for
higher levels of coverage, most insurers require blood tests and cursory health checks.

    To assess your risk, most insurers use standard mortality tables
that show the probability of dying at particular ages. Those who have
lower risk factors, such as women, nonsmokers, and people in certain professions, generally receive more favorable rates than those
who have a higher mortality risk. For example, using the standard

tables, a 45-year-old man has a 25 percent higher chance of dying before he reaches 46 than a 45-year-old woman does. At age 76, men have a 40 percent higher risk of dying before they reach age 77.

With term insurance, if you live to the end of the term of the policy, your beneficiaries will not receive anything. The insurance pays out only if you die, not if you *survive.*

Because your risk of dying increases as you age, the annual premium that you pay for term insurance will normally increase as well. The cost of buying term insurance when you are under 50 is fairly low, but term insurance can become prohibitively expensive for those at older ages. Since life insurance needs tend to decline after children are grown and savings levels are higher, you can lower your amount of coverage or drop the insurance.

Some variations on term insurance adjust either the premium schedule or the death benefit to accommodate individual needs for protection or affordability of premiums. Examples of common types of term include the following:

Increasing term: The death benefits increase over time according to a predetermined schedule.

Decreasing term: The death benefits decrease over time according to a predetermined schedule.

Level term: The death benefits stay the same, but the premium is set at a level amount for the period. You are basically paying more for your coverage than the true cost in the early years, so that in later years, as your risk gets more expensive, you can continue to pay the same level of premium. These policies are usually for five- to ten-year periods.

Renewable term: The policy is automatically renewable for a period of time without additional proof of insurability (e.g., a medical examination). If you were diagnosed with a serious illness during this period, the company would not be able to drop your insurance.

Permanent Insurance

Permanent insurance is life insurance for a longer period of time, often twenty years or more. In the traditional type of permanent insurance, called whole life insurance, the premiums are set at a level amount (as in level term) for the entire policy period. Since the risk of dying is much higher during the later years of the policy, premiums paid in the early years include extra money, and this money is invested by the insurer to help fund the later coverage. The variations on this type of insurance are related to the distribution of premium payments, how the extra premium dollars are to be invested, and whether the insurer allows the policyholder to benefit from better than expected performance of its pool.

The funds that are accumulating on behalf of the policyholder are usually called the *cash value*. Although you may have paid in $1,000 more than the cost of your death protection, the insurer never allocates all of that amount to cash value, since it still must cover its expenses, profit, and risk. As the cash value increases over the life of the policy, policyholders usually can borrow against it at favorable rates. Like universal and variable life, discussed later, whole life is usually marketed as a savings vehicle. Of the three, whole life generally provides the lowest return on investment. The cost of whole life premiums is generally several times the cost of the equivalent face value of term insurance.

Universal Life. This type of policy allows policyholders to participate in favorable experience of the insurer (e.g., if it has fewer deaths than expected or if its investment returns are higher than expected), and it allows flexibility in payment of premiums. If the cash value of the policy is high enough to cover the cost of providing the death benefits, you may have the option of skipping premium payments. The problem with this type of policy is that the lapse rates are very high. Human nature being what it is, too many people skip their premiums until they have no protection left at all. Few insurers market policies as "universal life" any more.

Variable Life. Like whole life, this type of policy offers permanent insurance coverage. However, the insurer allows you to assume the investment risk by designating your excess premium payments for particular investment funds (e.g., money market, bond, and stock mutual funds). Since the cash buildup will be dependent on the performance of "your" investment, the earnings and death benefits of the policy above a minimum guarantee will vary.

Adjustable Life Insurance. Adjustable life insurance provides permanent insurance but, like universal life, allows you some additional flexibility. Premiums and death benefits can be increased or decreased as your needs change.

Single-Premium Life Insurance. With this type of life insurance, you basically pay the full cost of the life insurance protection in one payment instead of paying it over time. The amount paid will be less than the total of the premiums you would have paid for whole life, since the insurer is getting the funds earlier and will have a longer time to invest them on your behalf. In some cases, you may be allowed a choice of investments, so that your death benefit and/or cash value might rise.

The Tax Benefits of Life Insurance

Using life insurance as an investment might seem like you are mixing two components of your financial portfolio that should be separate, but the tax benefits of investing through life insurance should not be ignored. Although you usually pay life insurance premiums with after-tax dollars, the earnings on the cash buildup in the policy are not taxed, and the death benefit that goes to your beneficiaries is also *tax-free*. Therefore, comparisons with other investments should take into consideration this substantial tax benefit.

So Which Kind Should You Buy?

Although there are some circumstances under which it will make sense for you to invest in permanent insurance, *term insurance* is my recommendation for most women. With term insurance, it is possible to purchase a large amount of death protection at relatively low cost. To keep the cost of permanent insurance within your budget, you will probably have to reduce your insurance coverage below the necessary level. Although permanent insurance represents enforced savings, there is the possibility that you will allow your policy to lapse because you are unable to maintain the required premium levels. This will adversely affect your financial plan. Furthermore, if you consider your permanent insurance as an investment and later borrow against it, your death benefit will be reduced by the amount of your loan, potentially resulting in insufficient insurance for your dependents.

Going back to the different scenarios I suggested earlier, let's look at each person to see what she should do.

Holly, the head of household with no children, is young enough that term insurance will be cheap. However, she and her husband have enough income that they could afford to purchase permanent insurance. If she begins a permanent policy now, she can lock in a premium rate that will become more affordable as time goes on. However, if she plans to quit work for a few years when her children are young, the higher payment may end up being too much for their reduced budget to handle. When I was in my early twenties and had no children yet, I talked to an insurance agent about my life insurance needs. My income at the time was about $20,000, and I could buy $100,000 of term life insurance for less than $100 per year, but for the equivalent face value in permanent insurance, the cost was about $1,000 per year (and would remain at that level until I was 65). Obviously, I couldn't afford to pay that much, so I had three alternatives: Buy a term policy, buy a smaller amount of permanent insurance, or don't buy insurance. Buying term insurance now and increasing her savings levels is probably the best bet for Holly.

Vickie, the head of household with children, is my case right now. When my children were born several years later, my husband and I both bought term insurance (at a higher cost, since we were then older), and we have increased our term coverage as our needs have increased. At present (ages 44 and 48), our term insurance is still relatively inexpensive, since we both qualify for good health non-smoker rates. I plan to maintain my term coverage until my children are independent, at which time my savings and retirement plan should be sufficient to provide for my husband's income replacement needs.

Jill, the homemaker, needs life insurance coverage sufficient to pay for the costs of her death and the lost support services to the family in the event of her death. These may include cooking, cleaning, before- and after-school care, among others. As in the other scenarios, if her household has adequate financial resources, life insurance may be unnecessary. Since support services will likely be unnecessary beyond the date when the children leave the home, term life insurance is most appropriate in this scenario.

Sue, the single woman with dependent parents, does not need as much coverage as Holly and Vickie. In addition, she may not need the insurance for her entire life, since it is likely that her parents will die before she does. She may decide to opt for a paid-up policy that will provide a specified level of income for her parents, or she could purchase a decreasing term policy and gradually buy additional amounts of paid-up permanent insurance. She must compare the cost of this option with the purchase of a whole life or variable life policy. Depending on her age, income, and health level, Sue may be better off just buying term insurance and investing additional funds to help offset the cost of higher term premiums in her later years.

Joan does not need life insurance, since she has no dependents. If she is following a reasonable financial plan, she will be saving for retirement in an employer plan or IRA, so she will not need the savings features or tax advantages offered by permanent insurance.

Should You Buy Term and Invest the Difference?

Notice that I have recommended term insurance for nearly everyone. Insurance professionals do not all agree on this point, so we should outline the pros and cons. Suppose that at age 20 I had bought the term insurance and invested the $900 difference between term and permanent insurance in a mutual fund each year. The cash value buildup in the early years of the alternative whole life policy would have been small, since the expenses of the insurer must be covered (and commissions often eat up 50 percent or more of the first year's premium).

Ask yourself: What would I have had to earn on the $900 investment to make it comparable to investing in the permanent life insurance? Since the earnings in the life insurance policy are tax-free, I would have to earn enough to cover the tax difference. Suppose that the life insurance illustration assumes that you will earn 7 percent. In order to earn 7 percent on an after-tax basis, a person in the 28 percent tax bracket must earn 9.8 percent on a taxable investment. This might be possible in a bond mutual fund or a diversified bond and stock fund, but it would be subject to the risk of market declines. In the early years, however, the mutual fund example will look better, since the insurance cash values will reflect the up-front costs of commissions and expenses on the policy.

You should also ask yourself: Do I have the discipline to invest this money every year? Do I have the discipline to not use the money for other purposes, such as vacations, cars, and other goodies? Some people opt for the life insurance savings instead of saving the money on their own because of the enforced aspect—you *must* pay the premium or lose the coverage. Although I don't like to assume that people will be irrational and choose a lower-yielding investment for this reason, I know it is true. If you need that kind of discipline, I would suggest that you set up your savings as an automatic withdrawal from your paycheck or from your checking account. If you are concerned about keeping your hands off the money, put it in an IRA or retirement fund so that there are penalties for early withdrawal. The tax benefits of IRAs, while not quite as good as those of life insurance, will mean that you do not need to target as high a return to make it comparable to the insurance option.

Insurance Policy Terms and Features

In this section, I summarize some of the features that might be available in your policy. Not all policies include these, so you need to read the contract carefully. When additional features are added to a standard policy, there will be "riders" attached to the policy document that become part of the legal contract.

Illustrations

Whenever you buy a long-term policy, the insurer will provide you with an estimate of the cash flows from the policy, including your premiums, the accumulating cash value, and the estimated death benefit at different ages. These are only estimates, however, and you should look at the assumptions carefully. If they assume unreasonably high interest rates and the market does not do well, your premiums may be higher, your cash value may be lower, and your death benefit may be lower. For those policies that are eventually paid up, the length of time you must pay premiums may be longer than that in the illustration.

Loan Provisions

Permanent policies allow you to borrow against your cash value at favorable loan rates. Until the loan is repaid, however, the death benefit will be reduced by the outstanding loan amount.

Guaranteed Insurability

Guaranteed insurability provisions allow you to increase the face value of your insurance in the future without a health examination. There is usually an age limit on how long this can be done, and the amount of increase per year is subject to a limitation.

Disability

Some policies include a rider that allows you to be paid a monthly income or a lump-sum amount if you become disabled during the policy period.

Suicide

Most policies do not pay the face value death benefit if the death was due to suicide within the first few years of the policy. Instead, the beneficiaries are entitled to receive only the total of the premiums that have been paid by the policyholder. If suicide occurs later, it will probably be covered. The purpose of this clause is to deter the purchase of a policy in anticipation of a suicide.

Fraud

If you lie on your policy application (e.g., if you claim to be a non-smoker when you are not), or if you fail to disclose a medical condition when asked, the insurer has a stated period of time, usually one or two years, to cancel the policy and refund your premium payments. After that *incontestability period,* the insurer cannot deny the coverage based on falsification of the application. Although this may seem on its face to be somewhat unfair to the insurer, it provides an incentive for the insurer to better investigate its policyholders' health status prior to entering into the agreement.

For misstatement of age, the usual remedy is that the insurer will pay the death benefit that would have been applicable for your age and the premium payments that you made.

I have acted as an expert witness on several cases where the policyholder has claimed that it was the agent who entered the false information on the application. While that may happen in some cases, keep in mind that, in signing your policy application, you are attesting to the truthfulness and completeness of the information provided. So don't sign it if you have not read it, and don't sign it if the agent has entered false information. The risk you take is that the policy will be contested after you are dead, and if the insurer wins, your dependents will have no insurance.

Double Indemnity

If the policyholder dies from accidental causes, some insurance policies will pay double the death benefit stated in the policy. While this sounds like a great deal, very few people die from accidental causes (and the additional cost of paying for these is factored into the insurance premium).

How to Research Insurance Options

Use the Internet

One of the great things about living in the "information age" is that we have so much information at our fingertips. Comparison shopping for life insurance (as well as for other types of individual insurance) has never been easier. Not only do companies' web sites give you the opportunity to get quotes for certain policies, but the larger insurers' sites have informational content that may help you analyze your insurance needs and make decisions between products.

Generally, it will be fairly easy to get quotes for simpler products such as term life, which vary little from company to company. Since there are so many variations on the policies that include investment components, legal restrictions require that insurers provide you with a lot more information, and so quotes are less likely to be available for permanent insurance.

Some interesting web sites for you to check out are:

http://www.insurance.yahoo.com. Yahoo's Insurance Center is a portal that links to lots of other insurance sites and includes educational information as well.

http://www.insweb.com. This site provides you with quotes from several companies for different types of insurance, including term life.

http://www.quotesmith.com. Similar to insweb, this site claims to represent 300 different insurers. Quotes are available for term life insurance; annuities; and vehicle, medical, dental, Medicare supplement, and workers' compensation insurance.

http://www.insurerate.com. This site is similar to insweb. Quotes are available for term life insurance; pet insurance; and auto, health, and homeowner's insurance.

http://www.financecenter.com/solutions/industries/insurance.fcs. This site allows you to compare life insurance policies and provides tips for homeowners, renters, and auto insurance.

Several insurers offer valuable information on their company web sites even though they don't actually provide quotes or sell insurance over the web. Two good examples are MetLife (*www.met life.com*) and Prudential (*www.prudential.com*). Prudential's web site includes several calculators that will help you to assess your insurance needs.

Once you have done your homework on the web, you can request the name of an agent who can take care of the actual purchase of the insurance. The lowest-priced term insurance will usually require a blood test, so it is unlikely that you will actually be able to complete the transaction over the Internet. It is possible that you can be approved subject to the blood test, however.

In some cases, other insurers will match the price that you get from a competitor (particularly on term insurance), so if you have a favorite agent that you use for other types of insurance, you may want to print out your quote and take it to your agent.

Financial Condition of the Company

Price should not be your only concern when you buy life insurance (or any other type of insurance, for that matter). You are purchasing a long-term product, and you are depending on the insurer to be there to pay your beneficiaries when you die. Just as you wouldn't want to put your hard-earned savings in a shaky bank, you should be sure to check out the insurance company you are sending your premiums to.

If you are considering life insurance with an investment component, you should beware the companies that promise unusually high rates of return. Higher return usually means higher risk, a rule that I discuss in more detail in Chapter 8. Although state insurance guarantee funds provide a measure of protection against loss of benefits, you are better off picking a company that will not have these problems.

Just because a life insurer is large is no guarantee that it is financially sound. A lot depends on the company's investment choices and general management.

Here are a few things to check out:

- *State of domicile.* New York has the most stringent laws, and it requires companies that do business there to follow the same rules in every state in which they do business.

- *Financial soundness.* Standard & Poor's Insurance Ratings Service rates the largest companies on their claims-paying abilities, with AAA being the highest rating. Moody's Investor Services rates publicly traded life insurers, with Aaa being the highest rating. These reports are likely to be available at any large library. You can write to the *Insurance Forum*, P.O. Box 245, Department CD, Ellettsville, IN 47429 to get a list of top-rated companies and a list of troubled companies.

- *Investment portfolio.* Companies will usually provide you with an annual report or other financial information that tells you how they are investing their assets. You can compare that to the industry averages in Table 6-3. Higher-risk portfolios should be providing higher returns.

Table 6-3 Investment Allocations of Life Insurers

Investment Class	% in General Account
Government securities	16.7
Corporate bonds	55.0
Common stock	3.9
Preferred stock	0.9
Mortgages	11.0
Real estate	1.5
Policy loans	5.3
Cash	0.2
Other invested assets	1.8
Noninvested assets	3.6
Total	100.0

Choosing a Life Insurance Agent

Although you may be able to get information and prices on the Internet, you will probably need to work directly with an insurance agent at some point, particularly if you are purchasing an investment-type product. Table 6-4 summarizes some of the characteristics that you should look for in an insurance agent. In some cases you may need to interview several before you find the one that's right for you. Since this is potentially a long-term arrangement (I've been using the same agent for ten years), you should take the time to pick carefully.

Check Credentials

There are several colleges and universities around the country that offer majors in insurance. An agent who has had several insurance courses will, in general, be more informed about the nature of insurance products and the options that are available. However, even a college degree in insurance does not guarantee that the person has had more than one course in life insurance, so this should not be the sole criterion that you use. Nor should it be an absolute requirement. There are thousands of well-qualified insurance agents who have never had a college course on the subject. In the western part of the

---

Table 6-4 Choosing a Life Insurance Agent

A good agent should be:

1. Educated
   Education, professional credentials, and certifications indicate that the agent understands the product he or she is selling and keeps current in his or her area of specialty.

2. Experienced
   More years in the business makes an agent better able to understand your needs.

3. Able to sell you a variety of products offered by different insurers
   Independent agents are not locked into selling only the products of one company.

4. Informative and responsive
   The agent should provide you with the information necessary to make good decisions.

United States, there are fewer schools offering these courses, so you will find that fewer agents can claim this credential.

There are also numerous types of professional certification that life insurance agents may have. Most states require a license to sell insurance. In addition, the agent may be a Chartered Life Underwriter (CLU) or be working toward that designation. This certification is issued by the American College in Bryn Mawr, Pennsylvania, to individuals who have passed a rigorous national examination after completing a series of courses on life insurance.

If the agent is claiming to be a financial planner, look for the Certified Financial Planner (CFP) designation, offered by the International Board of Standards and Practices for CFPs, Denver, Colorado. This is given only to experienced planners who have completed a series of courses on employee benefits, insurance, investments, estate planning, and tax planning. CFPs are held to a strong code of ethics and must meet regular continuing education requirements. Alternatively, the American College offers a Chartered Financial Consultant (ChFC) designation that covers financial, estate, and tax planning.

Finally, a life insurance agent may be a Fellow in the Life Management Institute (FLMI), a designation awarded by the Life Office Management Association to those who have completed a series of examinations.

Experience

It should go without saying that you should look for a more experienced agent. Although everyone has to start somewhere, I would rather that new agents practice on someone else. In my career as a teacher, I have seen many students head off to careers in insurance sales, many without ever having had a course in insurance. The licensing requirements in my state, while they cover the basics, do not ensure that a new agent is an expert.

I recommend that you require that your agent have at least ten years of life insurance sales experience, although she or he need not have worked at the same company for that amount of time. Sales experience in another type of insurance is not a substitute.

Independent Agent

There are two types of agents: those who sell the products of only one company, of which they are usually employees, and those who sell the products of many different companies, for which they are independent contractors. Employees may or may not receive compensation in the form of a commission based on sales, but independent agents always do.

The advantage of using an independent agent is that you are not locked into buying only one insurer's products. Your agent will be able to do the shopping for you to some extent. He or she may not be authorized to sell the products of every insurance company, so you still will not have an endless set of choices, but at least you will have more than one choice. Salaried employees do not have as great an incentive to provide you with good service, but they also may be less inclined to pressure you into buying insurance that you don't need.

Informative and Responsive

Since you are likely to be working with this agent for some time, you want to be comfortable with him or her. The agent should listen to you and respond to your requests for information and documents in a timely manner. He or she should be honest with you about the pros and cons of different insurance strategies. The agent may be the first point of contact for your survivors in the event of your death. You want to ensure that he or she will be helpful in the claims process.

Estate Planning and Life Insurance

Life insurance can also be an important feature of your estate planning. This subject is discussed in detail in Chapter 15.

Summary

If you have read this chapter and completed the worksheets, you should have:

- An estimate of your life insurance needs

- An understanding of the different types of life insurance products available to you

- A strategy for choosing an insurance agent

For most women, life insurance is a relatively inexpensive component of their financial plan, but it is nevertheless often overlooked. If you are like me, you will find that the peace of mind that your life insurance policy brings you will make the purchase well worth its price.

CHAPTER 7

Risk Attitudes and Risk Management

You need to read this chapter if:

- ✔ You would like to know what kind of risk taker you are.

- ✔ You would like to better understand the differences in the risk-taking behavior of men and women.

- ✔ You don't know the basic steps in risk management.

Taking risks is not something that always comes naturally to women. While younger women seem to be moving away from the stereotype, women in the baby boom generation and their parents generally find that there is some truth in the idea that risk taking is a male trait. However, even if risk *taking* doesn't come naturally to you, it is likely that risk *management* will. Women have always been household risk managers—making sure that there is food on the table, that the kids are clothed, and that homework is done; putting antiseptics on cuts and cold compresses on bruises. Risk management in the area of investments is not very different. The trick is

116

recognizing what the risks are and taking appropriate steps to reduce your exposure to acceptable levels.

This chapter will give you some insight into your own attitudes toward risk and show you how you are similar to or different from other women. I offer some explanations for why women and men might have different attitudes toward risk and then suggest a different way of thinking about risk in your financial planning.

What Is Your Attitude Toward Risk?

Although this will provide only a rough measure of your risk attitudes, take a few moments to complete the questionnaire in Table 7-1. If you have a male spouse or partner, it might be interesting to have him complete the questionnaire as well for the sake of comparison. Add up the number values of your answers (a = 1 point; b = 2 points; c = 3 points). Then compare your score to the following scale:

If you scored from 8 to 12, you are a *safety junkie*. You are cautious in most aspects of your life, perhaps to the extreme. Hopefully, with a little more knowledge about the rewards of investment risk, you might come out of your shell a bit in that area.

If you scored from 13 to 19, you are a *cautious risk taker*. You are generally cautious, but you will take a risk now and then. You will probably be very comfortable with riskier investments once you understand that they are not nearly as risky when they are looked at over the long term.

If you scored from 19 to 24, you are an *extreme risk taker*. Very few women ever get scores this high unless they are very young. When I give this quiz to my classes of college-aged men and women, there is usually at least one young man who scores a 24, but few women have scores that put them in this category.

In a national survey of household finances, individuals were asked a question similar to Question 6 in Table 7-1. A significantly

Table 7-1 Risk Attitude Questionnaire

For each of the following situations, choose the scenario that best describes you.

1. a. When driving a car, I never go faster than the posted speed limit.
    b. When driving a car, I think it's okay to go 5 mph over the speed limit.
    c. When driving a car, I like to get wherever I am going as fast as possible, so I pass any slow cars, even if I have to go over the speed limit.

2. a. I brush my teeth after every meal, floss every day, and see my dentist twice a year.
    b. I usually brush my teeth in the morning and before bed, floss when I remember to, and generally go to the dentist once a year.
    c. I brush my teeth at least once a day, never remember to floss, and avoid going to the dentist unless there's a problem.

3. a. I don't like to participate in sports.
    b. I like to watch sports on TV or go to games.
    c. I would much rather play a sport than watch it.

4. a. I would never participate in an activity that involved the risk of being injured.
    b. When I participate in dangerous activities such as backwoods camping and hiking, I make sure that I have all the equipment and knowledge necessary to limit my risk of serious injury.
    c. I love to participate in activities that give me a thrill—mountain climbing without ropes, bungee jumping, sky diving all sound like fun to me.

5. a. I never gamble.
    b. I sometimes buy lottery tickets or raffle tickets just for fun.
    c. I love to go to casinos and gamble.

6. a. In my investments, I am not willing to take any risk at all.
    b. In my investments, I am willing to take a little risk for a little higher return.
    c. In my investments, I am willing to take a lot of risk for a very high return.

7. a. I will work only for a company that pays me a guaranteed salary.
    b. I would prefer to get paid a base salary plus commission.
    c. I would prefer to have a job that was all commission so that I would be rewarded for how hard I work.

8. a. I usually take a lower dose of medicine than what is recommended on the package.
    b. I usually take the prescribed dose of medicine as recommended.
    c. If two Advil are good, then three must be better.

Questionnaire Scoring: a = 1; b = 2, c = 3.

higher percentage of women than of men said that they were unwilling to take any risk at all. Interestingly, even among those who said this, many had investments in risky assets.

Women and Risk

In my academic pursuits in the last several years, I have focused my research on the question of why women invest differently from men. When I first began looking at this question, the conventional wisdom (from pension sponsors and the financial-planning community) was that women were less inclined to take risk in their investments than men were.

While at first glance, taking less risk might appear to be a good thing, especially to those of you who don't yet understand the *value* of taking risk, the problem lies in a very basic finance principle: *More risk gives you more return.* So if you don't take the risk, in the end you will have less accumulated savings. That means less retirement wealth. And since women live longer than men, they will need to support a longer retirement period, which will require *more* savings, not less.

How Much Difference Does It Make?

For those of you who are thinking, "I don't care if I earn a little less on my investments than those risk-taking men," consider the following facts. During the unprecedented 1990s run-up in the stock market, the cost of *not* being in the market was extremely high. A dollar invested in 1990 in a CD or other low-risk investment would have been worth less than $1.75 at the end of the decade. That same dollar invested in a stock fund indexed to the S&P500 would have grown to more than $5.00. Inflation alone should have increased that dollar to $1.40 over that time period. "But look what happened last year!" you say. Even *with* the declines to mid-2001, the stock portfolio outperformed the CD!

Why (Some) Women Avoid Risk

Psychologists and sociologists offer many possible reasons for differences in risk attitudes between men and women. Although clearly none of these explanations are universally true (since every person is unique), and you may even find some of these ideas to be inflammatory or insulting to women in general, there is at least a ring of truth to most of them. But since these are conjectures, I am labeling them as hypotheses lest anyone later accuse me of stating that they are truths.

Hypothesis 1: Women Are From Venus . . . The most commonly offered explanation for differences in risk tolerance is that women are somehow inherently different from men. Evolution created men to be hunters and women to be gatherers and child rearers. The responsibility for children may have made women evolve into more cautious beings, whereas risk taking was an essential survival skill for men.

Scientists have found that women's brains have more connections between the right and left sides, whereas men tend to operate from one side at a time. This has been offered as an explanation for why women can multitask more easily, but it can also explain the facility that men have with math, science, and computers, subjects that may require prolonged focus on narrow problems.

Most parents will agree that there are differences between girls and boys that go beyond the way we treat them. Along with the usual trucks and Legos, I gave my boys dolls to play with, in the interest of not perpetuating male stereotypes. What did they do? They took off the dolls' heads and used the bodies as machine guns!

Even the TV networks recognize the differences between boys and girls and market different channels to each group. Boys like action, and girls like relationship stories.

Hypothesis 2: Women Have Less to Risk. Those who have more income and more wealth can more easily afford to risk it. Rich people are more likely to have large stock portfolios than people with more limited wealth. In one of my recent academic studies on working women's finances, I found that the ratio of women's earnings to men's earnings was only 57 percent in 1998. Given their lower income levels, it should come as no surprise that women's average accumulation in retirement accounts is less than half that of men. So it's a bit of the "chicken and egg" problem: You need to have the money to risk, but you need to take risk to get the money.

Hypothesis 3: Women Are Not as Good at Math and Science. When my two sons were in early elementary school, the stars of the math classes were always the girls. But when I was volunteering as a math enrichment teacher for the fourth grade, I was surprised to find that my group of "gifted" math students included nine boys and only one girl. I asked one of their teachers about this imbalance, and she said that it was related to the "boy-girl thing." Her assessment was that as soon as the girls started getting interested in boys, they stopped competing against them scholastically. I found that to be very sad.

While that sounds like something teachers could combat, there's another problem—the parents. When my boys started junior high school, all the students took a placement test to place them in one of three math levels. During the parent night for the new seventh graders, I spoke with the teacher of the group of seventh graders who were placed in ninth grade math and asked her how many girls were in the class. She said that there were only four out of twenty-eight, even though several more had been offered a spot in the class. Why weren't the others in the class? Their *parents* had opted to put them in the middle math level so that they wouldn't be overly challenged. Shame on them!

Hypothesis 4: Women Have Been Socialized to Avoid Risk. The conditioning of girls to risk avoidance, at least in previous generations, began in early childhood. While the days of "Don't get your dress dirty" seem to be giving way to girls' soccer teams and Girl Scout merit badges for career options and sports skills rather than sewing and cooking, adults still have some tendency to treat girl children differently from boy children. The math class example in the previous section is a clear case of this problem. We dress girls in cute pink frilly outfits and boys in overalls and miniature work boots. We take the girls to ballet lessons and the boys to peewee football.

Related to the issue of socialization is that of career choice. Women in previous generations were encouraged to find husbands and, in the short run, to pursue careers that were family-friendly, such as teaching or nursing. By the time my generation came of age in the 1970s, all this had changed, and I went to college believing that I could be anything I wanted to be. However, underlying my modern viewpoint, I still knew that I would ultimately want to have a family and that my career would play second fiddle to my children. I truly don't think that men are saddled with this duality of purpose.

As a woman in the field of finance, which is largely a male domain, I find career choice to be a particularly persuasive reason for gender differences in risk taking. Since we spend so much of our lives involved in our careers, it seems logical that skills that are honed in the workplace will affect our personal lives as well. Even if we all start out with equivalent skills, if you don't use them, you lose them. Women who choose careers in finance, economics, computer science, and mathematics are much more likely to be willing to take risk in their portfolios than those in "soft science" careers.

So You Aren't a Natural Risk Taker . . .

Regardless of how you got there, by the time you are an adult, your innate risk preferences are well established. Even before you took the Risk Attitude Questionnaire, you probably knew your "risk type," and so you weren't surprised by the results of the questionnaire. The key point is that you can learn to better understand and manage your financial risks.

The Risk Management Process

Table 7-2 outlines the process of risk management. This is the same process that business risk managers use, since risk management is the same whether we are looking at households or businesses. To illustrate the application of these principles, I will show you how to apply them for two types of risks that apply to nearly everyone. First, I want you to consider the risk management process as it applies to the risk of being injured in a car accident. Since we are all familiar with driving risks, this one is fairly straightforward. Second, I want

---

Table 7-2 The Risk Management Process

Steps:

   1. Identify the risk.

   2. Estimate the cost of risk.

   3. Identify and evaluate possible ways of managing the risk.

      a. Avoid the risk.

      b. Reduce the risk.

      c. Pass the risk on to someone else.

   4. Implement your risk management plan.

   5. Continually reevaluate your plan.

---

you to consider the financial risk of poor investment performance, an important aspect of your financial plan, but one that perhaps you are not as comfortable with. Since the ability to achieve your investment goals will depend on your investment choices, good risk management will require that you better understand your choices and the impact of these choices on your risk and return. The next three chapters discuss these issues in more depth, so I just deal with them in generalities for the moment.

Identify the Risk

What is risk? A very general definition is that a risk exists anytime the outcome of an event is uncertain. That pretty much defines our lives as being a bundle of risks, doesn't it? Most of the time, we aren't overly concerned with risks that result in better than expected outcomes. It's the risk of bad outcomes that we usually focus on.

Why do we take risks? Because there is some benefit to be gained from taking the risk. When you drive your car, you take the risk of being in an accident. The more you drive, the greater the probability of this happening. The trade-off is that driving allows you to get where you are going much faster than walking, and without being exposed to the elements.

In the area of investments, there are very few "sure things," so by choosing to make investments, you are voluntarily exposing yourself to risk. But the trade-off is that you are being "paid" to take the risk in the form of return on your investment: interest, dividends, or growth in the value of your investments. In general, the more risk you take, the greater the benefit you can potentially realize from your investment (an idea that I will discuss in more detail in Chapter 8). But risk isn't a one-way street. When you take a risk involving your investment, the investment may be worth more than you expect, or it may be worth less.

What exactly are the risks related to investments? Dividends or price increases may be less than you expected. The company you invested in may go bankrupt, resulting in a default on bonds or making your stocks worthless. The U.S. economy may take a downturn, causing inflation to soar and all of your investments to do poorly. Even if your money is in an insured account in a bank, the failure of the bank may cause delays in your ability to withdraw funds when you need them.

Estimate the Cost of Risk

In order to evaluate the ways you can manage a risk, you need to have some idea of what the cost of not managing it would be. You need to know what the possible outcomes are, how likely they are to happen, and how much they will cost you if they do occur. This is perhaps the most difficult step in managing any risk and, for many types of risks, it is impossible to do without help from professionals. If you misestimate the cost of risk, you will end up taking inappropriate steps to manage it.

A simple example of the effect of misestimating the risk is how people react to the risk of dying in an airplane crash. This risk is actually much lower than the risk of being injured or killed in a car accident, but because we have so little control in an airplane, as opposed to our illusion of control when we are driving a car, people tend to be overly worried about this risk. At most airports, you can buy accident life insurance that will pay out if you die on that particular flight. It only costs a few dollars, and therefore it seems like a good deal. But since people overestimate the risk, they pay far too much for this insurance, and the companies that sell it are laughing all the way to the bank.

Cost of Car Accident Risk. If you drive a car, the most likely scenario for any given year is that you will have no accidents. But if you are involved in a car accident, you may have significant medical bills and your car may be totaled. If you were responsible for injuries to a passenger in your own car or for injuries to people in another car and damage to property, you may have liability risk. The worst-case scenarios for car accidents can run into millions of dollars. Estimating the cost of risk therefore must take into account the small likelihood of the worst-case scenario. There are also nonmonetary costs that should be considered, such as pain and suffering, the inconvenience of having your car in the shop, and the distress associated with hurting other people.

Cost of Investment Risk. What happens if your portfolio of investments does poorly? Since investments are made for the long term, the immediate effect may be negligible. If your investment portfolio is earmarked for a particular purpose, such as providing retirement income, you may have to adjust your future savings program in order to meet your original goals. In Chapter 14, I provide some worksheets for you to use to estimate the cost of providing for your retirement. In the event that your investment portfolio declines significantly in value immediately before your planned retirement date or while you are enjoying your retirement, the cost of this risk could be very high. You may need to work for more years than you originally planned. You may need to curtail luxury expenditures such as travel and entertainment. But an important difference between investment risk and car accident risk is that the costs of investment risk are all monetary—there is no pain and suffering.

Identify and Evaluate Possible Ways of Managing the Risk

Depending on the type of risk you are managing, there will be many ways of approaching the problem. In this section, I give examples of the use of the risk management techniques identified in Table 7-2.

Managing Car Accident Risk. Applying the three methods of risk management to the risk of car accidents is pretty easy. You can avoid the risk entirely by not driving. (Of course, if you drive with others or take mass transportation, you are simply changing the nature of the accident risk, not totally avoiding it.) You can reduce the risk by driving carefully, keeping your car in good working order, and avoiding routes that are more dangerous. The last option, passing the risk on to someone else, is actually mandated by most states in that they require liability insurance. While you cannot pass on *all* of the costs of risk, insurance will take care of most of the monetary components of these costs.

Managing Investment Risk. Think about your reaction to the first option for managing the risk of an auto accident, that is, avoiding the risk by not driving. I doubt that you would seriously consider this option despite the risk. And yet many women avoid investment risks rather than attempting to manage them. The difference is the level of familiarity with the risks and rewards of investments and with the various risk management techniques that are available.

In the rest of this book, I familiarize you with some basic rules that will allow you to better understand the investment process and to manage these risks as easily as possible. You will find that the risk of bad investment performance can be significantly reduced by careful choice of investments and by reallocating between investment categories at different points in your life. If you have a large portfolio of investments of different types, it is unlikely that all of these investments will do poorly at the same time. As you approach retirement, you can divest yourself of the riskiest investments and emphasize those that will pay you a regular income and will not be subject to as much risk of default.

More sophisticated investors (and managers of mutual funds that you as an individual can invest in) may be able to pass on some of their investment risk to others by using "hedging" strategies. This simply means that they invest in specialized securities that can take advantage of adverse market movements. However, as you will learn in the next chapter, lower risk generally implies lower return, so these hedged portfolios will reduce their risk at a cost.

Implement Your Risk Management Plan

Your risk management plan will differ depending on the type of risk that you are considering. In the case of automobile risk, perhaps you will consider checking out the National Highway Traffic Safety Association collision ratings before you buy a new car (*http://www.nhtsa. org*). Or maybe you will replace your older vehicle with one that has airbags for the front seat occupants. You might check out your auto insurance coverage and think about increasing the limits.

For investment risk management, you should consider increasing the risk level of your portfolio. My experience tells me that most women would be better off taking a little more risk than they are comfortable with, particularly in their investment portfolio. Particularly for those who had fairly low scores on the risk attitude questionnaire, the best way to do this is in small steps. After reading the investments chapters in this book, a simple way to take a little more risk would be to reevaluate your 401(k) or IRA investment allocation and shift some of your funds into a diversified stock fund. Don't let yourself worry about short-run performance—let it ride. In the long run, your stocks will outperform lower-risk investments many times over. As you see this happening, you may gain the confidence to take even more risk (and reap the rewards).

Continually Reevaluate Your Plan

All risk management plans, and especially those involving your finances, should be reevaluated on a regular basis. When we get busy with other activities, it is often difficult to find the time to do this for our financial plan. You should make a habit of taking stock of your financial decisions on an annual basis—perhaps before you have an annual visit with your accountant, financial planner, or insurance agent. Just be sure you don't let inertia leave you in a plan that is no longer appropriate for you.

Summary

If you have read this chapter, you should know:

- Your level of risk tolerance

- The differences between men and women in risk taking and how the experts explain these differences

- The steps in the risk management process and how you can apply them to different types of risk

Your attitudes toward risk are an essential component of *who* you are. These attitudes will tend to change over your life cycle, as you marry, have children, approach retirement, or make other life changes. Your level of personal and financial risk taking will necessarily need to be adjusted accordingly.

CHAPTER 8

The Basics of Investing
Long-Term Growth Through Stock Investing

You need to read this chapter if:

- ✔ You want to know the most important rules of investing.

- ✔ You want to better understand the relationship between risk and return.

- ✔ You don't really understand what stock is or how people make money from investing in stock.

- ✔ You don't understand why stocks make the best long-term investments.

- ✔ You don't know how to buy stock.

You Should at Least Know the Most Important Rules of Investing

If you completed the Risk Attitude Questionnaire in Chapter 7, you now have a better feel for your own level of risk tolerance. Even if you think that you are not risk-tolerant enough to invest in stock, you should read this chapter anyway. I think that after you do, you will realize that taking a little more risk in your investment portfolio will help you to achieve your long-run financial goals.

The other reason to read this chapter is to learn the "lingo" of finance. Much of the mystery of investing will then be clearer to you, and you will be able to converse intelligently with all those friends, family members, and business colleagues who claim to be savvy investors.

In Table 8-1, I have boiled down the main investment concepts into a few rules that I believe are the most important things for you as a novice investor to remember. Interestingly, even some of the "experts" lose sight of these rules on occasion—to their detriment. In the following sections, I explain how these rules apply to you and how you can use them to your advantage.

More Risk, More Return

The most important concept in finance is that taking risk is usually associated with some kind of benefit. If you don't take any risk, you cannot expect to receive as much investment return. You, as the investor, are essentially being paid a premium for being willing to take the risk. If you invest in very safe securities such as government savings bonds, which are discussed in Chapter 10, you are subject to very little risk, so the government does not need to pay you anything extra and your return will be very low, just a little bit more than what you get on your FDIC-insured savings account at a bank. If you truly don't want to take any risk at all, then that might be okay for you.

Table 8-1 The Most Important Rules of Investing

1. Taking more risk gives you greater long-run return.
2. Don't put all your eggs in one basket—diversify.
3. Buy low, sell high.
4. Everyone else has access to the same information as you do.

But wouldn't you be willing to take just a *little* more risk for a few percentage points of extra investment return?

Before we go any further, we need to define what I mean by *return*. The best way of thinking about this is to consider all the benefits you get from an investment and compare them to the costs that you had to incur to be entitled to these benefits. There are two ways we can compare the benefits and the costs. If we subtract costs from benefits, we end up with a measure of our dollar gain, sometimes called "profit." In the investment community, however, it is more common to compare investments based on a ratio of the benefits to the costs. For example, we might calculate:

$$Annual\ Return = \left(\frac{Dollar\ Gain}{Amount\ Invested}\right) \div Number\ of\ Years\ Held$$

This equation is actually an oversimplification of the problem because it does not take into account the compounding of interest earnings over the time period (and thus overstates your actual return), but it is okay as a shortcut estimate.

> *Example: You bought a limited edition sculpture at an art show in 1985 for $200. In 2001, you find that it is now worth $400. In seventeen years, the artwork has doubled in value, earning you a 100 percent cumulative return. But the annual rate of return is less than 6 percent per year. Although it was better than inflation, you could have done much better in the financial markets over that time period.*

One way of thinking about the return you get for a given investment is to see it as a series of extra premiums that you charge for the different types of risk that you are being asked to bear. Whenever you invest in a risky security (and this applies not only to stocks, but to other investments as well), you may be subject to one or more of the following types of risk:

- *Inflation risk:* The risk that your money will not be able to buy as much in goods and services in the future. This risk is present in almost all investments, but the longer term the investment, the greater the risk.

Example of inflation risk: June loans her sister $1,000 and is paid back one year later. The $1,000 refrigerator that June was planning to buy with that money last year now costs $1,050. If she had charged her sister 5 percent interest, she would have just broken even. With no interest charged, June has lost purchasing power.

• *Liquidity risk:* The risk that you will not be able to get your money back promptly in the event that you need it. This risk is higher for investments that do not have an active resale market, such as privately held businesses, real estate, and some municipal bonds.

Example of liquidity risk: Mary invests $5,000 in her brother's latest business venture. One year later, she would like to back out of the partnership, but no other investors are interested. If her brother is unwilling or unable to buy out her interest, she has a completely illiquid investment.

• *Default risk:* The risk that the company issuing the securities will fail to pay you interest or dividends that are due to you or, in the most serious case, will go bankrupt.

Example of default risk: Elaine buys shares of stock in a high-technology company that has developed a new Internet business. So far, the company has not generated positive cash flows, and it does not pay any dividends to its shareholders. Elaine understands that there is a high probability that she will lose all of her investment.

• *Price risk:* The risk that the price of the security will go down between the time you bought it and the time you sell it. Unlike bank accounts and CDs, financial securities change in value over time, depending on such factors as the financial condition of the company, interest rates, and economic conditions.

Example of price risk: You own shares in Home Depot. The company announces that its earnings for the quarter are going to be lower than previously forecast. The stock price falls.

- *Market risk:* All investments are subject to common factors such as the general economic condition of the country, political unrest, exchange rates, and the balance of trade. Some investments will be affected more than others by these factors.

Example of market risk: The Federal Reserve announces an interest rate cut in early 2001. Stock prices fall and bond prices go up. Both of these reactions are examples of price risk and market risk.

Your required annual return on any investment should therefore include compensation for all the different types of risk that you are bearing.

The risk-return relationship can be seen very clearly by looking at the past history of returns for several categories of investments that differ in level of risk. Table 8-2 shows the average annual return on investment over time for a variety of investment categories, from riskiest to least risky. In the short run, as seen by the one-year performance of each group of securities, this relationship does not hold perfectly true, since government bonds had higher returns than long-term corporate bonds during 1997 and for the ten-year period 1988–1997. Small stocks also underperformed the larger market in 1997, even though they are generally considered to be more risky. However, in the long run, the riskiest investments will outperform the least risky, as can be seen by the average annual returns for the thirty-year period.

Another way to consider long-run performance, and one that is often used by financial professionals trying to convince new inves-

Table 8-2 Historical Return and Risk for Different Types of Investments

Investment Class	1 year 1997 Annual Return	1 year 1997 Cumulative Return	10 years 1988–1997 Annual Return	10 years 1988–1997 Cumulative Return	30 years 1968–1997 Annual Return	30 years 1968–1997 Cumulative Return
All stocks (standard dev.)	33.4%	133.4%	18.9% (14.4)	525.4%	13% (16.3)	3,093.6%
Small stocks (standard dev.)	22.8%	122.8%	17.8% (17.9)	458.9%	16.0% (23.7)	4,456.8%
Long-term bonds (standard dev.)	13.0%	113.0%	11.2% (9.2)	280.0%	9.5% (11.9)	1,277.7%
Government bonds (standard dev.)	15.9%	115.9%	11.7% (11.2)	289.7%	9.2% (12.0)	1,187.8%
Treasury bills (standard dev.)	5.3%	105.3%	5.5% (1.8)	169.8%	6.8% (2.6)	713.9%
Inflation (standard dev.)	1.7%	101.7%	3.4% (1.3)	139.8%	5.4% (3.2)	475.8%

Annual return equals the average of the annual returns for the period specified.
Cumulative return is the increase in the value of your investment if you had bought it at the beginning of the period and sold it at the end.
Source: Author's calculations.

tors to invest in stock, is to consider cumulative return. This tells you how much your initial investment will increase in value from its level at the beginning of the period. For example, suppose you invested $1,000 in a diversified stock portfolio at the beginning of 1997. At the end of 1997, your investment would be worth 133.4 percent of its original value, or $1,334. If you had invested $1,000 in a diversified stock portfolio in 1968 and left all your earnings in the fund to accumulate for thirty years, at the end of 1997 your investment would be worth 3,093.6 percent of its original value, or $30,936. A similar investment in low-risk Treasury bills would be worth only $7,139, about one-fourth as much.

By comparing the returns for the different types of investments, you can see how much the risk premiums are. Government bonds have no default risk, but long-term corporate bonds do, so the return on corporate bonds will usually be higher than that on comparable-length government bonds. The difference between high-rated bonds and lower-rated bonds is also due to default risk, with the lower-rated bonds giving a higher return to compensate for the greater default risk. These issues are discussed more fully in Chapter 9.

In the short run, the risk-return relationship is not as clear. For example, although the small stock group has outperformed all the others over the long term, its performance in the last decade has not been consistent because of troubles in the high-tech sector. In 1999, some investors made millions by investing in small technology stocks, but if they didn't sell these stocks before 2000, their technology stock portfolio may have lost as much as two-thirds of its value over the course of that year, and even more in 2001. This is important because it illustrates a corollary to the risk-return rule: Risk goes both ways. You need to be able to take the downs as well as the ups.

Table 8-2 also includes a measure called *standard deviation,* which is a way of looking at how much returns can deviate from the average. The higher the standard deviation, the wider the range of possible outcomes that can be expected. Comparing the different types of securities by their standard deviations, you can see that the risk-return relationship holds true for these ten-year and thirty-year periods. Although government bonds have a higher return for the ten-year period, they also experienced greater swings in value over that time, as evidenced by the standard deviation of 11.2 compared with only 9.2 for the corporate bonds. A little later in this chapter, I provide you with a way of interpreting the standard deviations more specifically.

The Benefits of Diversification

Another key concept in finance is one that comes from long-held women's wisdom: Don't put all your eggs in one basket. It wasn't until relatively recently that we have been able to mathematically verify the principle of diversification, but the logic is simple: If you have all your money in one investment, and that investment fails, you have nothing. But if you spread your money around into a lot of investments that are not dependent on each other, then the failure of one will not affect the viability of the others.

Example: Kenny and Molly each have $10,000 to invest. Kenny puts all his money in a new high-tech company, e-Video-games, which is selling computer games on the Internet. Molly also likes high-tech companies, but she puts $1,000 in e-Video-games and $1,000 each in nine other companies in different types of businesses. At the end of the year, e-Videogames stock is down to half its former value because sales are far below expectations. Kenny ends the year with only $5,000. Molly's other investments generate an average 20 percent return ($1,800), and so she ends the year with $11,300, a 13 percent average return, despite the poor performance of the one tech company.

Of course, this is a bit of a double-edged sword. Since you have reduced your risk by diversifying your portfolio of investments, you are also reducing your potential return.

Example: Suppose instead that e-Videogames does extremely well, so that at the end of the year the stock has doubled in value. Then Kenny's initial $10,000 investment will be worth $20,000, for a 100 percent return. Molly will also realize that gain, but only on her $1,000 investment. Her ending portfolio will thus be only $12,800, a 28 percent average return.

How Many Different Investments Is Enough?

As you add more securities to your portfolio, the overall risk of the portfolio declines. Does that mean that more is always better? Not really. The benefits of diversification can actually be achieved with a relatively small number of different securities if they are carefully selected to have different risk factors. Even if you choose a portfolio randomly (which you would never do), the risk reduction benefits of additional securities declines sharply when the portfolio has more than fifty different stocks in it. With careful selection, an investor can achieve diversification with as few as ten different securities.

A last point about diversification: If you invest in a lot of different companies, but those companies are subject to the same risk factors, you have not reduced your risk by diversifying. In the first investment example, if Molly had invested in ten different high-tech companies, rather than ten companies in different industries, her overall portfolio probably would have done as poorly as Kenny's.

The Power of Mutual Funds

Although I will come back to this later, any discussion of diversification must include mutual funds. You may have been wondering how in the world you can choose all the different investments that you will need in order to achieve the risk and return that you are comfortable with. Here's the answer: Let the professionals do it.

The idea of a mutual fund is to pool a whole lot of people's money and then hire a professional investment manager to make the day-to-day decisions about buying and selling securities for the pool. Each investor owns a proportionate share of the pool assets and is entitled to a proportionate share of the profits of the pool. There are literally thousands of mutual funds to choose from, with differing investment strategies and track records. Later in this chapter, I provide some tips for choosing among your alternatives.

Many people put their money into a number of mutual funds and assume that they have achieved diversification. First, you should understand by now that owning a single diversified mutual fund (as opposed to a fund invested in a single sector) is already sufficient diversification, assuming that you are comfortable with the risk and return characteristics of the particular fund. If you spread your money among several mutual funds with similar investment strategies—for example, all benchmarking the S&P 500 index—each of them will be invested in a similar mix of stocks. If one of them goes down, they will all go down, and you won't be any better off than you would have been if you had put all your money in one fund. Note, however, that you might want to invest in mutual funds with different characteristics, such as one that benchmarks the S&P 500, another that invests in international stocks, another that invests in real estate, and so on.

Buy Low, Sell High

The third rule of finance is one that seems very obvious, and yet we see violations of it all the time. You should always try to buy investments when their prices are low and sell them when their prices are high.

Unfortunately, the evidence shows that a large number of investors do exactly the opposite. As a stock's price keeps rising, more and more people buy it, presumably on the assumption that it will keep going up in value. Of course, it can't do this forever, and as the stock price begins to fall, investors start selling and continue to do so as the stock continues to fall in value. The result is that many of them buy at the high and sell at the low. One way to avoid being one of the investors who "follow the herd" is to adhere to a "buy and hold" strategy in your investing.

When I say "buy low, sell high," what do I mean by "low" and "high"? A price is low when it is less than what you think the stock is worth. But here's the rub: If the price is below what you think the stock is worth, then other investors must not have the same expectations as you do. If they also thought this was a good price, they would all be trying to buy it, and that would drive the price up. (This sounds like basic economics of supply and demand, doesn't it?) So either you are wrong or everyone else is.

Example: In early 2001, after the market had taken a sharp downturn, I got a call from a newspaper reporter who wanted my advice for her readers on what they should do with their pension investments in the down market. She was thinking that I would say that they should shift from stocks to money market funds or other lower-risk investments. It should come as no surprise to you that I told her that they shouldn't do anything. Pulling money out of long-term investments at the bottom of the market is the worst thing you could do. If the money is earmarked for retirement, then the portfolio can weather a short downturn.

No one can ever perfectly predict when a particular stock is at the lowest low it will go to, nor can anyone accurately pick the high points. If you choose to invest in individual stocks rather than follow my mutual fund advice, always keep the "buy low, sell high" advice in mind.

Everyone Else Has the Same Information as You (So You Can't Beat the Market)

Suppose that you read in *Business Week* or *Fortune* that a particular company is a "hot buy." Should you go out and buy a few shares? After all, the person making the recommendation probably has more expertise than you. The problem is that thousands of other people are reading the exact same article, and it only takes a few acting on that advice to drive up the price of the stock. Once the price has risen, the stock is no longer a good buy, and if you still act on the advice, you may end up being one of the people who violate my previous rule by buying high.

So the lesson in this section is simple: Assume that everyone else has *at least* as much information as you do, so you are unlikely to be able to make a killing on an investment. But that's okay—you don't need to make a killing. You just need to get sufficient return to compensate you for the risk that you are taking. So your goal should not be to "beat" the market—it should merely be to match the market.

There may be cases where you have access to information that is not available to the general public. That kind of information could help you net a large profit if you buy now and the information, when released publicly, causes the stock price to increase. However, keep in mind that if the information comes from an "insider" in a company, acting on that information by buying stock is illegal. And if it doesn't come from an insider, you need to question how reliable your source is.

What Is Stock?

Before you do too much more thinking about investment alternatives, you should be sure that you understand exactly what stock is, what cash flows are associated with stock, and what makes stock values go up and down.

Ownership of a Company

When you buy a share of common stock, you are actually becoming a part owner of a company. If there are 1 million shares outstanding (and large companies often have more than that), then you own one-millionth of the company. You are commonly entitled to one vote per share of stock—usually for election of the board of directors and for major changes in company direction.

As an owner, you are entitled to share in the profits of the company after all the company's costs have been covered. The board of directors may decide to pay out some of the profits in the form of a dividend each year. This is a small dollar amount per share that will be sent to you in the form of a check. But companies don't *have* to pay dividends. Instead, the company management may decide to use the profits to expand the company. If the company grows but the number of shares stays the same, the market price of each share of stock may go up. When companies are not making a profit, they will not pay a dividend, and they also will not have any extra money to reinvest in the business.

In the event of bankruptcy or liquidation, the common shareholders are entitled to a proportionate share of whatever is left over after all the debts of the company and the expenses of the bankruptcy are paid. Usually there isn't anything left to share.

Common Stock Versus Preferred Stock

Corporations can have two different types of stock. The type just discussed, and the one that you usually hear discussed in the financial news, is called *common stock*. The other type, called *preferred stock*, is actually more like a hybrid of stocks and bonds. Holders of preferred stock usually do not have the right to vote, and they are entitled to receive a dividend that is a predetermined percentage of the face value of the stock. So, for example, if the stock has a $100 face value, or "par value," and the dividend rate is set at 10 percent, then the stock will receive a dividend of $10 per year. This is guaranteed as long as the company has sufficient income to pay the dividends, and the preferred shareholders are entitled to be paid before any dividends are distributed to the common shareholders or any income is reinvested in the company. In the event that the company does extremely well, preferred shareholders generally do not get anything more than they were originally promised, the $10 dividend in my example.

The dividends on preferred shares are similar to payments of interest to bondholders except that, if the company doesn't have the money, it will not be in default if it does not pay the dividends. Since this type of stock has a more definite, and therefore less risky, cash flow stream, investors will require a lower rate of return than common stock investors.

Since individual investors rarely invest in preferred stock unless it is through a privately held or family business, the remainder of the discussion focuses on common stock.

Different Types of Common Stock

Generally, stocks are categorized by the industry that they are in, the marketplace that they are sold in, and their level of risk.

Industry Groups. Because common market factors affect the values of companies in particular industries, many analysts talk about "sectors" rather than specific companies within those sectors when making buy recommendations. The most important group in the last few years has been the technology sector. Prices of technology stocks skyrocketed during the latter part of the 1990s, but have since come back down to more realistic levels. Since many of these companies have yet to show a profit, they are not an investment for conservative investors. Even the few that seemed to be insulated from the general market trends have fallen in value in 2001. Most people who follow the technology sector agree that, once the dust settles, there will be a few companies that survive and a lot of failures over the next few years.

Other sectors include telecommunications (also fairly risky), retail, real estate, international, financial services, transportation, utilities, and industrial.

Market. There are many different marketplaces in which stocks are sold, and they are not mutually exclusive. In general, the stocks of most of the older, better-established companies in the United States are sold on the New York Stock Exchange (NYSE). Companies must meet certain size requirements in order to be eligible to trade on the NYSE. Smaller companies are generally traded on the NASDAQ stock exchange or on smaller regional exchanges. Nearly all the high-tech companies are traded on the NASDAQ, which is why there have been larger swings in value in the NASDAQ index over the last couple of years. Some companies, such as Microsoft, have voluntarily chosen to trade on the NASDAQ instead of the NYSE.

Risk

Historically, well-established companies in the transportation and utilities industries have paid higher dividends and have had less spectacular increases in value over time. These and other companies with long track records of solid performance have been lumped into a group called *blue chips.* This implies that investing in these companies will be a good long-term choice for investors who are unwilling to take the risk associated with start-ups and companies in more volatile industries. Dividend-paying stocks, which may or may not be blue chips, are often referred to as *income* stocks.

In general, smaller companies, assuming that they are successful, will have larger annual increases in value in the early years as they capitalize on growth opportunities. These companies will be unlikely to pay dividends, since they are plowing their earnings back into the company. You will hear them referred to as "growth" stocks.

How Do You Make Money From Investing in Stocks?

If a company is making a profit, there are two ways in which the common stockholders get a share of that profit. First, they may be given a dividend by the company, representing a proportion of the annual profits. Not all companies pay dividends, and those that do pay them generally do not give a very large one. One of the disadvantages of receiving your stock return in the form of dividends is that dividends are considered current income and are therefore taxable at your ordinary income tax rate. If you hold stock inside a tax-deferred vehicle such as a retirement account, however, the tax will not be payable until the money is withdrawn (e.g., at retirement).

The second way in which you can make money from stock investing is through the increase in the value of the stock itself, also known as a *capital gain*. However, in order to actually get the money, you will need to sell your shares. Also, unlike dividend income, the increase in share price may not be permanent. What goes up can also come down. If you sell a stock that you have held for more than a year, you will be subject to the more favorable capital gains tax rate, which currently has a maximum of 20 percent.

These two types of investment return—dividends and capital gains—are not mutually exclusive. Many companies pay small dividends, and investors in these companies may also realize appreciation in the stock price.

> *Example: Joan and Vickie decide to start a craft and sewing store. Each of them puts in $100,000 of her own money to lease a building and buy their starting inventory. They incorporate, and each receives 1,000 shares of stock. At the outset of the business, the company is worth $200,000, so each share is worth $100. If the company nets $20,000 after taxes the first year, Joan and Vickie can either put this into expanding the business or pay dividends to themselves of $10 per share. If they put the money back into the company, the company will now be worth $220,000, and so their shares will each be worth $110.*

What Causes Stock Prices to Go Up and Down?

The reasons for the ups and downs of stock prices are very complex, and there isn't anyone who can claim to truly understand them. In fact, if I knew exactly what caused stock prices to change, I would be a millionaire many times over. However, the basic idea is simple: The stock price should reflect the proportionate share of the underlying value of the company. If the company is doing better than expected, investors will want to buy the stock. More people buying the stock tends to drive up the price. If the company has experienced a decline, investors will not want to buy it, and some will try to sell their current shareholdings. People will not be willing to pay as much as the company was previously worth, so the price will have to fall.

The difficult part is estimating the underlying value of the company. Although finance professionals tend to agree that value is based on the potential for future cash flows, this is often difficult to estimate because of unknown factors. If you are looking at a company with a long history and an established market position, such as Wal-Mart, the future cash flows are fairly predictable. But what about an Internet company that has a good business plan but has not yet been able to realize a profit? This contrast illustrates an important factor affecting the riskiness of different stocks. A share of Wal-Mart will generate respectable returns over time and is unlikely to ever become worthless. The Internet company may or may not ever be profitable. If it does take off, the stock may eventually be worth many times its original value. But there is also a distinct possibility that it will be valueless in less than a year. So those who choose to take a chance on an extremely risky company may end up being millionaires or being bankrupt.

How Do I Measure Return on Investment?

The return on your investment is how much money you make for a given investment of dollars. In equation form, it is the dollars earned divided by the dollars you invested. So if a stock pays a dividend of $10 and doesn't otherwise increase in value, and you invested $100 per share, you have earned 10 percent on your investment. If instead of paying a dividend, the company plows the money back into the business, the change in the value of the stock is the amount earned, so that your return is ($110 − $100) divided by $100, or 10 percent.

If you have a small business, you usually cannot sell your stock, so the capital gain part of the return is only on paper. In addition, there will be a difference in after-tax return, since the dividend will be taxed at your ordinary income tax rate, which can be as high as 39.6 percent, whereas a capital gain is currently taxed at a maximum rate of only 20 percent. This goes a long way toward explaining why companies do not pay out a lot of dividends.

> *Example: Suppose you bought 100 shares of Sears stock on January 1, 2000, for $25 per share. Over the course of the year, you receive a dividend of 92 cents per share. On January 1, 2001, the value of each of your shares is now $35. You have earned a total return of 44 percent. The dividend yield was 0.92/25 = 4 percent and the capital gain (or price appreciation) was (35 − 25)/25 = 40 percent, for a total of 44 percent.*

How Risky Is Stock Investing?

Compare the Sears stock example to one in which investors didn't make out so well:

> *Example: Suppose you had bought Home Depot stock on January 1, 2000, for $70 per share. This stock paid only a 16-cents-per-share dividend in 2000, and on January 1, 2001, the stock price was $46 (although this was up from the $35 that it had dropped to during the course of the year). Your return on investment would have been −34 percent.*

Remember that the definition of risk is how different from the expected outcome the actual outcome can be. Suppose you looked at Table 8-2 and saw that stocks had returned an average of 13 percent over the last thirty years. If you start with that as an expectation, how likely are you to end up with a return on 13 percent or more on your diversified stock portfolio? A statistical measure of this aspect of risk is the standard deviation, which I mentioned in an earlier section of this chapter. Based on historical patterns, you have about a

95 percent probability of falling within two standard deviations of the average and a two-thirds chance of falling within one standard deviation of the average. Since the standard deviation for stocks is about 16 percent, two standard deviations is 32 percent, so you have a 5 percent chance of having annual returns of less than −19 percent (calculated by taking the return of 13 percent and subtracting two standard deviations, or 32 percent) or more than 45 percent. You have a one-third chance of having returns less than −3 percent or more than 29 percent. If you're a risk taker, that may look good to you, but for many of you who are not so inclined to risk taking, this may not seem like very good odds.

So why does anyone invest in stocks? The key factor here is *time.* If you hold your stock for longer periods, the ups and downs cancel out and, overall, the risk of your long-run return being more or less than expected gets smaller. This takes a strong stomach, and not everyone can do it. A recent study by two finance professors from the University of California found that women are actually better at this than men. They looked at the buying and selling behavior of men and women who had mutual fund investments. The men tended to trade a lot more frequently, and the women were more inclined to buy and hold. In the end, the men's portfolios had a slightly higher average return, but after accounting for the trading costs, the women were the winners.

Stock Mutual Funds

Take Advantage of Those Who Know More Than You

Despite the many books and articles touting surefire ways to make money in the stock market, stock investing is not something that should be undertaken lightly. Although I am a strong believer in taking risk in your portfolio in order to maximize your potential return, I do *not* think that the average person should do this on his or her own. As a busy woman, you are not likely to have sufficient time to spend tracking your portfolio and evaluating potential investments. Since there are people in the investment world whose full-time job is to stay informed about certain stocks and the economy, it is unlikely that you will ever have better information than they have.

If you invest through mutual funds with well-established track records, you will realize an average return that is appropriate for the level of risk that your fund takes on less the costs associated with paying professional managers. And if you hold these funds in a tax-qualified retirement (like an IRA), you can defer paying capital gains taxes on plan earnings. You will probably need to consult your accountant regarding the tax consequences of your investments. The different types of mutual funds are described in Table 8-3.

You Should Invest Only in No-Load Mutual Funds

Mutual funds can be load or no-load. A load fund is one that charges a fee when you initially invest (front-end load) or when you sell

Illustration by Kristopher S. Bajtelsmit

Table 8-3 Investment Characteristics

Aggressive Growth	Invest in highly risky companies that do not pay dividends. Sometimes called "small cap" because the companies they invest in are smaller. These newer companies may have potential for large gains in value, so the potential return is commensurate with the higher risk.
Growth	Invest in well-established companies that pay little in dividends and have potential for gains in value. Risk and return for these investments is moderately high.
Income	Invest in companies that pay most of their returns in the form of dividends. Growth potential will be lower, and the tax consequences of dividend income should be considered.
Index	Invest in a selection of securities designed to mimic a particular index, such as the S&P500, the Dow Jones, the New York Stock Exchange, or the NASDAQ. These funds' buy-and-hold strategies keep the administrative costs low.
Global	Invest in foreign companies or in U.S. companies with significant interests overseas. Some funds concentrate in particular geographic regions, such as Asia or Europe, and others are more broadly diversified.

(back-end load). These fees can range from 3 percent to 6 percent or more. Even with no-load funds, there will be other expenses. Each fund reports an operating expense ratio, and you should look at these in comparing different funds. The operating expense ratio is the ratio of the annual operating expenses and management fees to the net asset value of the fund. For no-load funds, this ratio shouldn't be more than 1.7 percent.

Index Funds Are a Good Choice for Long-Term Investing

An index fund is one that attempts to match a particular market index. An S&P 500 index fund will have all 500 stocks in it, and you will own a proportionate share. For index funds based on broader markets (such as the New York Stock Exchange, which has more than 2,000 different stocks traded, or the NASDAQ, which has several times as many), the funds will probably not own every stock in the market but will attempt to pick a set of stocks that closely mimics the index. Because these funds are not trying to outperform the market, and hence do not trade very much, they tend to have much lower expense ratios than actively managed funds—no more than 0.7 percent of the net asset value. There are a large number of index fund choices, so you can choose one that represents your risk and return preferences.

Choose Funds With a Good Track Record

Mutual fund prospectuses will always tell you "Past performance is no guarantee of future results," but there is still something to be said for experience. With so many mutual funds to choose from, and new ones being created all the time, it is important to see how the funds have weathered previous ups and downs in the marketplace. Since managers come and go, historical performance of more than five to ten years is probably not relevant, but the last several years will tell you a lot about how well the managers pick their portfolios and anticipate market movements. In the same way, you should not focus solely on very recent performance either.

If you choose an index fund, the question is whether the fund has accurately tracked the index that it is mimicking. In the case of actively managed funds, the goal is to do better than the indexes (otherwise you wouldn't want to be paying the extra fees), but in reality, only a small percentage of funds beat the market. Since the last year or so has not been great for the market, it is interesting to look at how well the different funds did in a down market.

If You Really Want to Invest in Individual Stocks

I am not a strong advocate of investing in individual stocks unless you have more financial savvy than average and are willing to spend a lot of time investigating particular companies. If you feel compelled to do so, here are a few tips.

Don't Invest Too Much in Your Employer's Stock

It is very tempting to invest in your own employer's stock. After all, you know more about that company and its management than you do about most other investments. Many companies have programs that allow their employees to invest in the company. The company's goal is to improve your productivity by giving you a stake in the outcome of your own hard work. In some cases, employers may even require that a large share of their contribution to your pension fund be in the company's stock. If you work for a great company with strong stock performance, this type of plan may seem like a boon, but you should remember the principle of diversification. If you have your investments, your retirement funds, and all your "human capital" tied up in the same company, where will you be if the company goes under?

Studies of pension fund investments show an interesting gender pattern with respect to company stock. Men are much more inclined than women to put their money into their employer's stock when given the choice. I'm not sure why this is the case, but my applause goes to the women.

Don't Invest Too Much in Any Single Investment

Again, you need to keep your diversification goal in mind. You should never have more than 5 percent of your total wealth invested in any single asset.

Invest in What You Like—But Do Your Homework

Several years ago, I taught an investments class for a group of fourth-graders. They were playing an investments game sponsored by the *Denver Post* in which they chose portfolios and tracked them for several weeks. After a couple of classes on the "ABCs" of stock investing, the students were given a chance to pick their companies. Their choices were somewhat predictable: ToysRUs, Coke, and Wal-Mart were the most popular.

Although the fourth-graders didn't know how to do any further investigation into these companies, their instincts were right. They reasoned that these companies had good products and services and would therefore be profitable. As an individual investor, however, you should do more than pick what you like. There are many resources on the Internet, several of which are listed in the appendix, that can help you track your portfolio, investigate different companies' track records, compare investments, and keep abreast of market developments.

Summary

If you have read this chapter, you now should know that:

- Taking more risk in your portfolio will give you more long-term return.

- Diversification is the key to achieving the best return for the least risk.

- Smart women don't follow the herd—they always try to buy low and sell high.

- You shouldn't be trying to beat the market.

- Busy women don't have time to be stock pickers—they let the professionals manage their money.

- Common stock is an equity ownership interest in a company and entitles you to a share in the profits of the company over time.

- Return on investment is a combination of current cash flows from dividends or interest and capital gains from the change in the value of the investment over time.

Most women (and many men as well, for that matter) have had the experience of suffering through a conversation with a neighbor or colleague who has to brag about the performance of his latest greatest investment. Maybe it's the guy in the next office who spends his lunch hour (and some of his work time as well) on the phone with his broker while you're eating lunch at your desk so that you can leave work early to pick up your son for soccer. Or it might be your neighbor's husband, who spends his evenings on the Internet tracking his portfolio while his wife makes dinner and helps the kids with their homework. The information in this chapter should be sufficient to let you critically consider this person's claims of investment success. In order to get the return, what kind of risk has he taken on? For each of his successes, how many failures did he invest in? How diversified is his portfolio?

More important, you are now armed with enough information to decide on your own strategy for stock investing. After reading a little more about investments with lower risk in Chapters 9 and 10, you will be able to make wise decisions that will put you on the path to achieving your financial goals.

CHAPTER 9

The "Fixed-Income" Misnomer
Municipal and Corporate Bond Investing

You need to read this chapter if:

✔ You don't know what a bond is.

✔ You are considering investing in bonds.

✔ You don't understand the different types of bonds and their risks.

When Anna was considering how to invest her contributions to her employer's pension plan, she attended a free information session offered by the plan sponsor. When she asked for advice on allocating her funds between bonds and stocks, the (male) financial adviser said, "Well, you're a woman, so you will probably want to invest mostly in bonds."

Believe it or not, this is a true story! Even if you don't feel you know much about investing, I hope that you can see the problem with the recommendation given to Anna. Being a woman, in and of itself, is not a reason to invest in a particular way. Perhaps this misguided man had observed in the past that women were less inclined to take risks in their portfolios. Or perhaps he simply had a predetermined notion that stock investing was a "guy thing." Whatever the reason, there is no excuse for this type of advice being given by a professional!

Although this chapter is focused on bonds, the basic investment principles from Chapter 8 also apply here. You still need to remember the basic rules of finance:

More risk means more return.

Diversification reduces your risk.

Buy low, sell high.

Everyone has the same information as you do.

Fixed-Income Securities

Bonds have often been called "fixed-income" investments because they pay interest at a rate that is set when the bond is first issued. In addition, the principal is completely repaid at maturity, unless the issuer defaults, so there is no risk of your not getting your money back. The assurance of a regular income may be very important to retirees or others without alternative sources of cash flow, and many investors are uncomfortable with the possibility of erosion of principal. However, these so-called safe investments have features that make them less attractive for long-term investing, in my opinion.

Bonds Are Risky, Too

Surprise! Despite their reputation as safe investments, bond prices are actually nearly as variable as stock prices. Take a look back at

Table 8-2—the standard deviations of returns are not quite as high as those for stocks, but the returns are lower, so, relatively speaking, bonds are nearly as risky. What makes bonds less risky than stocks is that they promise a certain cash flow from interest payments so long as the company has the money to pay it. But, even with this guarantee, you might not come out ahead of the game.

> *Example: Janet has $10,000 invested in bonds that pay 8 percent interest per year. Since her federal, state, and local income taxes total 30 percent, she nets 5.6 percent per year after taxes. If she needs to sell her bonds before maturity, they may not be worth the $10,000 she originally invested. And if inflation averages 4 percent per year, the buying power of her $10,000 in the future will be significantly less.*

What Is a Bond?

The Basics

In order to understand the pros and cons of bond investing, you need to understand the mechanics of this type of security. When you buy a bond, you have essentially loaned a company or a governmental entity the face amount of the bond, which is often in units of $1,000. In return, you are entitled to receive payment of interest at the "coupon rate," which is established at the time the bond is originally issued, from now until the end of the term of the bond, at which time you will also receive the face value of the bond back.

> *Example: Kmart needs money to finance the refurbishing of many of its stores and to expand some of them into "Super-Kmart" stores. Management estimates that the company will need $10 million. The company issues 10,000 twenty-year bonds with a face value of $1,000 each and a coupon rate of 10 percent. Mary buys one of the bonds for a cost of $1,000. She will receive a $100 interest payment (10 percent of $1,000)*

*per year for twenty years, and she will get the $1000 back at
the end of that period.*

The interest paid on the bond is your price for being willing to
let someone else use your money for the term of the bond. As long
as the company does not go bankrupt, you will be entitled to receive
that payment.

Risk

The risk of a bond depends on the soundness of the company or
governmental entity that issues it. Since a bond is essentially a loan
from the buyer (you) to the issuer (the company), you need to be
concerned about the company's ability to pay interest when it is due
and its ability to pay you back the face value at maturity (the end of
the term of the bond). Fortunately for investors, there are two independent agencies that regularly evaluate the creditworthiness of
bond issuers and rate them accordingly. Table 9-1 provides a summary of the rating system used by Moody's and Standard & Poor's.
Bonds that are rated AAA or Aaa are deemed to be the least likely to
default and will also generally give you a lower return. If you recall
one of our basic finance rules, more risk implies more return, so the
riskiest bonds will have to offer higher rates of return to attract investors and compensate them for the risk they are bearing.

Table 9-1 Measurements of Bond Risk

Creditworthiness, Risk Level	Bond Ratings	
	Moody's	Standard & Poor's
Highest grade, least risk	AAA	Aaa
High grade, low risk	AA	Aa
Good quality	A	A
Medium quality, moderate risk	BBB	Baa
Below investment grade, "junk"	BB	BA
Risky	B	B
Riskiest	CCC	Caa

Fluctuation in Bond Prices

When you put money in a CD or savings account, you are also being paid interest for letting the bank use your money during the time it is deposited. But if you decide to take your money out, the original amount that you invested is all there. With bonds, or any other type of security that has a market-driven price, the value will depend on what investors think it is worth at a particular time. So if you need to get your money back, you may find that your original investment has lost value in the interim.

Why do bonds lose value? When you first buy a bond, you make a judgment about the riskiness of the bond relative to other investment alternatives. If investors perceive a company as having a greater risk of default, they will require a higher interest rate to be willing to loan the company the money. If inflation is expected to be higher in the future, rates on newly issued bonds will rise along with the returns on all other investments in the marketplace to compensate for this risk. But since the coupon interest rate on a bond is fixed by the terms of the original bond contract, the amount of interest paid on an older bond cannot adjust to compensate investors for their greater (or lower) risk later in the life of that bond. The only thing that can change is the price.

Although I do not give you the mathematics of bond pricing here, a few simple rules will help you to understand what makes bond prices subject to price risk.

Change in Company Financial Condition. If you have locked in a long-term rate on a bond and circumstances change during the period the bond is outstanding, the interest paid on the bond will still stay the same, so you will be getting less (or more) return than the risk justifies. In order to compensate for this, the resale value of the bond will adjust to make the bond attractive to other investors. If the company's risk increases, the price will fall, and vice versa.

Example: Two years after Mary bought the bond in the earlier example, Kmart's financial performance is disappointing and the bonds are downgraded by the rating agencies (implying *that they have greater default risk). Mary thinks that she could get a 12 percent return on an investment with similar risk. She finds that the current value of her bond is only $854. Rather than take such a big loss, Mary decides to hold on to her bond in the hope that Kmart's performance will improve. Despite Kmart's poor performance, the company is still able to pay the $100 per year in interest.*

Change in the General Level of Interest Rates. Although company performance is certainly a major factor in the fluctuation in returns on a bond, much of that type of risk can be reduced by adequately diversifying a bond portfolio. If you hold bonds from many different companies, one may go down when another goes up, canceling out the ups and downs at the portfolio level. However, the overall level of interest rates generally plays a bigger role, and this affects all bonds to some degree, so that a diversified bond portfolio will still be subject to this type of risk. When the general level of interest rates goes up, bond values will decline across the board, and vice versa.

Example: In January 2001, the Federal Reserve decided to reduce interest rates in an attempt to avoid a recession. As a result, the required return for all bonds went down as well, although not necessarily by the same percentage. If required returns fall by ½ percent, then a bond with risk comparable to that of Mary's Kmart bond will provide a return of 11½ percent. The market value of her bond therefore moves to $887. Note that investors are still receiving the 10 percent per year coupon; they will receive the other 1½ percent of their required return in the form of a capital gain if they buy the bond at $887 and then get the $1,000 face value back at the end.

It's Not Always Bad News. Although we, as investors, are of course more worried about the downside risk, price fluctuations can operate in your favor as well. If you buy a bond at a time when the company is not highly rated and its ratings later improve, then the price will rise. This is because a lower-risk company will not need to pay as much in interest to attract investors. If you buy a bond when interest rates are high and they later fall, the price of your bond will increase, generating a capital gain to you. So your bond, with its higher interest guarantee, is now an attractive investment.

Don't get too excited, though. Most companies, when faced with the prospect of lower rates on bonds, will try to refinance their loans in order to reduce their annual interest expense, much as homeowners do with their mortgages during low-interest-rate periods. This is known as *calling* the bonds.

Types of Bonds and Tax Implications

Corporate Bonds

The examples that I have given all involved bonds issued by corporations to help finance their business operations. The holders of corporate bonds have essentially made a loan to the company and will be paid annual interest (often in semiannual installments). Corporate bonds can be issued with virtually any maturity date, but it is fairly common to see between fifteen- and thirty-year bonds. If you buy a bond from another investor, you may have a shorter maturity on your investment, since the bond may have been originally issued many years previously.

Interest paid on corporate bonds will typically be higher than that paid on less risky investments. The riskier the company, the higher the interest rate that will be paid. Bonds issued by corporations with ratings that are deemed "below investment grade" are often called *junk bonds*. These bonds have a much higher risk of default and therefore pay a higher rate of interest.

If corporate bonds are held in a nonretirement account, the interest paid to you will be taxable at your ordinary income tax rate. You will also be subject to taxes on gains made through buying and selling bonds, although if you hold them more than one year, you will be taxed at the lower capital gains tax rate.

Treasury Bonds, Notes, and Bills

The U.S. Government regularly borrows money to finance its operations. The difference between Treasury bonds, notes, and bills is the maturity of the security (or the length of time before the government pays you back your principal). Any Treasury securities with an original maturity of one year or less are called bills; those with maturity of up to ten years are called notes; and securities with longer terms are called bonds. Like corporate bonds, Treasury securities pay interest at regular intervals, and there is an active resale market. A further advantage is that the interest earned on these investments is exempt from state and local taxation.

Since all loans to the government are backed by the "full faith and credit" of the U.S. Government, these investments have a very low risk. As long as you hold them to maturity, the government has promised to pay you back the full principal amount when it is due. There is virtually no default risk, so the interest paid will be lower than that on corporate bonds with comparable terms. Generally, the longer the term, the higher the rate of interest you will earn, since you are subject to price risk and liquidity risk on longer-term investments.

Interest rates will have the same effect on Treasury securities as they have on other bonds: When rates go up, the value of existing lower-interest securities will fall, and vice versa.

Although it is fairly easy to purchase Treasury notes and bonds through brokerage firms or banks, Treasury bills are sold in large denominations and require that you participate in a government auction process in which you do not know what price you will pay until the auction is over. If you are interested in this type of investment, it is probably better to get into a mutual fund that invests in government securities rather than trying to do it on your own.

Municipal Bonds

State and local governments also finance their operations by borrowing money. In some cases, these bonds may be "general obligation" bonds, with proceeds that can be used for any purpose; in other cases, the funds may be earmarked for particular purposes, such as building schools, roads, or airports. Municipal bonds are usually issued with relatively long maturities, twenty years or more.

Interest paid on municipal bonds is usually exempt from federal taxation and may or may not be subject to state taxation. For this reason, you generally would not want to hold municipals in a retirement account, since you would be getting no additional tax advantage from the tax deferral. In addition, municipal bonds are generally priced with the tax benefit taken into account, so if you don't get the tax benefit, you will be paying too much for the bonds in the first place.

Interest rates paid on municipal bonds will depend on the viability of the governmental entity issuing the security. As with other investments, higher risk will imply higher return.

Example: When Denver built the Denver International Airport, it financed part of the construction with municipal bonds. As construction was nearing completion, there were problems with the new "state of the art" baggage-handling system, and the public became concerned that the airport would not open on time, therefore making default on the interest payments a possibility. The bonds were downgraded to "junk" status and prices fell precipitously. Investors who bought the bonds when their prices were low got a great deal, since the airport is now operating successfully.

A disadvantage of municipal bonds is that they do not have a very active resale market so, if you are concerned about the liquidity of your investment, the best way to invest in this type of security is through a mutual fund.

Zero-Coupon Bonds

A zero-coupon bond is an interesting type of bond that does not pay regular interest, but instead steeply discounts the price of the bond at the time it is issued. The interest is essentially all paid at the end when the investor receives the full face value.

Example: Phyllis is saving for retirement twenty years from now and therefore does not need or want to receive regular income from her investments right now. She has $50,000 to invest. She notes that twenty-year zero-coupon Treasury securities with $1,000 face value are currently priced at $250. If she puts all her money in this investment, she can buy 200 zero-coupon bonds, and in twenty years, they will pay her $200,000. This will be the equivalent of earning 7.2 percent per year.

A problem with zero-coupon bonds is that the IRS requires that, even though you have not actually received a payment of interest in a given year, you declare and pay tax on the interest earned annually rather than all at the end. In the previous example, Phyllis would have to pay tax on about $3,600 of "phantom interest" (7.2 percent of her original investment) each year. This can be avoided by holding the investment in a tax-deferred retirement account.

Zero-coupon bonds tend to have a lot more price variability than normal interest-paying bonds. This is primarily because they have no cushion of regular interest payments, so that any change in market rates must be entirely compensated for through a change in price. If you are a long-term investor, this should be of no concern to you, since you should be concerned only with receiving the face value at maturity.

Mortgage-Backed Securities

Although not technically called bonds, another group of securities with payment streams that resemble those of bonds is securities that are created by selling pieces of a pool of mortgages to individual investors. Commonly called *mortgage-backed,* this class of securities includes a lot of different types of investments that I will discuss only briefly here. The common factor among all of them is that the investors receive a proportionate share of the cash flows from the underlying pool of mortgages, much like a mutual fund. This will generally include a predictable stream of interest and principal payments. More complicated arrangements can also be created wherein some investors get the regular income and others get the capital gains.

Example: Suppose Nikki buys a house and finances it with a $100,000 conventional fixed-rate mortgage at 8 percent. The bank that originated her mortgage then sells the loan to a quasi-governmental agency that buys lots of mortgages. Examples include the Government National Mortgage Association (Ginnie Mae), the Federal National Mortgage Association (FannieMae), and the Federal Home Loan Mortgage Corporation (FreddieMac). Ginnie Mae may take one hundred similar mortgages and put them into a pool totaling $10 million. It then creates securities based on the pool of mortgages and sells them to investors. If each mortgage-backed security has an initial price of $100, Ginnie Mae could sell them to 100,000 investors. As Nikki and the others in the pool pay the interest on their mortgages, Ginnie Mae will pass through the payments to the investors, less a fee for management of the pool.

This type of security allows investors to participate in a diversified mortgage portfolio with low default risk (because the government guarantees against default), small minimum investments, and a fairly good rate of return. The downside is prepayment risk—when interest rates go down, you will not be able to maintain the rate of return on the pool in the long run, since the individuals in the mortgage pool will refinance their high-interest mortgages and the investors will simply get their principal back. And on the other side, if interest rates go up, you will be stuck with a lower-paying investment (and the resale price of your mortgage-backed security will fall as well). Another difference between mortgage-backed securities and bonds is that the payments to investors are not purely interest, but include some repayment of principal (since mortgages are amortized). To better understand amortization, check out Chapter 12.

If You Want to Invest in Bonds, Mutual Funds Are the Way to Go

You may be starting to see a pattern—I'm singing my favorite song again. As discussed in Chapter 8, it is probably not advisable for individual investors to attempt to manage a bond portfolio themselves unless they have a lot of time to do so. There are many bond mutual funds to choose from, differing in the types of bonds held, maturities, type of management (active versus buy and hold), and tax status. In general, bond fund managers add less value to your portfolio than stock fund managers, so an index fund may be the best choice.

Several differences between investing directly in bonds and investing in a bond mutual fund should be noted:

- A mutual fund will not have a maturity date, since the fund includes a mix of bonds with different maturities. In order to regain your principal, you will need to sell your shares in the mutual fund. The price of these shares will vary with market conditions in the bond market (when rates go up, prices go down).

- Your risk of default (not getting paid the interest or principal when due) should be lower, since it is diversified across all the bonds in the fund.

- Unless the fund is invested in tax-preferred securities or is held in a tax-deferred account, dividends paid by the mutual fund and capital gains on the sale of shares will be subject to regular taxation rules.

- The resale market for mutual fund shares may be better than the resale market for a particular bond. This will make it easier for you to get out of the investment if you need to for some reason—there is lower liquidity risk.

A Last Word About Bond Risk

The problem with bonds as investments is that individual investors often have the impression that they are "safe" investments. I hope you can now see that this is true only in a very narrow sense of the word. Bonds *do* pay a fixed rate of interest for a long period of time, so perhaps the word we should use is *predictable*. But this predictable stream of payments may turn out to be a bad deal (if market rates of interest increase or the creditworthiness of the company decreases), and you will not have the opportunity to renegotiate it. Furthermore, the taxability of bond interest reduces the net after-tax return to you.

The variability of bond prices in recent years has been almost as great as that of stocks, but the annual return from bond portfolios has been far less than that of stocks. Yes, it *is* true that bond portfolios far outperformed stock portfolios in the last year (when the stock market substantially declined), but when we look back at our portfolios over a longer time horizon, it is likely that the stocks will still have outperformed the bonds.

So what's the lesson for a long-term investor? If you are going to take on risk, you should get a return that is sufficient to compensate for that risk. For long-run investors (with investment horizons of ten years or more), a well-diversified portfolio of good-quality stocks will probably be a better bet. If you can't stomach the ups and downs of the stock market, buy into a mutual fund and never look at your statements.

Summary

If you have read this chapter, you now should know that:

- Bonds are not necessarily safe investments.

- Cash flows from bonds consist of regular payments of interest plus repayment of your principal at maturity.

- Bond prices fluctuate with market conditions, interest rates, and the financial condition of the company issuing the bonds.

- Increases in market rates of interest cause bond prices to fall, and vice versa.

- Treasury bills, notes, and bonds are U.S. Government debt and are the least risky type of fixed-income securities.

- Municipal bonds are issued by state and local governments and are generally exempt from federal income taxation.

- Corporate bonds are IOUs from corporations; the risk and return on this type of bond will depend on the risk of the company issuing them.

- Junk bonds are high-yield, high-risk bonds.

- Bond mutual funds are a good way for the average individual investor to invest in bonds.

In November 2000, I published a research study for the Employee Benefit Research Institute that I coauthored with my colleague Dr. Nancy Jianakoplos entitled "Women and Pensions: A Decade of Progress?" In that article, we compared the 1989 and 1998 investment allocations of working men and women in defined-contribution pension plans, using data from a national survey. The changes over the decade were encouraging. Whereas in 1989, about one-third of all men and women were invested mostly in bonds, by 1998, that number had fallen to 14 percent of men and 20 percent of women. The percentage that invested mostly in stocks rose from about one-fourth of both men and women to 44 percent of men and 41 percent of women. For women, the younger cohorts and those with greater wealth were more likely to be invested primarily in stocks. As more women take the time to educate themselves about their investment alternatives (and better understand the negative consequences of overly conservative investing), I expect that the differences between men's and women's portfolios will gradually cease to be a topic of conversation.

CHAPTER 10

The Price of Safety
Low Returns on Savings Accounts, CDs, and Money Market Securities

You need to read this chapter if:

- ✔ You think that low-risk investing is the way to build your wealth.

- ✔ You have more than a little bit of your portfolio in savings accounts, certificates of deposit (CDs), or other low-risk, low-return investments.

- ✔ You don't know the differences among the types of low-risk securities.

What Qualifies as "Low Risk"?

In this chapter, I discuss a class of investments called "cash-equivalent" or "money market" investments. This group includes bank deposits, Treasury bills, CDs, and money market mutual funds, all of which are short-term, are liquid, and have guarantees against default. As with the other investment categories discussed in this book, the basic rules of finance must guide your decision to invest some or all of your wealth in these assets. Based on what you have already learned, you should expect that lower risk will imply lower returns. The question you need to be asking yourself about these investments is, "Is safety worth the cost?" To answer this, you will need to understand the characteristics of the various assets in this category, their risks, and their rewards.

In Chapter 8, I outlined and defined a number of risks that you may be subject to when you invest: inflation risk, liquidity risk, default risk, price risk, and market risk. When you invest in stocks and bonds, you are exposed to all of these risks to some degree. In return for bearing this risk, you are rewarded with long-term returns in the form of current income and/or future growth. When you invest in cash-equivalent or money market securities, these risks are lower, and your returns will reflect that. Notice that I say "lower," not "eliminated." It is important to note that these types of investments are *not* risk-free.

In Chapter 9, you saw that bonds are riskier than they are often made out to be. Even though they are "fixed income," the issuer can default, the spending power of fixed cash flows erodes over time because of inflation, and the sale price of a bond sold before maturity may be less than the price at which it was bought. Because cash-equivalent investments have many characteristics similar to those of bonds, some of these factors will still be present, but to a lesser degree.

When It Comes to Your Savings, You Shouldn't Be Standing Still

Suppose you have been saving your extra dollars in a piggy bank, and you have accumulated the vast sum of $100 in August 2001. If you keep it in your piggy bank for another year and inflation averages 3 percent, that $100 will buy only the equivalent of what $97 would have bought you the year before. Inflation risk erodes the value of money over time, so that if you stand still, you lose ground.

What does that mean for your "safe" investments, that money that you have stashed in CDs and bank savings accounts? Well, it's pretty much like standing still. Depending on the rates of interest you are earning on these accounts compared to the rate of inflation, you may actually be losing ground. To see this clearly, think about the simple example of the piggy bank. Suppose you put your $100 in a savings account at the beginning of the year and earn 3 percent interest. If inflation averages 3 percent, you are back where you started, but at least you haven't lost any ground to inflation. The $103 now in your account will buy the equivalent of what $100 would have bought you the year before. But what if the goods or services that you need to purchase (such as medical care for retirees) have increased in price at a greater rate than average inflation? In that case, you will not be as well off as you were when you started.

Over the long run, "standing still" has a big cost. Table 8-2 showed that the annualized return on a stock portfolio averaged 7.5 percentage points more than inflation, whereas Treasury bills beat inflation by only 1.4 percentage points. Even long-term government bonds beat the money market investments by almost 4 percentage points. This means that, over time, an investment in stocks or bonds will result in a portfolio value that will be *several times larger* than the savings generated by a low-risk savings program.

The longer your time horizon, the greater the cost to you.

Example: Twin sisters Katie and Melody are both starting their first job after college and would like to begin saving for retirement. They each plan to put $2,000 into a retirement account each year for forty years and retire at age 62. Katie puts hers in a diversified stock fund, and Melody puts hers in a money market fund, currently earning 6 percent interest per year. After forty years of investment, here's the outcome:

Assuming that she maintains the 6 percent rate of return on her money market fund and reinvests all her interest, Melody's nest egg will be worth a little more than $300,000 when she retires.

By contrast, at an average return of 12 percent, Katie's in-

vestment will have grown to more than $1.5 million, five times that of her sister!

If you focus only on the short term, there may be times when low-risk investments will seem far preferable to stocks and bonds. For example, over the period from January through March 2001— only three months' time—most stock portfolios lost more than 10 percent of their value, whereas money market funds maintained their expected annualized return in the low single digits.

That's Why They Are Called "Money Markets"

Low-risk investments are often talked about as a group under the name "money market securities." All of these investments are similar to money in that they are liquid, they are often government guaranteed, and they don't fluctuate much in value in the short run. Regular bank accounts that pay interest have many similar characteristics and thus will offer returns that are similarly low. The primary difference is that, unlike money, bank savings accounts and money market securities do offer some protection against inflation risk by paying you a small annual interest rate. But, over the long term, these investments will not give you much more than that. And under some circumstances, inflation can still be a problem.

Example: Suppose that you expect inflation to be 3 percent in 2002. At the beginning of that year, you invest $10,000 in a bank savings account paying 4 percent interest. If your expectations turn out to be correct, the accumulated $10,400 in your account at the end of 2002 will provide you with 1 percent more spending power than you had when you made your deposit. But if inflation in 2002 ends up being 5 percent for the year, it will take $10,500 at the end of the year to buy the equivalent of what your initial $10,000 could have bought. You will have lost ground!

Types of "Safe" Investments

Bank Accounts

The easiest place to store your money is in a bank account. It's also just about the worst investment you can make. In fact, it's not really an investment at all, since it will not provide you with any growth over time. For that reason, you need to recognize the benefits and costs of these types of savings vehicles and compare them to the investment alternatives discussed in Chapters 8 and 9.

Checking accounts, passbook savings accounts, money market accounts, and short-term CDs all offer ease of opening the account, FDIC insurance up to $100,000, and easy access to your money for emergency purposes. Interest rates on these accounts vary from about 1 to 5 percent per year, depending on the restrictions that are placed on your ability to withdraw funds. Accounts with higher rates usually have more restrictions.

For example, banks may offer FDIC-insured money market deposit accounts that pay slightly higher rates than regular savings accounts. Although the rates are technically tied to the market, they will not respond to rising rates as quickly as you might hope. The price of getting the higher rate on your deposits is that you are usually limited to a certain number of withdrawals per month or per year. After inflation and taxes, even these accounts will lose ground over time.

Banks take the money that you have deposited and lend it out to other people. If they are able to make a mortgage loan at 7 percent interest, they get to keep the difference between this and the amount they pay you, an amount called the *spread*. Many people are surprised to find that they cannot automatically withdraw a large sum of money from their bank, but rather must give the bank a day or two's notice.

Certificates of Deposit

Short-term CDs offer slightly higher rates of interest than bank accounts but have some similarities. These securities are issued by banks and savings and loans and can have maturities that are very short (three months) or several years out. Like bank accounts, they are guaranteed against default, and there are no commissions.

The disadvantages of CDs relative to other comparable securities are related to taxes, fixed rates, and liquidity. The interest paid on CDs, like that on other bank accounts, is fully taxable by federal and state governments (as compared to Treasury bills, the interest on which is exempt from some taxes). So a 5 percent quoted interest rate will end up generating less than 3 percent after taxes. CDs lock in an interest rate for the entire period of your investment. If you invest in a CD when rates are rising, you will be stuck with that rate for the entire period (whereas rates on money market funds and bank accounts are usually adjustable). Of course, that can also work to your advantage if you lock in a high rate and rates later fall. Finally, although CDs generally allow you access to your money at any time, taking it out prior to maturity subjects you to an interest rate penalty.

Treasury Bills

Treasury bills, often called "T-bills," are short-term securities issued by the federal government and thus are free from default risk. Since Treasury securities are discussed in Chapter 9, I will focus here on the pros and cons of T-bills relative to other money market investments. Unlike the situation with bank accounts and CDs, interest is not paid directly to holders of T-bills. Instead, the T-bill is bought at a discount from the face value, and then the investor receives the full face value ($10,000) at maturity.

> *Example: The quoted yield on one-year T-bills is 5 percent. You purchase one T-bill with a face value of $10,000. The price you pay is $9,524. At maturity—one year later—you will receive $10,000. The difference between the purchase price and the face value is $476, which amounts to a 5 percent return on your original $9,524 investment.*

Relative to other money market alternatives, T-bills do have some disadvantages, particularly for small investors. Although the interest is exempt from state tax, which can result in substantial savings if you are in a high-tax-rate state, it is still subject to federal income taxation. T-bills have large face values, so it isn't possible to invest in small amounts. And, perhaps the biggest impediment for individual investors is that they are not that easy to buy. You must either mail in paperwork (in advance of a regular auction date) to the Federal Reserve or buy them through a broker.

Money Market Mutual Funds

Money market mutual funds are pools of money that are invested in a variety of short-term securities issued by corporations and government. To investors, these accounts operate much like bank accounts in that you can make deposits and withdrawals fairly easily by writing checks or using a debit card. The rate of return on the account fluctuates with market interest rates on a daily basis and thus can hedge inflation better than a fixed-rate bank account or CD. Accounts can be opened with small initial balances ($500 to $1,000), and subsequent additions can be even smaller. However, unlike bank accounts, money market funds are not insured or guaranteed in any way. These funds are available through most brokerage firms and are often used by investors as a temporary place to store money. Some money market mutual funds specialize in particular types of investments, such as municipal obligations or Treasuries, and therefore may offer some tax advantages that other funds will not have.

How Much and Which Type?

Most investment advisers will suggest that you have at least some amount of your portfolio in a cash-equivalent investment for emergencies. For young people, this should be kept to a bare minimum, since these investments are not going to contribute to your long-run wealth—they are just a temporary place to store some cash. If the car breaks down or you have an unexpected medical expense, you do not want to be in the position of having to sell stocks or bonds at a time when prices are low. Cash-equivalent investments will expose you to the least amount of price risk in these circumstances, and you will not be unnecessarily realizing taxable capital gains on long-term securities.

So how much should you have in cash equivalents? My suggestion is that you limit yourself to *two or three months* of your household expenses. If you have other sources of emergency cash, then you can reduce the amount you keep in cash equivalents even more. You want to have the cushion necessary to weather an emergency without overly limiting the growth potential of your portfolio. Keep in mind the purpose of this component of your portfolio and then choose your investment accordingly.

There is no need to diversify across different types of cash equivalents or different providers as long as you choose carefully in the first place. The purpose of this investment is to provide liquidity, which requires ease of deposit and withdrawal. So having multiple accounts adds unnecessary complexity. In my opinion, the best choice is a money market mutual fund from a well-established mutual fund group, brokerage house, or insurance company. The fund should have low expenses and a good track record (information available in the fund prospectus). You should not let yourself be lured by promises of extraordinarily high rates, since these will probably be associated with more risk than you want to take, either because the fund invests in longer-term securities or because it invests in lower-grade securities, neither of which you want.

Summary

If you have read this chapter, you should know:

- Low-risk securities will provide very low returns and will still expose you to inflation risk.

- You shouldn't have very much of your portfolio in cash equivalents—only as much as you may need to cover short-term emergencies.

- The common characteristics of cash equivalents are that they can be turned into cash quickly, they pay low rates of interest that is usually taxable (with the exception of state taxation on T-bills), and they have very low default risk.

- Higher yields on money market securities are associated with more restrictions or more risk.

There is a time and a place for low-risk investment. If you need liquidity for emergencies or if you are nearing retirement and cannot bear the risk of a volatile stock or bond market, then money market investments are clearly appropriate. But for those of you who are making investment choices to meet goals that are still fairly far in the future, assuming too little risk may mean that your goal will not be achievable or that it will take longer to achieve. Studies of investment differences between men and women have repeatedly come to the conclusion that women invest their portfolios more conservatively than professional money managers would advise. After reading Chapters 8 through 10, I hope you have come to realize that you may do yourself and your family a disservice if you do not consider taking more risk in your investment portfolio. This does not mean that you need to suddenly become a Wall Street expert. You can quite easily find a well-diversified stock mutual fund operated by a company with a good track record. And while you're at it, you can park a little emergency cash in a money market fund—but not too much.

CHAPTER 11

Planning for College

You need to read this chapter if:

- ✔ You have (or intend to have) children whom you plan to send to college.

- ✔ You don't know how much your children's education will cost.

- ✔ You would like to establish a savings plan that will be sufficient to cover future college costs.

- ✔ You don't understand the special types of investments that are available to fund higher education needs.

Aside from funding your retirement, sending your children to college will be one of the most expensive things you will do in your life. If you have no children or are beyond the child-rearing stage, you may not need to read this chapter. However, those of you who will eventually be grandmothers may want to take a closer look if you plan to help with your grandchildren's education expenses.

In this chapter, I help you to estimate the future cost of educating your children. Using this as a goal, you will be able to set up a plan to meet that goal.

The basic rules for college saving are fairly simple and are summarized in Table 11-1. Of course, as with most areas of your finances, saying this and actually doing something about it are two very different things. In this chapter, I provide a method for estimating your future education costs and developing a savings plan to reach your goal.

Start Early, and If It's Already Late, Start Now

If there's one thing that I hope will come across clearly in this book, it's the importance of beginning to save, for your goal, whatever it may be, as early as possible. With eighteen years of investing, the monthly payments necessary to produce a college fund can be manageable, but if you start later, the necessary level of payments will take a much bigger bite out of your budget.

Two Ends of the Spectrum

The Unprepared. When I started looking at colleges in 1974, my senior year of high school, I discovered that my parents had not been able to save much for my education. With five children (I am the oldest) and only one modest income, the costs of daily living had generally been a challenge, leaving little for savings. Through a combination of loans, help from my grandmother, and my own employment income, they were able to send me to the University of Virginia,

---

Table 11-1 Steps to Adequate College Saving

1. Start early.
2. Be realistic in estimating the costs.
3. Pay attention to taxes.
4. Set up a regular savings plan.
5. Stick with your plan.
6. Take advantage of government-sponsored savings programs and tax credits.
7. Make sure that your child contributes.

an out-of-state public university. Although I was an excellent student in high school, I didn't qualify for most scholarships because we were technically "middle income" and therefore didn't qualify for need-based financial aid. My mother completed her college education while I was in high school and began a career as an elementary school teacher, so the extra income was certainly a factor in my parents' ability to send all of us to college.

The Ultraprepared. Christie, a young woman in her twenties, is a member of a family with a clever method of saving for education. They have arranged a generation-skipping plan. The member of each generation, rather than saving for their own children, save for their grandchildren's education. Christie's education was therefore paid for by her grandparents, her own parents will pay for college for her children (and for her nieces and nephews), and she is currently saving for the education of her future grandchildren. This allows a much longer time to save—probably forty years or more. Of course, there could be problems if one generation has a lot more children than another, but presumably this can be worked out.

Where are you on the spectrum of preparedness?

I hope that, since you are reading this book, you will not be in as bad shape as my family was as my college years approached (with four siblings close behind), but you probably will not be in the enviable position of knowing that everything is taken care of, the way Christie was.

Be Realistic

There are two things you need to be realistic about. First, sending your kids to college will cost a lot of money. And second, it will not be that easy to get enough financial aid to make a significant dent in that cost.

Even though you have probably all heard the statistics about how much it will cost in the future to send your kids to college, most of you are probably not being realistic about how much you need to save to reach that goal. In the next section, I will help you to forecast how much it's going to cost, given the type of school you anticipate sending your child to and the level of tuition inflation. A warning here: You should be sitting down, because the sticker price is going to be a shocker.

Let's also start from the premise that, because you are developing a financial plan and saving for retirement, you will be financially healthy enough that your kids will not qualify for significant financial aid. There are a couple of exceptions to this. If you have a child who is a terrific athlete in a sport that is in demand at universities (such as football), a full ride might be in your future. (I have a nephew who is attending Princeton University under those circumstances.) Or, if you have a straight-A student who has a high SAT score and lots of extracurricular activities, there are various sources of scholarship money. But for the other 99.9 percent of you, planning for college should not be based on the assumption that financial aid will be forthcoming. Furthermore, assuming that you are doing this planning while your kids are still little, there's really no way to know whether your child will be one of the lucky ones, so you need to assume the worst-case scenario. Once college time rolls around, any financial aid you can get will be icing on the cake. (Check out *http://www.finaid.org* for financial aid information and *http://www.fastweb.com* for scholarship information.)

Finally, don't fool yourself into thinking that you will be able to get around the financial aid restrictions by playing games with your money. Some financial advisers will advocate various methods of hiding your money, making your kids look as if they are independent from you, etc. This is not a very good lesson to teach your kids, since it is in essence a form of cheating. But even apart from the moral issue, you may not want to shift the control of the money you have saved for college to the hands of an 18-year-old. More than one set of parents has been dismayed when their son or daughter decided to quit school and buy a hot rod or trek across Europe with "their" money.

How Much Will It Cost?

Are you sitting down? The way to estimate the cost of college in the future is to take the cost today and project it forward, using some assumptions about the inflation rate for tuition, fees, books, and room and board. Since there is wide variation in costs across types of educational institutions, you will also need to make some assumptions about where you plan to send your child to school.

Room and board does not vary that much from school to school, but tuition does. For example, tuition at an in-state community college today is likely to be less than $2,000 per year, whereas tuition at an Ivy League or other prestigious university for an out-of-state student can be more than $25,000 per year. Room and board is likely to run about $10,000 in either case, although you could clearly spend more than that, for example, for a private room, an apartment, more extracurricular activities, and travel. Many students who attend local colleges can save a lot by living with their parents.

Table 11-2 provides estimates for the cost of the first year of school for three different scenarios: an in-state public university, an out-of-state public university, and a private university. Since it is difficult to predict how much costs will rise each year, forecasts are provided for three different levels of annual cost increases: 2, 4, and 6 percent. The College Board estimates that tuition inflation is running about 4 percent for state schools and 5 percent for private schools, so these are relatively realistic values, barring unexpected future circumstances. You should take the first-year cost from Table 11-2 and multiply it by 4 to get an estimate of what you will need to have saved by the time your child begins college.

Future Cost of 1 Year of College (from Table 11-2) × 4

= _____

Example: Alex is the proud mother of a new daughter, Lana, and would like to begin a college savings plan. Using Table 11-2, Alex sees that the first-year costs for Lana will range from $17,139 for an in-state public education (if inflation in college costs is very low for the next eighteen years) to a high of

Table 11-2 Future Cost of One Year of College Tuition, Books, and Room and Board at Age 18, Assuming College Cost Inflation Averages 2%, 4%, and 6%

Child's Age Today	Public In-State School Annual College Cost Inflation			Public Out-of-State School Annual College Cost Inflation			Private University Annual College Cost Inflation		
	2%	4%	6%	2%	4%	6%	2%	4%	6%
18	12,000	12,000	12,000	18,000	18,000	18,000	35,000	35,000	35,000
17	12,240	12,480	12,720	18,360	18,720	19,080	35,700	36,400	37,100
16	12,485	12,979	13,483	18,727	19,469	20,225	36,414	37,856	39,326
15	12,734	13,498	14,292	19,102	20,248	21,438	37,142	39,370	41,686
14	12,989	14,038	15,150	19,484	21,057	22,725	37,885	40,945	44,187
13	13,249	14,600	16,059	19,873	21,900	24,088	38,643	42,583	46,838
12	13,514	15,184	17,022	20,271	22,776	25,533	39,416	44,286	49,648
11	13,784	15,791	18,044	20,676	23,687	27,065	40,204	46,058	52,627
10	14,060	16,423	19,126	21,090	24,634	28,689	41,008	47,900	55,785
9	14,341	17,080	20,274	21,512	25,620	30,411	41,828	49,816	59,132
8	14,628	17,763	21,490	21,942	26,644	32,235	42,665	51,809	62,680
7	14,920	18,473	22,780	22,381	27,710	34,169	43,518	53,881	66,440
6	15,219	19,212	24,146	22,828	28,819	36,220	44,388	56,036	70,427
5	15,523	19,981	25,595	23,285	29,971	38,393	45,276	58,278	74,652
4	15,834	20,780	27,131	23,751	31,170	40,696	46,182	60,609	79,132
3	16,150	21,611	28,759	24,226	32,417	43,138	47,105	63,033	83,880
2	16,473	22,476	30,484	24,710	33,714	45,726	48,047	65,554	88,912
1	16,803	23,375	32,313	25,204	35,062	48,470	49,008	68,177	94,247
0	17,139	24,310	34,252	25,708	36,465	51,378	49,989	70,904	99,902

$99,902 for one year at a private university (assuming that costs rise at a rate of 6 percent annually). Since Alex feels that a public university education is more realistic, she decides to target saving for something between these two extremes. Assuming inflation at 4 percent, an out-of-state public university education will cost $36,465 in the first year. Multiplying this by 4, Alex estimates that she will need to save $146,000 by the time Lana is 18.

Although this estimate ignores the fact that your accumulated funds will continue to earn interest for you while your child is in college, it also ignores the fact that college costs will continue to increase over the four years that your child is in school. If you assume that your funds will at that time be in a relatively low-return, low-risk investment, your investment should earn approximately enough to cover the annual increase in costs.

Now That You Know the Bad News, What Can You Do to Get There?

The next step is to estimate how much you need to save each month or year to achieve the college fund goal. This will definitely be easier if you are starting early than if you begin when your child is getting closer to high school.

The College Fund Factor. Table 11-3 provides a set of factors that will allow you to calculate your monthly payment. Since the amount that you need to save each month depends on the investment return that you will get on that money, you need to make an assumption about your annual after-tax return on investment. I have provided factors for a range of investment return assumptions, but it is probably a good idea to make conservative assumptions, particularly if your son or daughter is no longer an infant, and you don't have a long investment horizon.

Pay Attention to Taxes

In comparing alternatives for college saving, there are definitely ways to reduce the tax impact. Since taxes can take a big chunk out of your savings, you should always consider alternatives based on the end result. In the latter part of this chapter, I outline some of the tax-preferred methods of saving for college, such as education IRAs and qualified state tuition plans. But in the end, you need to have a certain number of dollars saved. If you have to pay taxes on the investment returns of the college fund, those dollars will not be available to you later, so the amount that you have after taxes is the relevant figure.

> *Example (continued): Alex thinks that she can earn an after-tax rate of return of 6 percent in a moderate-risk investment.*

Table 11-3 Monthly College Fund Factor
(Multiply factor by college fund goal to get monthly payment required.)

Child's Age Now	Months to Goal	Assumed After-Tax Investment Return				
		4%	6%	8%	10%	12%
17	12	0.081817	0.081066	0.080322	0.079583	0.078849
16	24	0.040092	0.039321	0.038561	0.037812	0.037073
15	36	0.026191	0.025422	0.024670	0.023934	0.023214
14	48	0.019246	0.018485	0.017746	0.017029	0.016334
13	60	0.015083	0.014333	0.013610	0.012914	0.012244
12	72	0.012312	0.011573	0.010867	0.010193	0.009550
11	84	0.010335	0.009609	0.008920	0.008268	0.007653
10	96	0.008856	0.008141	0.007470	0.006841	0.006253
9	108	0.007708	0.007006	0.006352	0.005745	0.005184
8	120	0.006791	0.006102	0.005466	0.004882	0.004347
7	132	0.006043	0.005367	0.004749	0.004187	0.003678
6	144	0.005422	0.004759	0.004158	0.003617	0.003134
5	156	0.004898	0.004247	0.003664	0.003145	0.002687
4	168	0.004450	0.003812	0.003247	0.002749	0.002314
3	180	0.004064	0.003439	0.002890	0.002413	0.002002
2	192	0.003727	0.003114	0.002583	0.002126	0.001737
1	204	0.003431	0.002831	0.002316	0.001879	0.001512
0	216	0.003169	0.002582	0.002083	0.001665	0.001320

Using Table 11-3, she locates the appropriate factor for a newborn at 6 percent return—0.002582. Multiplying this times her goal of $146,000, Alex calculates she will need to save $376.97 per month. She notes that if she can increase her after-tax investment return to 8 percent, she will be able to fund the account with payments of only $304, and if she can earn 10 percent, the payments will be only $243.

Be Creative in Your Tax Planning. Once you focus on the tax implications, you may find that traditional saving is not the way to go at all. In order to earn 8 percent after taxes, Alex must invest in a relatively risky asset earning 11 percent or more per year. What if instead of putting the money in her college fund, Alex added the contribution to her 401(k) plan instead? Most retirement plans allow participants to borrow from their accounts to fund educational needs at relatively favorable rates. The contributions are deductible from current income, and the later borrowing does not trigger taxation, since it is not a "withdrawal."

> *Example: Assume that Alex has a marginal tax rate of 28 percent. She contributes an additional $417 per month to her 401(k) plan in pretax dollars (the equivalent of $300 after tax). In addition, she will save the taxes she would have paid on the earnings in the fund each year. Alex will be able to accumulate $281,029 in eighteen years of investing in the 401(k), compared to $144,025 in a comparable taxable savings account. Alternatively, Alex could contribute $217 per month to the 401(k) to meet her goal of $146,000.*

What if you didn't plan ahead?

> *Example: Sally is a single mom with two kids, Ryan, age 6, and Susan, age 8. She has been struggling to make ends meet and has no savings. She has just received a promotion that will mean about $600 more per month in after-tax income, and she wants to begin a college fund for her kids. She realistically expects that her kids will need to go to an in-state college. Using Table 11-2, she estimates that Susan's education will cost $19,212 per year and Ryan's will be $17,763 per year, or about $77,000 and $71,000 for four years.*
>
> *Using Table 11-3, Sally is dismayed to find that, because she has started saving so late, the monthly payment required to meet her goal, assuming an after-tax return of 6 percent, will be $76,000 × 0.004759 = $362 for Ryan and $71,000 × 0.006102 = $433 for Susan, for a grand total of $795. Although her raise is not quite sufficient to meet this goal, Sally figures that some of the college costs will be covered by her children's savings from jobs, and she also knows that she will receive further raises in the future, so she will be able to increase her monthly contribution to the fund in the future.*

Help on the Internet

As an alternative to using the tables in this chapter, there are also resources available on the Internet. A particularly easy tuition savings calculator is located at *http://www.banksite.com/calc/tuition*. You can enter the current tuition of any school, an estimate of annual tuition inflation, the number of years until your child goes to college, your current savings, and your annual contribution to determine whether you are saving enough. A similar calculator, as well as additional tips on saving for college and finding scholarship money, is available at *http://moneycentral.msn.com/family/home.asp*.

Stick With Your Plan

Many people begin saving with great intentions, but find reasons to dip into college savings accounts. Bills need to be paid; the car breaks down; the family really needs a vacation. Whatever your excuse, you should keep in mind that if you take the money out, you lose all the power of compound interest and you will need to put a lot more money in later to make up for the dollars you have siphoned off. In tax-preferred savings plans such as IRAs, withdrawals trigger taxes and penalties as well.

Getting Government Help

Recognizing the difficulty that families have in saving for college, the federal government and many state governments have created programs that make it easier and cheaper to plan ahead. In this section, I outline several of the alternatives, but you will probably want to consult more detailed references on these topics. Your financial planning professional may also be a good source of information on the pros and cons of alternatives in your jurisdiction.

Education IRA

The Education IRA, which isn't really an IRA at all, was established under the 1997 Taxpayer Relief Act. The federal government allows you to invest up to $500 per year in a custodial account or trust, usually maintained by a financial institution, exclusively for the purpose of paying for qualified higher education expenses for the named beneficiary of the account, who must be under the age of eighteen.

The contribution limit is phased out for those with higher incomes, so that you can take the $500 maximum only if your adjusted gross income (AGI) for federal taxes is less than $95,000 for singles and $150,000 for joint returns. If your AGI is more than $110,000 ($160,000 for joint returns), no contribution can be made.

The tax advantages of the education IRA are that the contributions are tax-deductible at the outset and the distributions are not taxed when withdrawn unless the amount withdrawn exceeds the qualified education expenses for that year.

Hope Scholarship (HOPE) Credit and Lifetime Learning Credit

Also established under the 1997 Taxpayer Relief Act, the HOPE credit and the Lifetime Learning Credits allow a taxpayer to claim up to $1,500 per year per student as a credit. The HOPE credit is 100 percent of the first $1,000 of qualified tuition and related expenses plus 50 percent of the next $1,000, and it is available only for the first two years of undergraduate education. The Lifetime Learning Credit is 20 percent of up to $5,000 in education expenses for you, your spouse, or any dependent, for a current maximum of $1,000. To qualify, the student must be enrolled in a degree or certificate program on at least a half-time basis.

The HOPE credit will increase with inflation beginning in 2001. The maximum Lifetime Learning Credit will change to 20 percent of $10,000 beginning in 2003, but it will not be indexed to inflation.

If an expense is claimed as an education deduction or if the student receives any tax-exempt distribution from an education IRA in a given year, these credits cannot be taken. The HOPE credit and the Lifetime Learning Credit can be used in the same year as long as they are covering different qualified expenses.

Both credits are subject to the same earnings limitations: The full credit is available for singles with up to $40,000 in AGI and joint filers with up to $80,000, and the credits are phased out after an AGI of

$50,000 for singles and $100,000 for joint returns. Those who are married filing separately cannot use the credit.

Section 529 State-Qualified Tuition Plans

Qualified state tuition plans are state-based, although the statutory authority for establishing them is laid out in the IRS Tax Code Section 529. Because states have some leeway in establishing the rules for these plans, there is wide variation in the plans offered. Many states allow nonresidents to participate, and there is active competition to attract investors. To compare different states' offerings, check out *http://www.savingforcollege.com.*

There are two main types of 529 plans: savings programs and prepaid tuition programs. This section outlines the features of these plans and then provides some more details on how the plans operate.

Common Features of 529 Plans. Both prepaid tuition plans and savings programs provide federal tax deferral for the earnings on plan assets until withdrawal, at which time they are taxed at the beneficiary's tax rate. Most states also allow deferral of state income taxes for residents, and some even allow a deduction for contributions made.

Unlike most federal tax relief for college expenses, Section 529 plans are not subject to income limitations, and they have fairly high maximum contribution levels. You can use the HOPE and Lifetime Learning Credits in the same year that you use Section 529 dollars to fund educational expenses. However, Education IRA contributions cannot be made if you contribute to a Section 529 plan.

The donor also has the advantage that he or she maintains control of the account. The beneficiary does not even have control over the withdrawals, and, in the event that you need the funds for other purposes, you can even reclaim the funds under most state plans. If your child chooses not to go to college, the account can be transferred to a different beneficiary.

Your contribution to the Section 529 plan is treated as a gift to the beneficiary, but it is subject to some special gifting rules. The

normal gift tax limitation of $10,000 per year per recipient is acceler-
ated to allow a contribution of $50,000 in a single year covering the
next five years of gifts. This can be particularly beneficial to anyone
who is trying to reduce the size of his or her estate for estate tax
purposes.

Prepaid Tuition Plans. In a prepaid tuition plan, the state allows you
to purchase tuition units by making a lump-sum payment today or a
series of payments until your child goes to college, that will be sufficient to cover a unit of state tuition. For example, the state may take
current tuition levels and divide by 100 to determine the value of one
tuition unit. To fully pay for four years of tuition, the donor would
need to purchase 400 units of tuition.

The estimated future cost of tuition is used to calculate the "fair"
value of that tuition today so that the payments into the fund will be
invested to meet that goal. The advantage of this plan is that, if tuition inflation exceeds the estimate made by the state fund, you are
still guaranteed the number of units of tuition that you have paid for.

*Example: June has a daughter, Lyn, who is 12 years old. Her
state has a guaranteed tuition plan that requires a payment
of $215 per month for six years to guarantee four years of tu-
ition for Lyn. Tuition for a four-year state college currently is
$3,000 per year.*

Although the assumptions made by the state plans vary, they are
generally conservative, estimating higher tuition inflation and lower
investment returns, so that your net investment return will be relatively low. In the previous example, a payment of $215 is consistent
with an assumed 6 percent tuition inflation rate and an investment
return of 3 percent. If it turns out that the fund earns a 5 percent
return on investment and tuition increases at a rate of only 5 percent,
the state will have collected more from you than it needed to, but
the only thing that you have bought is the right to have your tuition

paid for by the state. In other words, you don't get the benefit of good performance.

A last but important point about prepaid tuition plans: In computing your eligibility for financial aid, the prepaid tuition will be counted as an asset to your child. Since college aid formulas presume that your child is contributing a substantial portion of his or her wealth to educational costs, this will reduce his or her eligibility for aid. Parents are not expected to contribute as large a percentage of their wealth for college, so the same investment held in your name would have less effect on financial aid eligibility for your child.

State College Savings Plans. This type of plan generally allows parents to save money for college in a special account that operates like a mutual fund. Since the plan assets are professionally managed and regular contributions are often set up as automatic withdrawals or payroll deductions, it is an easy way to invest. Most plans offer alternative investment options with varying degrees of risk and return.

> *Example: The Colorado Scholars Choice College Savings Program, initiated in 1999, does not require residency, but it charges an additional $30 fee for nonresidents. Program management fees are less than 1.3 percent. The maximum contribution is $150,000, and contributions are fully deductible from Colorado taxable income. Minimum contributions are $25 for the initial contribution and $15 for subsequent contributions, but payroll deduction deposits can be lower. The investment options can be age-based but also include 100 percent equity and 100 percent fixed-income options.*

The college savings plans are generally preferable to prepaid tuition programs. Although these investments are clearly riskier, particularly if you invest in equities, they will generally provide a better rate of return. This means that you will be able to fund the same amount of tuition costs with a lower contribution level. More important, the assets are counted as belonging to the donor, not the beneficiary, for financial aid purposes.

Borrowing the Money

So what happens if the day of reckoning comes and you don't have enough money to send your child to the school she or he wants to attend? Assuming that you have already weighed the pros and cons of school choices and now are simply looking at the financial question of how to do it, there are few alternatives, and they all involve borrowing money.

Should You Take a Second Mortgage?

For many families, their single largest asset is the family home. For women, housing equity makes up an even larger percentage of wealth. If you purchased a home when your children were young, let's say fifteen years ago, you will have paid off about 25 percent of the principal and your home will probably have appreciated significantly in value. If you estimate conservatively that your home appreciated 5 percent per year, it will have more than doubled in value over the fifteen years.

A lender will generally allow you to take a second mortgage on your home that brings your total mortgage indebtedness to 75 to 80 percent of the value of the home. Subject to the limitations on income that are discussed in Chapter 12, you may borrow the difference between 80 percent of the home's value and the current mortgage balance. Second mortgages often have shorter terms than first mortgages—for example, fifteen years instead of thirty—so the monthly payment will be higher than that for a comparable thirty-year mortgage.

Example: Suppose that Alex, in the first example in this chapter, didn't manage to save any money toward college for Lana, but instead had purchased a home for $100,000 fifteen years ago. At that time, she borrowed $95,000 at 8 percent for thirty years. Her home is now worth $208,000 (an increase of ap-

proximately 5 percent per year), and the remaining balance on her mortgage is about $73,000. The maximum that her bank will lend her is 0.75 × $208,000 = $156,000 minus the other mortgage amount of $73,000, for a total of $83,000. The payments on a fifteen-year mortgage of that amount at 9 percent will be about $842 per month, and she will still have to make the payments of $697 on her first mortgage, for a total of $1,539.

It may be preferable to simply refinance your first mortgage for the larger amount rather than keeping the first mortgage and paying for a second mortgage on top of that. A fifteen-year mortgage in the amount of $156,000 at 8 percent will require a payment of only $1,490. If you refinance for a longer period, the payment will be lower, but you will have to pay it for a longer period of time. In any case, the obvious downside to using a mortgage to pay for educational needs is that long after your child is self-supporting, you will still be making those payments. If you are 50 when your child starts college, a fifteen-year mortgage will require payments until you are 65, which may be well past your planned retirement age. However, the tax deductibility of the interest payments makes them preferable to other types of loans that do not share that feature, provided that mortgage rates are reasonable.

The Tax Advantages of Using Home Equity

Just as you can use your 401(k) to store away college savings, you can use your home mortgage as a tax-preferred method of saving. Increases in the value of your home are essentially tax-free under current tax law. Interest paid on mortgage loans is tax deductible. These two advantages make your home a valuable college saving resource. If, instead of contributing to a college fund, you make extra payments on your mortgage, thus increasing the equity in your home, that money will be available to borrow against at a later date.

Example: Suppose that Alex had made an additional $300 contribution to her mortgage payment each month instead of *putting it into a college fund for Lana. This additional amount is not tax deductible in the year she makes the payment because it is a payment of principal rather than interest. However, her entire mortgage will have been paid off in year 13 of the loan. This will mean that she can take a new first mortgage before Lana goes to college, and all the interest she pays on that loan will be tax deductible.*

What About Student Loans?

Student loans are available through most savings institutions and usually offer rates of interest that are lower than those on alternative unsecured loans. Interest rates may vary depending on credit record and financial resources. In most cases, no payments will be due until the student is no longer a full-time student. Some loans do require that interest be paid prior to graduation.

The loan is technically the responsibility of the person who is receiving the education—that is, your child. However, parents must be cosigners, since the student generally has no means of support.

Your Child's Contribution to His or Her Education

In Table 11-1, I listed several important steps in saving for college. The last one was to make sure that your child contributes to his or her education. The reason this is important is not simply because it cuts down on the amount you need to save. Generally speaking, the amount of money that teens can earn toward their education is only a small fraction of the total cost. However, if your child contributes, he or she learns that college requires sacrificing of other expenditures. I recommend that at least half of every dollar that a teenager earns should be required to go into the college fund, whether or not you think that his or her money will be necessary. Even if you are independently wealthy, you should want your children to take some responsibility for their education.

In my own case, my parents told me that I had to save enough for my incidental expenses. In 1975, we estimated that about $15 per week would be required for these expenses, so that meant that I needed about $500 for the school year. This doesn't sound like a lot until you remember what the minimum wage was twenty-five years ago. And it turned out that $15 was far too little. Although I didn't *need* to eat out, since I had a meal plan at school, college social life often centered around food—going out for pizza or to parties. And there were numerous activities that required small extra fees. The college admissions office will usually give you an estimate of expected incidental expenses, but you should expect that these may be higher, especially if your son or daughter pledges a fraternity or sorority.

My own children, at ages 15 and 16, are quickly approaching their college years. I am using the 50 percent rule for them, and their attitudes toward this restriction differ because of their very different money personalities. Kristopher, my oldest, is a spender, and Kyle is a saver. After many years of having limited resources and spending nearly every dollar that has come his way on CDs, video games, collectibles, and guitar paraphernalia, Kris is resistant to being forced to save his hard-earned money. Kyle, on the other hand, has saved nearly $1,500 over the years from birthdays, Christmas presents, and jobs. He takes pride in his thriftiness, and I doubt we will need to monitor his behavior to ensure that 50 percent of what he earns goes into the college fund. He is likely to relish his increasing account balance more than he would enjoy any of the things he could buy with it.

You may end up with kids who are more like one or the other of my two sons, but the important thing to keep in mind is that they probably will not change their attitudes toward money while they are in college. You should expect to have to ration money to the spender, perhaps by depositing a certain amount in a checking account each month, whereas you can probably delegate responsibility for money management to the saver.

Summary

If you have read this chapter and completed the worksheets, you now should know:

- How much your child's college education is likely to cost in the future

- How much you need to be saving each month to meet your college fund goal

- The costs and benefits of various government-sponsored savings alternatives

- The costs and benefits of borrowing to cover college costs

The realities of the high-tech world we live in make a college education a prerequisite for our children's financial success. But the costs of higher education are high enough that it isn't reasonable to expect children to be able to foot the entire bill by themselves. With this in mind, your financial plan needs to include adequate savings to meet the expected costs of your children's, and/or your grandchildren's, education. Absent such a plan, as your children head off to college, you may find yourself dipping into resources that are earmarked for other purposes. If your child later qualifies for scholarships, goes to a less expensive school, or chooses not to go to college, your savings can easily be shifted to other needs.

CHAPTER 12

Buying a Home

You need to read this chapter if:

- ✔ You don't know whether you should rent or buy a home.
- ✔ You have never bought a home or are unsure about the process.
- ✔ You don't know how to choose a real estate agent.
- ✔ You don't know how to choose between types of mortgages.
- ✔ You don't know how much mortgage you can qualify for.
- ✔ You don't know how much house you can afford to buy.
- ✔ You don't understand what will happen at the real estate closing and what your potential costs will be.

Your home is probably the biggest purchase you will ever make. Many of you may have already purchased one or more homes over your lifetime. If so, then you know that it is a complex transaction involving many steps and decisions. Understanding this process and the choices that you need to make can save you many thousands of dollars. Women face special challenges in this financial process because they may not have adequate credit or work history, and they may find that mortgage lenders and realtors are suspicious of their ability to carry a large loan on their own. All of these problems can be alleviated or avoided by doing a little financial homework and having the correct answers to questions that will be asked by professionals with whom you must deal. In this chapter, I provide you with all the basic information you need in order to make the process of buying a home more understandable and, hopefully, less costly to you.

Table 12-1 provides you with a basic outline of your decision process. The explanations and worksheets in the remainder of this chapter are the tools that will allow you to make an informed decision when you choose a home, whether you are a renter, a first-time home buyer, or a bigger-home buyer.

Should You Rent or Buy?

Deciding whether to rent or to buy is not always an easy decision, and there are many factors to consider. Home ownership has come to be an expectation of the baby boom generation, and the "bigger is better" mentality has resulted in a building boom in some areas of the country. In my town, most new homes are in the $250,000 and up price range, many with a square footage of 3,000 and more. (Think about the cleaning!)

When we first moved to Fort Collins in 1991, my husband and I could not afford to buy a house because we had not been able to sell our previous house in New Jersey. I was surprised to find that I was actually embarrassed to admit to people that I was renting, particularly as the situation dragged on for several years. However, after owning our own homes for many years previously, my husband and I found that there were certain advantages to being renters. After a couple of years, we probably could have bought a smaller home and waited until we unloaded the New Jersey property to move up, but instead we decided to buy some land and continue to rent until we could build the right house. We made this decision not for financial reasons, but for personal reasons, such as where our kids would go

Table 12-1 The Financial Steps to Home Ownership

Requirements:

    a. Calculator

    b. Pen or pencil

    c. Your basic financial information

1. Decide whether to rent or buy.
2. Determine how much you want to and can afford to spend on housing. (Use the worksheet in Table 12-2, Step 1.)
3. If you plan to buy,

    a. Calculate the maximum mortgage you can afford. (Use the worksheet in Table 12-2, Steps 2 and 3.)

    b. Calculate the maximum house you can afford. (Use the worksheet in Table 12-2, Step 4.)

4. Investigate your mortgage choices and choose the right mortgage for you.
5. Learn about the real estate purchasing process.
6. Choose a real estate agent.
7. Choose a home.
8. Learn about the closing process and estimate closing costs.

to school and the time and aggravation of moving. To help you in your decision, the following list summarizes the advantages and disadvantages of renting and buying. Some of these are financial and others are personal, so each of you needs to weigh the relative merits for her own circumstances.

Rent

Advantages

- There are usually no maintenance or repair costs on building or appliances.

- It is easier to relocate on short notice.

- Rent is usually cheaper than financing costs for a comparable-sized property.

- It is easier to move up to a nicer home.

- The landlord sometimes pays for certain utilities.

- Renter's insurance is cheaper than homeowner's insurance (since it covers only your personal possessions).

Disadvantages

- Rent increases over time, sometimes faster than the rate of inflation.

- Rent is not tax deductible, although some states give state tax credits to renters.

- You usually are not guaranteed to be able to stay beyond the term of the lease.

- Renting does not provide you with any investment return.

- The landlord can restrict your usage of the property.

- You usually cannot upgrade the property (and if you do, the landlord will own any improvements that you make).

Buy

Advantages

- Interest is tax deductible.

- Capital gains on sale are not taxed (up to a limit).

- The value of the home increases over time (usually faster than inflation).

- Monthly mortgage expense is usually fixed for thirty years.

- You can make improvements to the property and reap the benefits.

Disadvantages

- You must generally have a sum of money saved for a down payment.

- You must pay for repairs.

- The mortgage expense is often higher than rent in the early years (for a comparable-sized house).

- Home prices sometimes depreciate, so you may lose money if you have to sell.

- Relocating is more difficult and costly.

- Your home value is somewhat dependent on the quality of your neighborhood and how well your immediate neighbors take care of their property.

After looking at the advantages and disadvantages of each, you should make your own decision as to whether to rent or buy. In the later sections of this chapter, I elaborate on some of the financial aspects of buying that might influence this choice.

For most of the problems in this chapter, I use the following example (and there is space on the worksheets for you to do calculations for your own financial situation):

Example: Mary is single and earns $45,000 per year ($36,000 take-home pay). She rents a condominium ($1,000 per month, which includes the condo fee of $100) but would like to buy a house. Mary has just found out that her rent will increase to $1,100 per month for the next lease period. When she first rented her condo five years ago, the rent was only $850. Mary's total monthly expenses, not including housing costs, are $1,500 per month, including payments on her credit cards and a car loan payment of $350 per month. Her accumulated savings amounts to $15,000. Mary does not itemize deductions on her taxes.

How Much Mortgage Can You Afford?

Many people roughly estimate how much house they can afford and then proceed to look for one before doing a more careful consideration of the expected expense, and this often leads to disappointment. Mary, for example, might assume that she can afford a mortgage payment of about the same amount as her rent. If she decides to buy a condominium, however, she must remember that the cost of condo fees, which were included in her rent, will have to be paid in addition to the mortgage. Condo fees are costs assessed by the condominium association to cover maintenance of the common areas shared by all the owners. These common areas may sometimes include such things as pools or health club facilities. There are also other costs associated with home ownership, such as property taxes, regular maintenance, and repairs, that must be considered.

If you underestimate your expenses or the costs of home ownership, you will overestimate the home price that you can afford. It is much better, and not very difficult, to make a more careful judgment up front as to what price range you should be looking at and stick to it. Completing the worksheet in Table 12-2 will give you a better idea of what you can afford to buy. The first column shows the calculations for Mary's case; the second blank column is for you. For all figures, you should use monthly information.

Even though lenders consider gross pay rather than take-home pay in measuring your ability to pay, it is important that *you* consider your true cash flow. Rough rules of thumb do not work very well because your expenses may be greater than those of the "average" person. For example, I have a husband and two teenage sons with incredible appetites, leading my food bills to be much higher than normal. I must therefore budget for a larger food expense than more typical families of four.

In filling out the information for Step 1, it will be helpful to refer back to the cash flow worksheet in Table 2-4 and the budget that you developed in Table 4-2. Since mortgage payments are normally fixed for a long period of time, whereas your income and other expenses will be increasing, be sure to use your forecasted values for these numbers rather than past information.

If you currently are renting, you are probably not responsible for regular upkeep on your home. Unless you buy a new home, you can anticipate that there will be additional expenses, such as exterior and

Table 12-2 How Much House You Can Afford to Buy

	Mary's Example	Your Case
Step 1: Maximum monthly house-financing expense		
a. Your total monthly take-home income	$ 3,000	_____
b. Expenses (not including rent) and savings	1,800	_____
c. Expected additional utilities/repairs	100	_____
d. Total available for principal, interest,		
taxes, and insurance (PITI) ($= 1a - 1b - 1c$)	1,100	_____
Step 2: Maximum mortgage payment		
a. Expected monthly property taxes	200	_____
b. Expected monthly homeowner's insurance	40	_____
c. Maximum principal and interest ($= 1d - 2a - 2b$)	860	_____
Step 3: Maximum total mortgage amount		
a. Mortgage factor (Table 12-4)	136.3	_____
b. Maximum mortgage you can afford ($= 2c \times 3a$)	117,218	_____
Step 4: Maximum house you can afford		
a. Down payment available	10,000	_____
b. Gifts from parents or others	0	_____
c. Expected closing costs	2,000	_____
d. Maximum house you can afford ($= 3b + 4a + 4b - 4c$)	$125,218	_____

interior painting or replacement of appliances. The older the home you anticipate buying, the larger the amount that you should budget for these expenses (so you may need to come back to this worksheet later as you narrow down your search for houses). If you are not handy yourself (or if you don't have the time) and have no convenient handyman (like my husband), you must budget for the costs of minor repairs as well. Utilities will be more than you are currently paying if you are buying a home that is bigger than your current one, or if your landlord currently pays some of the utilities. Examples of expenses that might increase or that you might not have previously paid are cable, electric, gas or oil, water, sewer, homeowner's association dues, road maintenance fees, telephone, and lawn care.

The abbreviation PITI is commonly used to refer to the payment of the mortgage principal (P) and interest to the lender (I) plus the monthly portion of property taxes (T) and homeowner's insurance

(I). Because these latter two expenses generally are due in large lump sums, lenders find that it is more convenient for homeowners to pay part of the amount each month with the mortgage. The lenders then take care of paying these expenses as they come due. This process of collecting the funds in advance and taking responsibility for paying the bills is called *escrow.* As property taxes and insurance costs increase over the life of the mortgage (often thirty years), the lender will adjust the amount that it collects, which means that your payment will increase.

What Are Property Taxes and How Are They Calculated?

Property taxes can, in some areas of the country, be a very large expense. These taxes, which are generally used to fund local school systems, road improvements, and local government, depend on the budgetary needs of the local taxing authority (usually a city or county) and are therefore adjusted annually. They are calculated based on the value of the home that is being taxed, so a cheaper house will also have lower property taxes than a more expensive house in the same community. Areas with high population growth often require a lot of new schools and road work, so taxes can sometimes increase substantially from year to year. However, if a lot of new homes are being built, particularly if they are more expensive than the average for the community, you may even find that your property tax bill will decline (since you are sharing the budget with more people). You can call your local taxing authority or a local realtor to get an idea of what the average tax is in your community. The annual property tax for an average home may vary from as little as $1,000 in some areas to $7,000 in others.

The actual calculation of property taxes is sometimes confusing to homeowners. The taxing authority will periodically assess the market value of your home. *Assessed value* is an estimate of market value, but it is not the same thing as an appraisal, which is a valuation done for the purposes of justifying the amount of your bank loan. The assessed market value may then be adjusted by using an *assessment ratio*, which is a percentage value that is applied to all properties of a certain type, to arrive at a *taxable value*. The actual tax is then calculated by applying a *tax rate*, sometimes called the *mil rate*, a dollar amount to be paid per thousand dollars of taxable value. Your local taxing authority will probably have a flier that provides the assessment ratios and tax rates for your local area.

> *Example: Molly currently owns a home with a market value of $120,000. Based on information provided by the county assessor's office, she knows that the assessment ratio is currently 50 percent and the mil rate is $35 per $1,000 of taxable value.*

The calculation of Molly's property tax is worked out in Table 12-3, which also has space for you to do calculations for your own situation.

Why are there so many steps? The general reason is that the tax assessor is trying to achieve equity among newer and older homes and to fairly distribute the tax burden between homes and commercial properties. Since the properties in a taxing district are not all assessed annually, it is likely that a large percentage of homes are not currently assessed at their true market value. Suppose that in the example just given, Molly bought her house for $120,000, but her

Table 12-3 Calculation of Property Tax

		Molly's Example	Your Case
Step 1:	What is the market value of the home? (Use sales price if recently sold.)	$120,000	_____
Step 2:	Calculate taxable value. Determine the assessment ratio. Taxable value equals #1 × #2.	50% $60,000	_____ _____
Step 3:	Calculate property tax. Determine the tax (or mil) rate. Property tax equals #2 × #3.	$35 per $1,000 or 0.035 $2,100	_____ _____

next-door neighbor bought his identical house five years ago for $95,000. Would it be fair to make Molly pay taxes based on a higher amount? Districtwide reassessments are very expensive, so the tax assessor's office adjusts for changes in market value by applying a reduction factor to the more recently sold homes. The 50 percent figure in Table 12-3 implies that most homes in that area are assessed at 50 percent of their market value. If home prices are increasing in your area, this percentage will decline from year to year. When the assessment ratio starts to get very low, the tax assessor's office will generally try to get approval for the costs of doing a reassessment (this usually happens every five years or so). At that time, the assessments will be brought up to market value (i.e., the assessment ratio will be 100 percent) and the mil rate will be reduced.

If your house was recently assessed and you feel that the market value determined for your home is unfair, there is generally an appeal process whereby you can request a reevaluation of your particular case. When I bought my first house, it was a real "fixer-upper" duplex, with broken windows, a bad roof, and other problems. The sale price was $45,000, but the market value assigned by the assessor's office was $95,000. Since the owner had been in financial trouble, she had not paid any taxes for several years and so had not been entitled to appeal the assessment. My husband and I researched the values of homes in the area and went to the appeal fully prepared to argue our case. As it turns out, we never had to say anything—the assessor's office simply reduced our assessment to $45,000 based on the sales price. We eventually subdivided the duplex into two units, remodeled them both, and sold them for $95,000 and $89,000, respectively, for a nice profit.

Do You Need Homeowner's Insurance and How Much Will It Cost?

Yes, you will need to buy homeowner's insurance. This insurance covers losses to your home and personal possessions in the event of a fire or theft. It also covers you against liability for your own negligent acts (if someone slips on ice on your front steps, for example). Homeowner's insurance premiums differ by state, community, and value of home. Homes that are in crime-prone areas, or where coverage for weather-related damage (such as Florida hurricanes) is necessary, will have higher rates.

You will also pay more for your homeowner's insurance if you have special items that need to be insured, such as valuable jewelry, collectibles, art, or antiques. There are limits on these items in the standard homeowners policies that will not generally be sufficient (e.g., a $1,000 limit on jewelry coverage), so insurance companies offer riders, or addendums to the insurance contract, to cover these risks for an additional premium charge. The standard policy will only pay you for the *depreciated* value of items that are lost. If you lost everything you owned in a fire, the amount that you would receive in insurance would not be sufficient to replace everything, since your "used" belongings are worth less than what it will cost to replace them. For career women, the cost of replacing a wardrobe of work clothes would be substantially more than what you would get for your closetful of "used" clothes. My husband and I pay extra for a rider that provides us with replacement cost insurance.

Calculating the Mortgage Amount

For the final step in the process, you should refer to Table 12-4, which provides an easy reference for translating a monthly payment into the mortgage that it will be sufficient to pay for. Banks and realtors often use similar tables or financial calculators with built-in tables such as these. Keep in mind that this is only a rough estimate, since mortgage rates may not be quoted in increments of 0.5 percent. If you want a more exact estimate, several web sites offer mortgage calculators. For example, you can enter the mortgage rate and the number of months of the mortgage to arrive at the projected payment on the following site: *http://www.debtfreeforme.com/tips/budget.htm*

On the worksheet in Table 12-2, I estimated that Mary's annual mortgage rate would be 8 percent and that she would choose to fi-

Table 12-4 Mortgage Factors
(Maximum Mortgage = Maximum Payment × Factor.)

Annual Mortgage Rate	Term of Mortgage	
	15 years (180 months)	30 years (360 months)
6.0%	118.50	166.80
6.5%	114.80	158.20
7.0%	111.30	150.30
7.5%	107.90	143.00
8.0%	104.60	136.30
8.5%	101.50	130.00
9.0%	98.60	124.30

nance over thirty years. In that case, $860 per month times the mortgage factor of 136.3 from Table 12-4 equals $117,218. Mary can afford to borrow a maximum of $117,218.

You can also use Table 12-4 to calculate a mortgage payment if you know the amount of the mortgage. You simply work the problem backward: Divide the mortgage amount by the mortgage factor to arrive at the necessary payment of principal and interest. For example, if I knew that I wanted to borrow $100,000 for thirty years at 8 percent, I would divide $100,000 by 136.3 to get a payment of $733.68.

Financial Benefits of Owning a Home

Tax Deductibility of Interest

The most important financial benefit of home ownership is that interest payments are tax deductible, whereas rent is not. Some financial advisers suggest that when you analyze your payment ability, you should consider your after-tax cost of borrowing, rather than the full mortgage payment. The effective cost of tax-deductible interest payments is the interest cost less the taxes you would have paid on that amount of income.

If Mary has a payment of $860 per month, she will pay $10,320 to the bank each year. This is not *all* tax deductible, however; only the portion of the payments that constitutes interest can be deducted. But, in the early years of a mortgage, most of the payment goes to cover interest. In Mary's case, the interest paid in the first year of the mortgage will be $9,342 (which will be reported by the bank to her after December 31). If she deducts this on her taxes, she will save 28 percent of this amount, or $2,615, in federal income taxes, for a net cost of $6,727. Since interest charges are based on the outstanding loan balance, the interest deduction will decrease each year of the loan (although the payment remains the same, with a larger proportion going to pay back the principal loan amount).

Does this mean that Mary's $860 available cash per month will actually be sufficient to cover a larger monthly payment? Perhaps. The problem with looking at it this way is that even people who don't itemize deductions get to take a standard deduction, so the after-tax income we considered in the original worksheet already reflects some tax savings from deductions. However, to the extent that Mary will have higher take-home pay as a result of lower taxes, she may be able to afford a slightly higher mortgage.

Favorable Capital Gains Tax Treatment

Another tax benefit of homes as investments is that the Taxpayer Relief Act of 1997 now allows you to keep $250,000 profit (or $500,000 for a couple) from the resale of your home tax free regardless of whether you buy another home. Since gains in value on other assets are taxed at 20 percent (the capital gains tax rate), this makes your home a tax-preferred investment. Prior to 1998, the IRS allowed you to roll over gains on the sale of one house into another, more expensive house, and then gave you a onetime exclusion of $125,000 in capital gains after age 55. The new rule is much more liberal and virtually guarantees that low- and middle-income homeowners will never have to pay capital gains tax on their homes.

As an example, suppose you bought a house in 1998 for $100,000 and you sell it in 2000 for a net price (after commission) of $120,000.

If you have not made any capital improvements on the property, you have made a capital gain of $20,000 in two years. If this had been a $20,000 gain on a stock portfolio, you would owe the IRS $4,000 in federal income taxes (at the 20 percent capital gains tax rate) and you would possibly owe state taxes as well, for an after-tax net gain of less than $16,000.

Leveraging of Investment Returns

Applying a concept from the investments chapters in this book, we can estimate your investment return as follows:

$$Annual\ Return = \left(\frac{Dollar\ Gain}{Amount\ Invested}\right) \div Number\ of\ Years\ Held$$

If you consider the $100,000 purchase price as your initial investment, then the investment return on this house was approximately 10 percent per year ($20,000/$100,000 divided by 2). But your true investment in this home was probably much lower, since you borrowed most of the funds used to purchase it. What if your down payment was $20,000? You earned $20,000 on an investment of only $20,000, which looks like a return on investment of 100 percent, or 50 percent per year. But you need to take into account the cost of borrowing. At an 8 percent mortgage rate, you will have paid $12,696 in mortgage interest over the two years, or about $9,000 after taxes. So your actual dollar return on your $20,000 investment was $20,000 less the $9,000. The annual return was therefore 27.5 percent per year, and that doesn't even take into account the fact that you got the use of the house for those two years.

This illustrates the benefit of *leverage*, or borrowing funds to purchase investment assets. If you use someone else's money, you will make a bigger return on your investment. The tax benefits of home investments are a bonus: after-tax interest costs and no capital gains tax on the sale! It shouldn't come as any surprise to you that home equity is a large component of wealth for most households. For women, it is an even larger proportion of their portfolio. Although this implies that their portfolios are probably less diversified than they should be, at least they are reaping the rewards of taxes and leverage.

Different Types of Mortgages

Shorter-Term Mortgages

If you plan to take a shorter-term loan, or if mortgage interest rates are different at the time you are making this calculation, you should look for the appropriate value in Table 12-4. For example, if Mary would like to pay off her mortgage in only fifteen years, then the $860 payment would only be sufficient to cover a total mortgage of $89,440 ($860 times the mortgage factor of 104.6). For the $117,218 mortgage amount, she would have to make a payment of $1,120.63 per month for fifteen years. Notice that the mortgage payment is only $260 more per month, but the mortgage will be completely paid for in half as many months. This difference may be even greater if the lender offers a lower rate for the shorter-term loan, which is often the case. For example, if the fifteen-year loan is offered at 7$\frac{1}{2}$ percent interest, the payment would be $1,087 per month ($33 less than at 8 percent interest).

If you prefer to take a shorter loan, you can achieve the same objectives without obligating yourself to the higher payment by making larger payments each month voluntarily. Any extra amounts that you pay will be allocated to repayment of principal and will reduce your future interest charges and the term of your loan.

Another alternative that has been offered by lenders is the biweekly payment loan. In these loans, instead of making the monthly payment of $860 per month, Mary would make a half-payment of $430 every two weeks. Under this scenario, Mary would pay off her loan in 16$\frac{1}{2}$ years instead of the originally contracted thirty-year period. However, this is not the deal that it seems to be. With biweekly payments, Mary has actually paid twenty-six half-payments per year, which amounts to the equivalent of thirteen months instead of twelve! She has made an extra payment each year. Again, this same result can be achieved without locking yourself into it contractually by simply making an extra payment once a year. Before you make extra payments, however, you should check with your lender to be sure that there are no prepayment penalties.

Adjustable-Rate Mortgages

An adjustable-rate mortgage, or ARM, can be a way to reduce your monthly payment at the outset of your mortgage, since most lenders offer below-market "teaser" rates to entice borrowers. For example, in a market where fixed-rate mortgages are averaging 8 percent, you might find that lenders would be willing to give you an ARM at 6 percent. This could allow you to finance the same mortgage with a lower payment, or it could allow you to qualify for a larger mortgage. In Mary's case, her $117,218 maximum mortgage will now cost her only $703 per month. Alternatively, her $860 per month payment will now qualify her for a 6 percent mortgage of $143,448 (from Table 12-4: 166.8 × $860).

But *beware* of this temptation! It involves significant risk. Adjustable-rate mortgages give you this low introductory rate for only the first year or two; after that, they fluctuate based on market rates. Depending on the loan, they may be fixed for a period of time, but afterward, their rates and your mortgage payments will change annually or every two years. The rates are usually linked to the prime rate or a government borrowing rate, and the annual rate of increase generally has annual and lifetime caps. In a period of rising rates, it is likely that a low-rate ARM will require a substantially higher payment at its next adjustment date. If rates are falling, lenders may not offer ARMs with as attractive terms.

> *Example: In 1986, I took out an ARM to buy a condominium with the following contract terms. The introductory rate was 7½ percent for one year (at a time when rates were averaging 9 percent), and thereafter the loan could adjust up to 2 percent per year (based on the Treasury bill rate plus 3 percent). The lifetime cap was a 6 percent increase, which means that the maximum mortgage interest was my original 7½ percent + 6*

percent = 13½ percent. When I bought the property, I had intended a quick turnaround, so I thought that I had little risk of being exposed to these higher rates. However, the real estate market took a nosedive, interest rates increased, and I lost a lot of money on my investment. The rate eventually adjusted up to 11½ percent, which made my mortgage payment nearly double the original amount!

As an illustration of a different problem, let's suppose that Mary decided to borrow the full $143,448 that she could afford with her $860 payment per month and a 6 percent rate. If her annual cap is 2 percent per year, even if overall rates have not increased, her below-market rate would at least adjust to 8 percent in the following year. This would bring her monthly payment to approximately $1,052. (Remember that you can use Table 12-4 to calculate the payment by dividing the mortgage balance of $143,448 by the appropriate mortgage factor of 136.3.) This isn't exactly correct, because Mary actually only has twenty-nine years to go on the mortgage at this point and she has also paid a small amount of principal back to the bank already, but it's pretty close. If the Treasury bill rate goes up again the next year and the mortgage adjusts to 9 percent, the new payment will be approximately $1,154. This is almost a $300 difference per month in just two years. It is doubtful that Mary's salary will have increased by as much.

It should be obvious to you by now that in periods when rates on fixed-rate mortgages are very low, it is probably best to lock in a long-term mortgage with the lowest rate you can get. If rates are high, then an ARM will allow you to qualify for a little more mortgage, and the risk of increasing rates will be fairly low. If rates decline, your ARM rate will also decline, and you can think about refinancing to a fixed-rate mortgage at that time. For banks, the preference is just the opposite because of their different risk exposures. In periods of high rates, they would prefer that you take a fixed-rate loan, and when rates are low, they would like you to take an ARM. For this reason, the teaser rates on ARMS during periods of very low rates that are expected to rise may be very attractive, and you shouldn't dismiss them without doing a more thorough evaluation of your potential costs. The savings in the early years might offset the increased costs in later years, particularly if you do not plan to stay in the home for a long period of time.

Should You Buy Down the Interest by Paying Points?

Many lenders offer fixed-rate or adjustable-rate mortgages with lower rates but require the payment of points. A *point* is an up-front charge of 1 percent of the mortgage amount. Although it may seem like a good idea to get a lower rate, and hence a lower mortgage payment, you need to think about whether it makes sense to pay what is essentially interest on something for which you have not yet received the benefit. Is it better to pay $1,000 now or a slightly higher rate spread out over thirty years? If you plan to sell the house in less than ten years, it is probably not cost-effective to pay the points. The mortgage market is competitive enough that, with a little searching, you can probably find a lender who will give you the lower rate without the points.

How Large Should Your Down Payment Be?

Most lenders require that you pay at least some minimum portion (usually 10 percent) of the purchase price in cash before they will allow you to borrow the rest. This ensures that you have some stake in the property and makes their loan less risky. If they let you borrow 100 percent of the purchase price and home values in your neighborhood subsequently decline, you might have an incentive to simply walk away from your investment, leaving the bank with a house that is worth less than the mortgage loan. The larger the down payment, the better the banks like it. There are some special deals for first-time home buyers that allow them to make smaller down payments, but this is not always a good idea.

If your loan is more than 80 percent of the purchase price, the bank will often require that you buy mortgage insurance. This insurance guarantees the payment of principal and interest to the bank in the event that you default. It generally costs an extra $1/4$ to $1/2$ percent in loan interest, which is very expensive, since there is very little likelihood that you will default. A down payment of at least 20 percent will avoid this additional cost.

The size of your down payment will depend on:

- The equity you have in your current home (if any)

- Your total savings and investments

- How much money you need to keep as reserves for emergencies

- The expected expenses of fixing up your new home

- Whether you have any other sources of cash (from parents or others)

- The expected costs of moving to the new home

- Your return on alternative investments (if this is greater than the mortgage interest rate, it might be best to keep your money in the investment rather than make a larger down payment)

- Penalties for early withdrawal of funds from CDs or pensions

In Mary's case, she has $15,000 in available savings. She cannot use all of this, however, since she needs to keep some in reserve for emergencies, and, if she buys an older home, she will undoubtedly have additional costs of fix-up. In Table 12-2, she allocated only $10,000 for the down payment. Since she is not putting 20 percent down, she will have to pay the extra amount for mortgage insurance.

Can You Qualify for the Mortgage?

Now that you have determined what you *can* afford to borrow, you must still contend with the bank's requirements. Lenders have particular rules that determine whether they can easily sell your loan to other financial institutions or investors. The two rules that are most important are as follows:

1. Your principal, interest, taxes, and insurance (PITI) can't be more than 28 percent of your gross monthly income.

2. Your PITI plus all other monthly debt payments (car loans or leases, credit cards) cannot be more than 36 percent of your gross monthly income.

These percentages are the most common, but some lenders may be more or less restrictive.

Let's see how well Mary meets these requirements:

Gross income: $45,000/year or $3,750/month

Maximum affordable monthly PITI: $860/month

Other credit expenses (car + credit cards): $350/month

If she borrowed the maximum, her PITI would be 23 percent of her gross income ($860/$3,750), so she is well within the 28 percent maximum for that ratio. Her total credit expenses would be 32 percent of her gross income [($860 + $350)/$3,750], which is also less than the 36 percent maximum. However, you should note that this second ratio is often a problem, since car loans and leases often exceed $300 per month and even moderate credit card debt can result in minimum payments that are $100 or more per month.

Another way to use these ratios is to back out the maximum PITI you can qualify for by using your financial information. Mary could estimate the maximum mortgage payment she qualifies for by determining the *smaller* of the following two values:

$$\text{Maximum PITI} = \text{Gross Monthly Income} \times 0.28$$

$$= \$3,750 \times 0.28 = \mathbf{\$1,050}$$

$$\text{Maximum PITI} = (\text{Gross Monthly Income} \times 0.36) -$$

$$\text{Other Credit Expenses}$$

$$= (\$3,750 \times 0.36) - \$350 = \underline{\mathbf{\$1,000}}$$

Notice that it would have been a mistake for Mary to simply assume that it was appropriate for her to use the bank's maximum as her maximum affordable mortgage. She would be $140 short every month if she committed to a $1,000 per month payment when she has only $860 per month available!

Using a Real Estate Agent to Buy a Home

How to Choose

Once you have decided to buy a home and have determined the price you can afford, it is time to begin looking. Some people are lucky enough to find the perfect home immediately, but it often takes much longer, particularly when the real estate market is tight (which means that there are not a lot of homes for sale, so the good ones sell very fast, often before they even are advertised). A real estate agent is not always necessary, but an agent can be very helpful in narrowing down your search.

Table 12-5 identifies some characteristics that you should consider in choosing your agent. As in other areas of your finances, women may face special challenges in dealing with professionals. In the real estate business, its the conventional wisdom (probably identified by a man) that "men okay the price and women okay the house." With this in mind, in your initial contacts with agents, be sure that the agent appears to be responsive to your opinions and concerns related to the financial aspects of your home purchase. A good agent will be aware of the properties that are for sale in your area and can make arrangements to show them to you at your convenience.

Your Legal Relationship with the Broker or Agent

Many home buyers are under the mistaken impression that the real estate agent who shows them properties is actually working for them. Under the law in most states, real estate agents are actually agents for the seller, whether or not they have even met the seller. After all, the commission is being paid by the seller and not by you. There are

---

Table 12-5 Characteristics of a Good Real Estate Agent

1. Experienced

   An agent who has been selling homes for a long time will be more familiar with the area. Generally, only the agents who are good at what they do will survive the ups and downs of the real estate market over time.

2. Full-time

   There are many agents who moonlight at real estate. These agents may not have as much time to give you, may not have as much experience, and will not necessarily be able to show homes at times that are convenient for you.

3. Sales Track Record

   An agent who has sold a lot of homes in the last few years is probably good at matching buyers with appropriate homes.

4. Good Reputation

   Check with friends who have recently sold homes in the area. Ask them about service, dependability, personality, and other factors that you deem important.

5. Mid- to Large-Size Broker's Office

   Larger offices will have more in-house listings, which will be more important if houses are in tight supply.

6. MLS Subscriber

   Since most properties are listed on a computerized data service called the multiple listing service (MLS), an agent whose office subscribes will have access to the most current information on available homes and recent sales in the area.

7. Responsive to Your Needs

   Buying a home is a very personal decision. An agent should listen to what you want and show you appropriate homes.

---

some states that allow you to hire an agent who will work exclusively for you, called a buyer broker or buyer agent. This may require that you pay your own commission (often 3 to 3^1/$_2$ percent of the purchase price) over and above the commission paid by the seller to his or her agent.

If you do not hire a buyer broker, you should keep the agent's loyalties in mind when you are negotiating a sales price and other terms of the sales contract. Do not assume that any information you give to the agent will be confidential. For example, suppose you would like to make an offer on a property that is lower than the asking price. If you say to the agent, "I want you to offer $98,000, but I could go as high as $102,000," then you can be pretty sure that the sellers will be told that $102,000 is your maximum price. Instead, you should tell the broker, "I refuse to pay a penny more than $98,000!" and sound like you mean it. This information will get back to the seller and may help you to get the lower price.

Commissions

Real estate agents usually get a commission of 6 to 7 percent on the sale of a home, but this is paid by the seller. The commission is split between the listing agent (the seller's representative) and the selling agent (your representative). The agents share their half with the broker who owns the office out of which they work. On a typical $100,000 home, this means that an agent will get about $1,750 ($7,000/4), out of which he or she must pay income taxes, office, and car expenses. For this fee, the agent will show you as many homes as you want to see (and as many times as you want to see them), submit your offers and counteroffers on particular homes, prepare the purchase contract, walk through the property with you on the day of closing, come with you to the closing, and explain the documents to you if necessary. An agent may show houses to ten potential clients for every one that actually ends up in a sale. For this reason, agents will generally try to avoid showing you homes that are out of your price range or homes that you probably will not like. The better you describe your requirements, the better job the agent can do for you.

Using More Than One Agent

Unlike the seller, who must generally sign a listing contract with one agent, you are not limited to using only one agent. The only restriction is that whichever agent *first* shows you a particular property will be the one who is entitled to the commission. For this reason, agents may be reluctant to work with you if they know that you are also using another agent. They don't want to waste their time. If you are looking in several different towns or areas, you might consider using different agents in each if you feel that they might have more specialized knowledge.

Using an Agent to Sell a Home

Most people will use the same agent for selling their home and buying a new one if they are not relocating. Even though your agent has listed the house for sale, it will probably be another agent who actually finds the buyer. However, it is still important to try to select an agent who will make an active effort to find a buyer for your property, rather than one who will simply put it on the MLS and wait for someone else to sell it (for which your agent will still receive a portion of the commission as the listing agent).

My husband and I have bought and sold several properties over the years, and we have generally had pretty good experience with the real estate agents we have hired. The method that works best for selecting a selling agent is to identify the best sellers in the area and ask each of them to do a market analysis and selling plan for your property. This plan will identify comparable properties and their values and, based on the unique characteristics of your home, will recommend a selling price for your home. It will also include a proposal for marketing your property, usually through MLS listing and advertising in newspapers and other media. After each realtor has presented a plan to you, you can choose one of them based on the quality of the agent's proposal and your judgment of his or her personality and ability. Or you may decide you don't like any of the agents. Despite the work they have done for you, you are under no obligation at this point.

The first time my husband and I sold a house, we followed this strategy, and it was a real eye-opener. There were large differences among the three agents we interviewed, even though all of them came highly recommended and had good sales records. The first one (who was the one we had previously thought would be the best, since he was the top seller in the area) was fifteen minutes late for our appointment and then sat in his car obviously throwing together some information at the last minute. Needless to say, his market analysis was not very thorough, and we did not feel confident in the selling price that he suggested to us. We decided on the spot that he wasn't right for us.

The second agent was prompt and pulled up to the house in a

BMW. His market analysis was very professionally put together in a folder and included color photos of our house and several others that he had identified as comparable. He showed us his evaluation of how our property differed from the others in size, location, and other characteristics. He pointed out to us that he had his own personal secretary (which made it easier for potential buyers to contact him) and that his broker gave him a 75-25 split on the commissions (due to the volume of business he brought into the office). Although we were impressed with his credentials and his analysis of the market, we were disappointed when he suggested a selling price that was several thousand dollars lower than what we had hoped to get.

The last agent we spoke with was the least experienced of the three and worked out of the same office as the first agent. His market comparison was similar to the second agent's, but he suggested a price that was about 5 percent higher than the second agent. Now here's the dilemma: We wanted to sell the house for the highest price possible, and there was a discrepancy of about $8,000 between the two agents' suggestions. We liked both of the agents and felt that each of them would do his best to sell our house. We ended up choosing the third agent because we liked him better (and because we thought he was correct about the price). The house sold for the full asking price within one week of listing it (which made us wonder if we could have gotten more). Our instincts had been correct in this case, but it is often the case that agents will initially suggest higher prices to entice you to list with them. When the house doesn't sell right away, they come back to you and suggest that you lower the price. So don't necessarily pick the one who suggests the highest price. Look carefully at the market analysis and consider your own knowledge of recent home prices in your area.

What Is Title and Why Do I Need Title Insurance?

Title means legal ownership of an asset. You may recognize it as the word we use for ownership of a car. In the case of a car, the title is an actual piece of paper that represents legal ownership (and will be held by a bank if you have borrowed money to pay for your car). In the case of real property, title has a more complex meaning. It describes what kind of ownership interest you have in a property as well as the history of ownership of the property. Before a real estate sale, banks require that the title of the particular property be researched to determine that there are no potential unknown claims on the ownership. The title insurance company researches the title, clarifies any potential problems (such as ownership after a divorce or tax or mechanic's liens against the property), and then insures it against defects in title. The fact that liens are often required to be paid at closing can be beneficial for individuals or organizations that are having trouble collecting from homeowners. For example, it is common for taxing authorities, homeowners' or condominium associations, and contractors to file liens for nonpayment.

> *Example: A title search for a home that we had contracted to purchase several years ago turned up two liens against the property. One was for $25,000 in unpaid property taxes to the town, and one was a mechanic's lien in the amount of $5,000 for aluminum siding that had not been paid for. The title insurer noted these "clouds on title," and as a result our lender agreed to finance the loan only on the condition that the liens be paid for and removed at the closing. In such a case, to ensure that this happens, the title-closing agent, acting as a representative of the bank, processes the paperwork and files the appropriate releases.*

There may be defects in title that are more difficult to fix:

> *Example: While I was president of the homeowners' association for our neighborhood, we had an interesting problem arise. At the entrance to our rural neighborhood, there are a small building that is used for shelter when children wait for the bus and several mailbox units on concrete pads, all of which had been in place for ten years or more. The adjoining*

neighbors had their home surveyed for a refinance and discovered that both the building and the mailboxes were over the property line by a few feet. The least-cost solution was to redraw the property lines and pay the neighbor for the part of the property that we had encroached on.

The Closing

The closing is the meeting at which the seller signs the documents to turn the property over to you and you pay all the costs associated with the sale and your mortgage. Although closings can be done through the mail, it is more common to have a single meeting at which the parties transact this business. The seller, the buyer, the attorneys for each party, a person representing the title company, and one or more real estate agents are likely to be present. In most states, the title insurance agent stands in as a representative of the

Table 12-6 Closing Costs

1. Mortgage-related costs:

   Application fee (usually paid in advance)
   Credit report fee (usually paid in advance)
   Mortgage points (one point = 1 percent of total mortgage)
   Mortgage insurance premiums ($1/4$ to $1/2$ percent of mortgage)
   Loan origination fee (for processing the mortgage)
   Attorney's fee for bank documents
   First mortgage payment (or interest to end of month)

2. Property tax escrow (2 to 3 months)

3. Homeowner's insurance escrow (2 to 3 months)

4. Appraisal fee

5. Survey (sometimes paid by seller)

6. Home inspection

7. Title insurance and title search (usually paid by seller)

8. Title company charge for closing agent and meeting room

9. Your attorney's fees

10. Commission (paid by seller unless you use a buyer's agent)

11. Fees for legal recording of deed and mortgage

bank and will make sure that all necessary bank documents are signed before money and property can change hands. Prior to that time, you are required by law to be notified about the expected costs of closing, which are generally 2 to 5 percent of the total cost of the home. The items in Table 12-6 are examples of typical costs that must be paid on or before closing.

Summary

If you have read this chapter and followed the worksheets, you now should know:

- The factors to consider in deciding whether to buy a home
- The steps to follow in buying a home
- How to figure how much mortgage you can afford
- How to figure the total house price you can afford
- Whether you can qualify for a mortgage
- What property taxes are and how they are calculated
- What types of mortgages are available
- How mortgage payments work
- How to select a real estate agent
- What is meant by title
- What a mortgage closing is and what the potential costs of closing will be

Since the purchase of a home is probably the biggest, and possibly the best, investment you will ever make, understanding the content of this chapter is an important element in achieving your goal of financial success and independence.

CHAPTER 13

Buying a Car Without Being "Taken for a Ride"

You need to read this chapter if:

- ✔ You do not know how to get essential car-buying information from the Internet.

- ✔ You do not understand the difference between buying and leasing a car.

- ✔ You need to better understand the mechanics of car loans and where to get them.

- ✔ You need to better understand the mechanics of car leases and how to select the best one.

- ✔ You don't understand how a trade-in works.

A car is one of the few "investments" you make that is guaranteed to go down in value. In fact, your new car loses value the moment you drive it off the lot. With price tags as high as some houses, car purchases are extremely important and often complex financial decisions. Too many people focus on the affordability of the payment rather than on the overall cost of the car in making comparisons between alternatives.

This chapter does not tell you how to choose a particular car. That is a decision that you must make based on your own needs and wants. Several resources that may be useful to you in this selection process are provided in the appendix.

However, there are some financial considerations that you should take into account before you decide to make such a large purchase. Table 13-1 outlines the basic steps, each of which is more fully discussed later in this chapter. The most important point is that your financial ability to buy a car should be the *first* consideration. Despite the steep cost of new cars, it is an unfortunate truth that many people make automobile purchases on impulse. They happen to stop by the lot; they fall in love with a particular car; and before they know it, they are signing papers that obligate them to make large monthly payments for the next five years. In many cases, these individuals have not shopped alternative dealers or alternative financing!

Example: Several years ago, my housecleaner Debbie came to me for advice regarding a purchase agreement on a new truck

---

Table 13-1 The Steps in Buying a Car

1. Determine how much you can afford to spend on the car.
    a. What payment can you afford?
    b. How much can you borrow?
    c. What total cost can you afford?
2. Make a list of cars that meet your needs and are affordable.
3. Identify dealerships or individual owners with available cars.
4. Negotiate the price and terms of the deal.
5. Investigate your financing options.

she had just purchased. Although she thought that the agreed-upon price was $24,000, the invoice was for $28,000 at a 10½ percent interest rate. She was concerned about the extra $4,000, but I was more worried about the financing. She had signed an agreement obligating her to pay more than $600 per month when she didn't even make that much in take-home pay!

Why would Debbie agree to such terms, and how could the dealer allow her to borrow that much when she did not have the income to support it? I discovered later that she left town shortly afterward to get away from an abusive husband, so perhaps she lied on her financial application. The sad truth is that people are able to buy cars that they cannot afford. Financing charges are generally higher for those with bad credit or low income, and those people cannot negotiate good deals on price, so the dealers and lenders make more money. And if the buyers don't make the payments, the cars can be repossessed.

A word of warning to women car buyers: This is an area where it may pay to get help from a male relative or friend. "Undercover" buyer tests have shown that male buyers tend to get more attention from car salesmen and end up getting better deals on the cars that they buy. The generally adversarial context of car buying is not one that women feel particularly comfortable with, and they are therefore less likely to negotiate effectively. Automobile sales is one of the few remaining areas in which it is *expected* that the buyer will attempt to negotiate a better price than what is indicated on the sticker.

No matter how nice the salesperson seems, his or her livelihood depends on taking advantage of uninformed buyers. The lesson in this is that you must become sufficiently informed to be able to win at the salesperson's game. This chapter does not cover the steps in negotiation but focuses on getting you up to speed on the financial aspects of the car purchase. In the appendix, I have included several resources that will be helpful in the negotiation part.

To illustrate the points in this chapter, I build on the following example:

Example: Molly has $5,000 from the sale of her old car and would like to buy a new van that can accommodate her growing family. She estimates that she can afford a monthly payment of $300.

How Much Can You Afford?

Financial planners suggest that as a rule of thumb, your total car expenses (including car payments, repairs, licensing fees, and insurance) should be 10 to 15 percent of your budget. Rather than assume that this will work for you, you should look at the budget you developed in Chapter 4 to determine your ability to pay for a car.

As with buying a house, the larger the down payment that you make up front, the smaller the amount that you will have to pay per month. In fact, you could pay for the car outright and have no monthly car payment. However, you should consider this decision in light of some of the investment principles discussed in earlier chapters.

Since cars are not really investments, because they decline in value over time, it is possible that you might be better off taking the same money and investing it in an earning asset. If the interest rate on your car loan is lower than the rate you can earn with that money, you might be better off borrowing. For example, if Molly were to borrow the additional $5,000 at 8 percent for 60 months, it would cost her an additional $101 per month. These payments will be sufficient to pay back the $5,000 plus a total of $1,083 in interest over the life of the loan. If Molly invests the $5,000 in a mutual fund that earns 10 percent per year (moderate risk) before taxes and reinvests the after-tax earnings each year, she will have $7,078 after five years (assuming a tax rate of 28 percent). Alternatively, she could use the earnings of the mutual fund to offset her car payment costs each year.

For the moment let's ignore the investment alternative and assume that Molly will use the $5,000 from the sale of her old car as a down payment on the new one.

Table 13-2 provides a simple way of figuring out the amount of car that can be bought with a particular amount of monthly pay-

Table 13-2 How Much Can You Borrow?
(Multiply your affordable payment by the value in the table.)

Annual Rate	Term of Loan (Months)			
	36	48	60	72
0.0%	$36.00	$48.00	$60.00	$72.00
1.0%	$35.45	$47.03	$58.50	$69.85
2.0%	$34.91	$46.09	$57.05	$67.79
3.0%	$34.39	$45.18	$55.65	$65.82
4.0%	$33.87	$44.29	$54.30	$63.92
5.0%	$33.37	$43.42	$52.99	$62.09
6.0%	$32.87	$42.58	$51.73	$60.34
7.0%	$32.39	$41.76	$50.50	$58.65
8.0%	$31.91	$40.96	$49.32	$57.03
9.0%	$31.45	$40.18	$48.17	$55.48
10.0%	$30.99	$39.43	$47.07	$53.98

ment. Since most car loans are for between three and six years, the table provides estimates for these loan terms. Select the interest rate in column 1 and look across to the number of months you expect to finance the purchase. The longer the loan term you choose, the smaller the payment per month, but you will pay more interest over the life of the loan. The amount shown in the table is the total amount you can finance (purchase price plus tax and charges less any down payment you make) for each dollar of monthly payment. Multiply the amount in the table by your affordable monthly payment to arrive at the amount you can finance.

Example (continued): How much can Molly afford? If her bank is offering a rate of 8 percent per year for sixty months, the amount in the table shows that she can finance $49.32 for each dollar of payment. Therefore, a $300 payment will be enough to finance $300 × 49.32 = $14,796. Since Molly also has a down payment of $5,000, the total cost of her new car with taxes and fees must be less than $19,796.

Table 13-3 provides a summary of the steps in this calculation so that you can figure out the amount for your own car purchase.

Table 13-3 Calculation of Maximum Total Car Costs

	Molly's Example	Your Case
1. Amount of payment you can afford (Use tables in Chapter 4 to determine available cash flow.)	$300	_____
2. Value from Table 13-2 based on estimated terms of loan	$49.32	_____
3. Affordable loan amount (#1 × #2)	$14,796	_____
4. Available down payment	$5,000	_____
5. Maximum total costs (#3 + #4)	$19,796	_____

The Interest Rate Doesn't Make That Much Difference in Monthly Payments

While we are talking about interest rates on loans, you should take a look at how little difference the rate actually makes on your monthly payment. Many dealers will advertise low loan rates, even as low as 0.9%, and you might wonder how they can do that. You can be sure that if they are not getting enough interest to compensate them for the risk (remember the risk and return rule from Chapter 8), they will make up for it somewhere else. If you have shopped around and can get a lower rate from one place than another with exactly the same terms, then by all means go for it.

Let's compare the difference in payments that results from differences in loan rates:

Example (continued): Suppose Molly finds that the dealership where she is negotiating for a car is offering a low-rate loan at 6 percent. Her total car costs including taxes and fees are $19,000. She is planning on making a $5,000 down payment and financing $14,000. From Table 13-2, Molly knows that her monthly payment would be a little under $300 if the loan was at 8 percent. Here are the required payments at several different interest rates:

8% $283.87

6% $270.66

4%   *$257.83*

2%   *$245.39*

The moral of this story is that you shouldn't be overly influenced by dramatically lower rates on loans. The amount of money that you finance makes far more difference in your payments than the rate of interest over such a short loan period. At 8 percent interest, decreasing the amount that she borrows to $13,000 instead of $14,000 will reduce Molly's payment by $20 per month. Note that a two percentage point decrease in interest reduces her payment by only $13. Beware of dealers who offer good rates but don't negotiate much on price.

Of course, if you can get a lower rate without giving up anything else or paying higher fees, you should do so.

Tricks Used by Car Dealers

In order to spot the tricks dealers play on unsuspecting car buyers, you need to understand the different sources of potential profit for the dealer and the individual salesperson. As many people believe, dealers make money by selling the car for more than they paid for it. But, in addition, they often receive special kickbacks from the manufacturer for selling particular models and warranty plans. They also benefit from arranging the financing, either through the manufacturer's financing company or through local banks. All car dealers add on a charge for "Delivery," "Dealer Prep," or "Destination Charges," and this can vary from $200 to more than $1,000. In many cases, the salesperson makes no mention of this charge until you see the final papers, and then he or she will argue that this is nonnegotiable and that all buyers pay it. A joke that introduces the web site *http://www.carbuyingtips.com* asks, "What do you call a person who pays sticker price for a car? Answer: A victim."

With so many sources of potential profit, salespeople often confuse buyers by making offers that incorporate one or more of these elements in return for a lowered price. Knowing the budgetary focus of most buyers, they will emphasize payments rather than other terms of the deal or the loan. Just because your monthly payments are lower does not mean that you are getting a better deal.

Use the Internet to Simplify Your Car-Buying Experience

The availability of information on the Internet has made it much more difficult for car dealers to take advantage of buyers. It has turned out to be the "great equalizer" for women, who have often felt themselves at a disadvantage in this adversarial setting.

> *Example: Lyn and her husband were in the market for a new car. Since Lyn works part-time and was likely to be the primary driver of the new family vehicle, she agreed to take on the responsibility of researching the possible alternatives and arranging for financing. Lyn was somewhat apprehensive, since her previous car-buying experience many years before had been about as much fun as getting a tooth pulled. Lyn's first stop was the Internet, where she was able to look at vehicle safety records (http://www.nhtsa.com); check reliability ratings; and, best of all, determine the trade-in value of her old car and the dealer's invoice cost on the car she was considering (http://www.edmunds.com). She and her husband decided on a Subaru Forrester, and Lyn arranged for preapproval of a loan through their local lender at a favorable rate. With computer printouts in hand, they went to a local dealer and made an offer of $200 over the dealer cost. The offer was accepted, and they drove out with their new car.*

The key factor in this example was that the dealer recognized that Lyn was an informed buyer who was not willing to play the games that are "business as usual" in car sales. Since the financing was taken out of the negotiations, there was no opportunity for the dealer to play "payment" games. I suspect that as time goes on, the industry will become more competitive, and only the less creditworthy buyers will be taken advantage of.

Should You Lease or Buy?

You might notice that I didn't put the "lease versus buy" section earlier in this chapter but began with examples assuming that you were buying the vehicle. This was intentional. In nearly all cases, it is preferable to buy rather than to lease. Leases are another one of those gimmicks used by car dealers to make extra money off unsuspecting consumers. In comparing leasing versus buying, too many consumers focus on payments, which are almost always lower with leases. Ask yourself this: How can the dealer/manufacturer afford to give you the car for a much lower price per month? The answer should be obvious: The dealer/manufacturer is making money on you somewhere else, usually from the down payment, the end-of-lease charges, and the value of the vehicle at the end of the lease.

Understanding the Basic Components of a Car Lease

The essential terms of a car lease are:

Up-front fees: This is often called a down payment, but in fact it is not really a down payment, since you don't own the vehicle. So the money is a throw-away.

Monthly payments: These are often much lower than the payments on a loan on the vehicle, but that is because you are not repaying principal and you are not accumulating any equity in the vehicle.

Lease term: Traditionally leases were two years, but many are now being extended to lengths that resemble car loan terms. Note that longer-term leases add risk, since it is more difficult to estimate the end-of-lease value and the condition of the vehicle.

Mileage limitations per year: The lease usually limits you to 10,000 to 15,000 miles per year. The lower-mileage leases are cheaper because the car will presumably be worth more at the end of the term if it has not been driven as much.

Penalties for overmileage: Many consumers take the lower-mileage leases to get the lower monthly payments, but they are then socked with big charges at the end of the lease for exceeding the limits.

Trade-up value of car at end of lease: At the end of the lease, you can usually opt to either buy the leased car or lease a newer car. Assuming that you have not put excessive wear and tear on your vehicle or exceeded your mileage limits, you can usually apply some amount of "value" to the new car value to determine the lease amount. This amounts to a transfer of your down payment to the new vehicle.

To compare leasing versus buying, you also need to estimate the value of the vehicle at the end of the lease, since you will own the equity in the vehicle if you buy the car. Dealers will often provide you with these estimates, but you would be wise to use outside sources. You can check residual values in the Automotive Lease Guide provided at *http://www.carwizard.com.*

Trading In Your Old Vehicle

Both new-car and used-car dealers are willing to give you money toward a new car if you turn over the title to your old car. This is called a *trade-in.* However, the amount the dealer will give you for your car will be based on the wholesale value of your car, not the retail or Blue Book value of your car. Therefore, if you have a car that you can sell on your own by placing an ad in the paper, you will probably make out better than if you trade it in. In addition, a trade-in gives the dealer one more way to take advantage of you.

Example: You have a five-year-old vehicle that has a retail value of $10,000 and a wholesale value of $8,000. The car you want to buy has a sticker price of $20,000, but the dealer is willing to sell it for $17,000. If the salesperson perceives that you are primarily concerned with getting the best trade-in you can for your old car, he or she might tell you that the dealer *will give you $10,000 for the trade but then only negotiate the new car price down to $19,000.*

If you have a car that would be difficult to sell privately (e.g., it is an unpopular model or has high mileage), it may be best to use it as a trade-in, but you should be sure to keep the trade-in negotiation separate from the negotiation for the new purchase. For some additional tips on negotiation, check out the books and web sites listed in the appendix.

Summary

If you have read this chapter and completed the worksheets, you should know:

- The steps in buying a car

- How to determine the amount of car you can afford to buy

- The tricks that car dealers use to make money on unsuspecting consumers

- Why the Internet is the car-buying woman's best friend

- The advantages and disadvantages of leasing

- How trade-ins work

Buying a car has historically been an unpleasant experience for women. The games played on unsuspecting consumers by car salespeople are numerous. But the Internet is the car-buying woman's best friend, leveling the playing field so that we can get a fair deal. With just a little effort, you can easily determine which car is best for you, how to get the best financing terms, and what you should be paying for the car. But despite all this, don't forget the most important rule: You should make your car purchase decision in the context of your overall financial portfolio. Don't buy more car than you can afford.

CHAPTER 14

Planning for a Comfortable Retirement

You need to read this chapter if:

- ✔ You have not set a retirement goal.

- ✔ You do not know how much you will need to meet your retirement goal.

- ✔ You want to know more about the benefit you will receive from Social Security.

Even though I love my job as a college professor, I think I would also love to retire early. Since there are so many things that I would like to have more time to do, I suspect I will be busier in "retirement" than I am now. (But I probably still won't get my Christmas cards done on time.)

How about you? My definition of early retirement may not be the same as yours, but consider this: Prior to the development of the

Social Security program in 1934, most people worked *until they died,* or until they were too sick to work. When they could no longer work, the elderly were dependent on their extended families for support. Even as recently as a few decades ago, this was the norm, and in some families it still is. In my family, Grandmother Barwick lived with us during my teenage years until she eventually went into a nursing home. Grandmother Herring was able to live on her own until the age of 96, at which time she moved in with my dad and eventually passed away at home.

What's Different Today?

"Live Long and Prosper"

The Vulcan salutation (from *Star Trek*) seems to have been a forecast of the future for Earth as well. We are living longer all the time. Your grandmother's life expectancy wasn't much more than what we currently call the "normal retirement age"—around 65. Baby boomer women, on average, will live to be 80. More and more people are making it to age 100 with every generation.

Living longer is great if you are healthy and wealthy. Taking care of both of your physical health and your financial health will go a long way toward improving your quality of life in your later years. One of the problems with longevity is that it will cost a lot to support you in retirement. And women live considerably longer than men, on average, so this is a bigger issue for us. If we retire at 62 and live to be 97 as my Grandmother Herring did, then we need to have the financial resources to support thirty-five years of retirement.

"Girls Just Want to Have Fun!"

Another difference today is that older people have much more active lifestyles—travel, golf, volunteer work, and even seeking further education are not uncommon retirement goals for people today. These activities are a lot more expensive than sitting around the fire knitting socks, so retirement planning must incorporate the cost of meeting these goals.

The Double-Edged Sword of Medical Progress

Last, and perhaps the least pleasant aspect to talk about, there is the cost of health care. Although medical science has figured out ways to help us live longer, these life-extending miracles are expensive. As a result, the cost of health care in retirement can be beyond the means of many people. While Medicare is available after age 65, its coverage is insufficient at best. Good retirement planning should include the cost of both health insurance and health care, as well as long-term care needs. Most people will eventually spend time in a long-term health-care facility such as a nursing home, and the nice ones are extremely expensive.

This chapter follows up on several themes that I have introduced in earlier chapters. An important component of your financial plan is to set long-term goals and develop a plan for reaching them. Most of you will probably have listed a comfortable retirement as a long-term goal. Although you will need to decide what your personal retirement will look like, and I can't tell you when to retire or where to live in retirement, this chapter will help you to develop a realistic plan for meeting the financial needs of retirement—how much you will need to save in total and how much you will need to put away each year to meet that goal. The steps outlined in Table 14-1 are actually fairly easy, especially if you have already done some short-term budgeting in the earlier chapters. But even if you haven't done this, you can get a rough idea of what you should be doing now and you can refine your retirement savings plan as you get older and consider the various options available to you.

Making a Complex Problem Simple

Because of the complexity of this problem, this chapter provides tables that simplify the calculation. The chapter provides a method for estimating your retirement savings needs; identifies the different types of retirement savings vehicles; and explains payment options, tax advantages, and what to do with lump-sum distributions from plans. There are also lots of web resources in the appendix that can substitute for or supplement the calculations in this chapter.

Table 14-1 Steps to a Comfortable Retirement

	Jessica's Example	Your Case
1. Estimate your annual pretax retirement income needs (see Table 14-2).	$119,963	$_____
2. Estimate your expected annual Social Security income (see Table 14-3).	$33,000	_____
3. Estimate retirement income available from other benefit plans.	0	_____
4. Estimate your additional income needs (#1 − #2 − #3).	$86,963	_____
5. Estimate amount of wealth needed at retirement (Additional Income Needs × Factor from Table 14-4).	$1,647,340	_____
6. Estimate the future value of current savings and retirement plans (Current Savings Amount × Factor from Table 14-5).	$753,335	_____
7. Estimate additional wealth needed (#6 − #7).	$894,005	_____
8. Estimate necessary annual savings to achieve goal (Additional Wealth Needed × Factor from Table 14-6).	$9,090	_____

Although establishing your retirement income goal is one of the most important steps in the retirement-planning process, most people skip it. The reason is simple: This is a pretty complicated issue. Many people aren't sure what their expenses will be next year, let alone how to figure them out for an unknown period of years from now.

But just because something is hard does not mean you shouldn't even attempt it. The method that I outline for you here is relatively easy because I have precalculated lots of scenarios and provided multiplier factors that you can use to simplify the problem. In a few minutes, you can have a better idea of how much you should be saving to meet your retirement goals. Don't be surprised if it's more than you expect. Several recent studies suggest that the people in the average baby boom household are saving about one-third to one-

Illustration by Kristopher S. Bajtelsmit

half of what they should be saving in order to maintain their lifestyle in retirement.

Step 1: Estimate Your Annual Retirement Income Needs

One of the most difficult things for people to estimate is the impact of inflation on their income and expenses. Table 14-2 shows you how much your current income will be in future dollars, assuming average wage growth of 4 percent, which is pretty close to the long-run estimates used by the federal government in forecasting Social Security and other government programs. If your income generally grows with inflation, then you can use this table to estimate how much you will be making when you retire. This is a good starting point for determining how much retirement income you will need.

When considering your retirement income *needs*, keep in mind that you will not necessarily need to match your preretirement *income*, since your *expenses* may be far less than your income. You should consider how much of your current income is eaten up by

Table 14-2 Estimate Your First-Year Pretax Retirement Income Needs (Assumes 4% wage inflation per year to retirement.)

Current Pretax Income	Years Until You Retire							
	5	10	15	20	25	30	35	40
$25,000	$30,416	$37,006	$45,024	$54,778	$66,646	$81,085	$98,652	$120,026
30,000	$36,500	$44,407	$54,028	$65,734	$79,975	$97,302	$118,383	$144,031
35,000	$42,583	$51,809	$63,033	$76,689	$93,304	$113,519	$138,113	$168,036
40,000	$48,666	$59,210	$72,038	$87,645	$106,633	$129,736	$157,844	$192,041
45,000	$54,749	$66,611	$81,042	$98,601	$119,963	$145,953	$177,574	$216,046
50,000	$60,833	$74,012	$90,047	$109,556	$133,292	$162,170	$197,304	$240,051
55,000	$66,916	$81,413	$99,052	$120,512	$146,621	$178,387	$217,035	$264,056
60,000	$72,999	$88,815	$108,057	$131,467	$159,950	$194,604	$236,765	$288,061
65,000	$79,082	$96,216	$117,061	$142,423	$173,279	$210,821	$256,496	$312,066
70,000	$85,166	$103,617	$126,066	$153,379	$186,609	$227,038	$276,226	$336,071
75,000	$91,249	$111,018	$135,071	$164,334	$199,938	$243,255	$295,957	$360,077
80,000	$97,332	$118,420	$144,075	$175,290	$213,267	$259,472	$315,687	$384,082
85,000	$103,415	$125,821	$153,080	$186,245	$226,596	$275,689	$335,418	$408,087
90,000	$109,499	$133,222	$162,085	$197,201	$239,925	$291,906	$355,148	$432,092
95,000	$115,582	$140,623	$171,090	$208,157	$253,254	$308,123	$374,878	$456,097
100,000	$121,665	$148,024	$180,094	$219,112	$266,584	$324,340	$394,609	$480,102

expenses and which expenses are likely to change in retirement. Some of this may be a wash. For example, you will no longer have children in the home, but you may want to spend money on grandchildren. You may have your house paid off, but your home will be older and need more repairs. You will no longer have the expenses related to employment, but you will have higher leisure expenses, such as golf fees and vacations. The biggest expense to consider is health care. You may have fairly low health-care expenses now, but in retirement, you will not have an employer paying your insurance and you will have higher doctor and prescription drug costs. Keep in mind that most of your expenses (utilities, food, clothing, leisure activities, health care) will go up in cost at the rate of inflation or higher.

My recommendation is to estimate high so that you will not underestimate your savings needs. If you currently spend most of your after-tax income, then I recommend that you estimate your retirement needs directly from Table 14-2. You can also try using the retirement expense calculator offered at *http://www.moneycentral.com/ investor/calcs/*.

To illustrate the use of the tables and how to do the basic calculations, I will use Jessica's example:

> *Example: Jessica is an accountant and currently makes $45,000 per year. She is a single professional who is 37 years old. Jessica has accumulated $100,000 in a 401(k) plan from her employer (to which she contributes 7 percent of her pretax salary), and she has $10,000 saved in an IRA.*
>
> *Step 1 for Jessica: Jessica currently spends about 90 percent of her after-tax income each year, with the remainder being available for saving and nonnecessities. In order to be conservative in her estimates, Jessica uses Table 14-2 and finds that if she plans to retire at age 62 (twenty-five years from now), her income will be $119,963 if it grows 4 percent per year until retirement. She enters this amount in Table 14-1.*

Step 2: Estimate Your Expected Social Security Income

Most people can expect to receive something from Social Security in retirement. Despite all the hype to the contrary, Social Security is such a political "hot potato" that it is highly unlikely that Congress will do away with it. Congress may, however, change the rules, so you cannot assume that it will definitely be as generous in the future. But with 99 percent of all working adults currently contributing to the system, it would be political suicide to radically increase taxes or reduce benefits. Those readers who are nearer to retirement are most likely to get the benefit of the current system, and younger women should expect that there may be some changes in structure (e.g., you may be allowed to invest some of your payroll taxes). If you don't want to rely on Social Security's being available to you in retirement, you can skip this section (enter a zero in Table 14-1) and go on to step 3.

How Does Social Security Work?

Social Security is actually a combined set of programs that cover retirement needs, health insurance, disability insurance, and survivors' insurance. I talk only about the retirement part here. Of the 7.65 percent payroll tax that you pay and the equal amount that your employer pays (for a total of 15.3 percent of nearly all payroll in the United States), 5.3 percent from you and 5.3 percent from your employer goes to pay for the retirement portion. The maximum amount of income on which you pay your tax is $80,400 in 2001, and that amount increases at about the average wage growth rate each year. The money flowing into the system is used to pay benefits to the people who are currently entitled to receive them, and the remainder of the funds, if any, is invested in a special type of Treasury security that pays the Social Security trust fund interest each year.

Is Social Security Really in Financial Trouble?

Yes. The problem stems from the design of the program and the changing mix of ages in the population. In its original design, Social Security was intended to be a "pay as you go" system. Current payroll taxes are collected and then distributed to the current retirees. This worked really well when the system was first started because there were seventeen workers contributing to the system for each retired person. Currently there are less than four workers per retiree, and in a couple of decades, there will be only two! With more old people in the country relative to young people, a different sort of financial arrangement is obviously needed. But the reality is that changing such a massive program is very difficult. According to the estimates done by the Social Security Administration Board of Trustees, the system will be bankrupt in less than twenty years if something isn't done to fix it.

What Are the Most Likely Social Security Reforms?

Although I cannot guarantee this, of course, my study of this issue leads me to the conclusion that politicians will tweak the system in order to keep it alive a little longer without making any *major* changes. For example, a simple change that will extend the system considerably is to increase the retirement age. Currently it is scheduled to rise to 67 gradually over the next several years. Why not make it 70 or 75? The idea of the original program was to help people out in the last few years of their life, but the retirement age has never been radically adjusted to take into account changing life expectancies. Any change of this type will be gradually implemented, so only younger people will be affected.

Another easy fix is to increase the amount of payroll that is subject to tax. This is already the case for Medicare, since we pay the tax on our entire income for that program and most people don't even realize this. This change wouldn't affect the vast majority of people, since only the top 5 percent of families make more than $75,000.

Decreases in benefits or increases in payroll taxes are also obvious fixes, but less politically popular. However, a small increase in the payroll tax or a small decrease in benefits (e.g., reducing the amount that is given to higher-income people) would keep the system afloat for many more years.

Although both presidential candidates in 2000 included Social Security reform proposals in their campaign promises, complete privatization (basing benefits on the performance of individual investment accounts instead of giving a benefit based on salary) is not likely to occur in the near future. The difficulty is in the details of how the new plan would provide benefits for older workers while still allowing younger workers to siphon off some of the payroll taxes to individual investment accounts. I do think that some type of privatization plan is on the horizon, but it is likely to be a small supplement to a promised benefit, rather than a substitute.

Estimating Your Social Security Income

Social Security is, for the time being, a type of *defined-benefit pension* (as described in Chapter 5). The benefit that you eventually receive is based on a formula that is defined in the law. (Contrast this with a *defined-contribution* plan, where your employer promises to make a specific contribution, but your ultimate benefit is determined by accumulations in your investments.) Because the main purpose of Social Security is to prevent poverty in old age, the benefit is a larger percentage of preretirement income for poor people and a smaller percentage for the rich. Since we cannot be sure about changes in the future, this section assumes that the basic structure of the program will be the same in the future.

Recently, the Social Security Administration began sending benefit information to participants summarizing their past covered earnings and estimated future benefits. If you are over 25 years of age and have paid Social Security tax in the past, you should receive a statement about three months before your birthday each year. If you can locate that information, use the estimate of benefits in future inflated dollars. Alternatively, Social Security also has a very easy to use web site that includes a calculator to help you forecast your future benefit at *http://ssa.gov/OACT/COLA/benefitEx.html.*

On the web site, you can enter your current age and earnings and request the inflated future dollars estimate of benefits. Although the calculation is based on your income increasing at the rate of average wage growth, you also have the option of entering alternative scenarios. For example, to be more realistic, you might want to include some years in which you do not work or work part-time. Or if you have achieved larger than average gains in income over time or expect to in the future, you can adjust for this.

In Table 14-3, I have summarized the results of these estimates for selected ages and incomes in 2000 if you want to take a shortcut. These figures are given for two assumed retirement ages: 62 and 67. Age 62 is the earliest that you can begin to receive benefits; if you retire at this age, the benefit amount is reduced to account for the fact that you are paying in for five fewer years and collecting benefits for five additional years. Age 67 is the normal retirement age for most of the ages in the table. (It is 66 for people age 50 and age 55, and age 66 and 2 months for people age 45. This is because the normal retirement age is being increased each year at a steady rate until it reaches 67.) Notice that if you make more than the Social Security maximum earnings level in every year of your working career ($76,200 in 2000), you will receive the maximum annual benefit shown in the last two rows of the table. While these dollar amounts look large, keep in mind that they are adjusted for future inflation

Table 14-3 Estimate Your Annual Social Security Benefit at Retirement

Current Income	Retirement*	Current Age						
		25	30	35	40	45	50	55
$20,000	Early	31,656	25,644	20,772	16,824	14,448	11,832	9,624
	Normal	54,048	43,788	35,472	28,740	22,428	18,168	14,760
$25,000	Early	36,492	29,568	23,952	19,404	16,656	13,644	11,088
	Normal	62,412	50,568	40,956	33,180	25,884	20,976	17,040
$30,000	Early	41,340	33,492	27,132	21,984	18,876	15,456	12,564
	Normal	70,764	57,336	46,440	37,620	29,340	23,772	19,320
$35,000	Early	46,188	37,416	30,312	24,564	21,084	17,268	14,040
	Normal	79,128	64,104	51,936	42,072	32,808	26,580	21,588
$40,000	Early	51,036	41,352	33,492	27,132	23,292	19,080	15,516
	Normal	87,480	70,884	57,420	46,512	36,264	29,376	23,868
$45,000	Early	54,408	44,076	35,712	28,932	24,828	20,340	16,536
	Normal	92,328	74,808	60,600	49,092	38,388	31,104	25,272
$50,000	Early	56,676	45,912	37,200	30,132	25,872	21,192	17,184
	Normal	96,252	77,976	63,168	51,180	40,008	32,412	26,340
$55,000	Early	58,944	47,760	38,688	31,344	26,904	22,032	17,784
	Normal	100,164	81,156	65,748	53,256	41,628	33,732	27,372
$60,000	Early	61,224	49,596	40,176	32,556	27,948	22,824	18,348
	Normal	104,088	84,324	68,316	55,344	43,248	35,040	28,356
$65,000	Early	63,492	51,444	41,676	33,756	28,980	23,616	18,888
	Normal	108,000	87,504	70,884	57,432	44,868	36,348	29,316
$70,000	Early	65,760	53,280	43,164	34,968	30,012	24,372	19,392
	Normal	111,924	90,684	73,464	59,508	46,488	37,656	30,228
Maximum	Early	68,952	55,932	45,300	36,660	31,368	25,296	20,016
	Normal	117,420	95,256	77,184	57,299	48,744	39,312	31,368

*Early retirement is at age 62; normal retirement is at age 66 to 67, depending on current age.
Source: Social Security Administration web calculator at *http://www.ssa.gov.*

levels and are worth a fraction of that amount in today's dollars. (At 4 percent inflation per year, $100,000 forty years from now is only worth about $20,000 today.)

Unlike many employer defined-benefit plans, which base benefits on final salary, Social Security bases your benefit on an average of nearly all of your years of income, adjusted to current dollars. So if you worked part-time for some of your working years or took off time from work to raise your kids, your benefit will be lower as a result. In addition, you must participate in the system (i.e., pay Social Security tax) for at least forty quarters (ten years) to be eligible for benefits, although you may still qualify for benefits on your spouse's income.

> *Step 2 for Jessica: Using Table 14-3, Jessica estimates that since she is 37 and makes $45,000, her Social Security benefit (in future dollars) will be between $28,932 and $35,712 if she retires at age 62, or between $49,092 and $60,600 if she waits until she is 67 to collect Social Security. Since she wants to retire at age 62, she enters an estimate of $33,000 in Table 14-1.*

Step 3: Estimate Annual Retirement Income From Other Sources

Although employers are less likely to offer defined-benefit pensions now than in the past, some still do. If you have a pension plan that promises you a benefit upon retirement based on some formula such as 50 percent of final salary, then you should take this into consideration in your calculation of savings needs. Some defined-benefit plans are "integrated" with Social Security. This simply means that your pension benefit and your Social Security benefit together will replace a specified percentage of preretirement income. In that case, you should calculate the total benefit (based on the percentage of your final income) and subtract the estimated Social Security benefit to arrive at the estimate for the pension benefit. Keep in mind, however, that plans may differ, so it is a good idea to consult your employer's benefits office for the specific details. You may have a union plan that will provide a small additional defined benefit. Enter the total amount of these expected benefits in Table 14-1, line 3.

As was discussed in Chapter 5, women and younger people are much less likely, on average, to have this type of pension for a few reasons. One is simply that they are not as likely to work in the types of companies that have traditionally offered them. A second is that defined-contribution plans (such as 401[k] and profit-sharing plans) have become very popular among workers, who value the control that they have over the plan and the ability to take their pension with them when they leave the job. Employers like these plans because they are not subject to the investment risk.

Step 4: Subtract Your Expected Income From Your Retirement Income Needs

Steps 3 and 4 for Jessica: Jessica's employer does not have a defined-benefit plan, so she leaves line 3 on Table 14-1 blank and calculates that she will need an additional $119,963 − $33,000 = $86,963 per year.

Step 5: Estimate the Amount of Wealth You Need to Accumulate by Retirement

The amount of wealth that you will need to have accumulated by the time you retire in order to fund the income requirements that you have estimated depends on several factors. You need to make assumptions about how long you will live (longevity), how much your income needs will change over your period of retirement (inflation), and how much you will earn on your investments while you are retired (investment return). Most financial planners simplify this problem by assuming that you will be living off the investment return only, but, in fact, you may have no need to do so. That assumption requires you to have a lot more saved for retirement than you may actually need.

You can use Table 14-4 to calculate how much wealth you will have to have in order to provide yourself with enough income to support your needs, assuming that your income will have to increase at a 4 percent rate to cover inflation each year. This is approximately the rate of increase in Social Security benefits each year as well.

Take the first-year retirement income that you calculated in Step 4 and multiply it by the factor in Table 14-4, taking into account how long you expect to be retired and the after-tax rate of return that

Table 14-4 Estimate Your Required Retirement Wealth
(Multiply additional retirement income needs by the Retirement Wealth
Factor for your estimated years in retirement and
average annual investment return.)

Years in Retirement	Retirement Wealth Factor Investment Return during Retirement			
	4%	6%	8%	10%
1	0.9615	0.9071	0.8399	0.7636
2	1.9231	1.8690	1.8176	1.7686
3	2.8846	2.7771	2.6762	2.5812
4	3.8462	3.6681	3.5030	3.3495
5	4.8077	4.5423	4.2992	4.0759
6	5.7692	5.4000	5.0659	4.7627
7	6.7308	6.2415	5.8042	5.4120
8	7.6923	7.0671	6.5151	6.0259
9	8.6538	7.8772	7.1997	6.6063
10	9.6154	8.6720	7.8590	7.1550
11	10.5769	9.4517	8.4939	7.6738
12	11.5385	10.2168	9.1052	8.1644
13	12.5000	10.9674	9.6939	8.6281
14	13.4615	11.7039	10.2608	9.0666
15	14.4231	12.4265	10.8067	9.4811
16	15.3846	13.1354	11.3324	9.8731
17	16.3462	13.8310	11.8386	10.2436
18	17.3077	14.5134	12.3260	10.5940
19	18.2692	15.1829	12.7954	10.9252
20	19.2308	15.8399	13.2475	11.2384
21	20.1923	16.4844	13.6827	11.5345
22	21.1538	17.1168	14.1019	11.8144
23	22.1154	17.7372	14.5055	12.0791
24	23.0769	18.3459	14.8942	12.3293
25	24.0385	18.9432	15.2685	12.5659

you expect to earn on your investments *during* retirement. To be conservative, you should assume a lower rate of return and a longer retirement period, since you don't want to outlive your resources.

Step 5 for Jessica: Since Jessica has estimated her income needs to be $86,963 and she assumes that she will live longer than *average, she considers the factors in the last row of Table 14-4 (assuming twenty-five years in retirement).*

At a 4 percent return, she will need to have $86,963 × 24.038 = $2,090,417.

At a 6 percent return, she will need to have $86,963 × 18.943 = $1,647,340.

At an 8 percent return, she will need to have $86,963 × 15.269 = $1,327,838.

At a 10 percent return, she will need to have $86,963 × 12.566 = $1,092,777.

Jessica decides to be relatively conservative in estimating her investment returns and enters $1,647,340 on line 5 of Table 14-1.

Step 6: Estimate Future Value of Current Savings and Subtract From Goal

If you have already accumulated retirement funds, these will continue to earn returns for you until you retire. Use Table 14-5 to estimate how much your savings and retirement accounts will accumulate to by the date of your retirement. Take the current total balance in all your retirement investment accounts and multiply by the appropriate factor from Table 14-5 (depending on your estimated years to retirement and your estimated long-run annual return).

Step 6 for Jessica: Jessica has $100,000 in a 401(k) plan and $10,000 in an IRA. Assuming that she can earn a relatively conservative 8 percent annual return on these funds, they will be worth $753,335 in twenty-five years ($110,000 × 6.8485).

Step 7: Estimate Additional Wealth Needed at Retirement

You now have an estimate of the amount of wealth you will need to accumulate by the time you retire (Step 5). You also know how much

Table 14-5 Future Value of Current Retirement Savings (Multiply the appropriate factor below by the current value of your current retirement savings.)

Years to Retirement	Future Value Factor				
	Average Annual Investment Return				
	4%	6%	8%	10%	12%
5	1.2167	1.3382	1.4693	1.6105	1.7623
10	1.4802	1.7908	2.1589	2.5937	3.1058
15	1.8009	2.3966	3.1722	4.1772	5.4736
20	2.1911	3.2071	4.6610	6.7275	9.6463
25	2.6658	4.2919	6.8485	10.8347	17.0001
30	3.2434	5.7435	10.0627	17.4494	29.9599
35	3.9461	7.6861	14.7853	28.1024	52.7996
40	4.8010	10.2857	21.7245	45.2593	93.0510

of that can be met from your current savings (Step 6). Subtracting the latter from your overall goal, you now have an estimate of the additional wealth you need to accumulate.

Step 7 for Jessica: Jessica subtracts her expected accumulation from her current savings of $110,000 ($753,335) from her retirement wealth goal of $1,647,340 to arrive at the remaining goal of $894,005.

Step 8: Estimate Annual Savings Required to Meet Your Retirement Wealth Goal

How can you save enough to retire? If you have completed the calculations so far, you may be getting nervous about being able to meet such large goals. In this section, I help you figure out how *much* you need to save, but it will be up to you to get started as soon as possible and to stick with it. At this point, you should look back at the budget that you set for yourself in Chapter 4 and consider whether you need to reevaluate your current spending in order to meet your retirement savings goals.

The amount that you need to save each year will depend on how long you have until your retirement date and on how much you can earn on your investments. You can use Table 14-6 to calculate the amount of annual savings that will give you the amount of wealth that you will need to fund your retirement income goals. Simply take the amount of additional wealth you need to have at your retirement date and multiply it by the factor in Table 14-6, given your estimated years to retirement and your expected after-tax return on investment. Note that if you are planning on investing in a tax-deferred retirement plan, you can use your pretax return (after any costs associated with management of plan assets).

Although your investment options are discussed more fully in Chapters 8, 9, and 10, Table 14-6 provides a really great example of the power of compounding returns. If you consider an investment goal of $1,000,000 for someone with forty-five years to retirement, that person would need to invest only $386 per year if he or she can earn 14 percent per year for the whole forty-five years. Of course, that

Table 14-6 Estimate Your Annual Savings Required
(Multiply retirement wealth needed from Table 14-1 by the Retirement Savings Factor, given your estimated years to retirement and annual investment return.)

Retirement Savings Factor

Years to Save	Investment Return Preretirement					
	4%	6%	8%	10%	12%	14%
5	0.184627	0.177396	0.170456	0.163797	0.157410	0.151284
10	0.083291	0.075868	0.069029	0.062745	0.056984	0.051714
15	0.049941	0.042963	0.036830	0.031474	0.026824	0.022809
20	0.033582	0.027185	0.021852	0.017460	0.013879	0.010986
25	0.024012	0.018227	0.013679	0.010168	0.007500	0.005498
30	0.017830	0.012649	0.008827	0.006079	0.004144	0.002803
35	0.013577	0.008974	0.005803	0.003690	0.002317	0.001442
40	0.010523	0.006462	0.003860	0.002259	0.001304	0.000745
45	0.008262	0.004700	0.002587	0.001391	0.000736	0.000386

rate of return is unlikely on average. Assuming a more reasonable 8 percent rate of return, he or she would need to invest $2,587 per year. At 4 percent, he or she would need to invest $8,262 per year. Taking a little more investment risk can make a *big* difference!

But time is the other important factor. If you wait until you have thirty years to retirement to begin saving, earning an 8 percent return, you will need to save $8,830 per year (compared to $2,587 if you start saving fifteen years earlier).

Step 8 for Jessica: Jessica has estimated that she will need an additional $894,005 at her age 62 retirement. At age 37, she has twenty-five years to retirement and feels that she can afford to take some risk with her portfolio. If she can average 10 percent return in a tax-deferred account, she needs to be saving $9,090 per year, or $758 per month ($894,005 × 0.010168 from Table 14-6). While she is currently contributing 7 percent of her salary ($3,150) to her 401(k), Jessica estimates that she needs to increase her retirement contributions substantially if she hopes to meet her goals.

But That's Impossible!

As with the problem of saving for future educational expenditures, many people who work through this problem experience a degree of sticker shock. If your current level of savings is far too low and you don't have a lot of leeway in your budget to increase your retirement savings, there are a few things you can consider.

First, you may need to reconsider your retirement goals. It may not be realistic to retire early or to plan on maintaining the same lifestyle in retirement. You can significantly reduce your retirement expenses by downsizing houses, cars, and vacations. Retiring a few years later will reduce the number of years of retirement you must support and will allow you more years to contribute to your account and to build up your Social Security eligibility. In Jessica's case, if she assumes that she will retire at the normal retirement age of 67, she will need to contribute only about a third as much per year to reach her goals.

Second, you may want to consider changing jobs. There are many employers out there that offer generous pension plans. If your current employer does not contribute to your plan, but a new employer provides a guaranteed match, this can make a world of difference. If Jessica, in my example, was getting another 7 percent from her employer, she would probably be in good shape for retirement, given that both her own and her employer's contributions would increase with her salary over time.

Similarly, you should remember that the estimate you did in this chapter assumed that you would contribute the same amount to your retirement for each year of work. It may be more realistic to assume that you will contribute smaller amounts in earlier years and more as your income increases. You should balance that type of saving plan with the understanding that early contributions make the most impact on your ultimate retirement wealth as a result of the power of compounding.

Finally, you should consider the possibility of taking a little more investment risk. In the example, we assumed only an 8 to 10 percent rate of return on investment. Allocating a larger percentage to stocks would increase this return, and since Jessica has a long investment time horizon, she can afford to take a little more risk. If she retires at age 62, but her investments earn an average of 12 percent, which is a little less than the long-run average for the S&P 500 index, she will need to save one-third less per year to reach the same goal.

Retiree Health Insurance

Ensuring that you and your family have continued health coverage after retirement is a significant factor in retirement decisions. You have several choices of postretirement health coverage. If you are lucky, your employer may have made arrangements for your postretirement health insurance, usually by setting aside sufficient money throughout your working career to cover the higher costs later. In other cases, employers make the insurance available, perhaps with less generous deductibles and coinsurance, but require that the retiree pay the full premiums. A study based on the Survey of Income and Program Participation showed that, in 1992, nearly half of all nonworking retirees age 55 and over were covered through the health plan of a former employer. However, the trend is for employers to eliminate or reduce the generosity of their retiree health coverage. With longer retirement periods and increasing medical costs, these programs represent a significant cost to the company. In addition, because of a change in accounting rules in the early 1990s, companies are now required to report the present value of this expense as a liability on their financial statements, making it more apparent to investors that certain companies (those with an aging workforce) have made large commitments to their future retirees.

After age 65, you will be eligible for the Medicare program (which you paid for through a portion of your Social Security payroll tax). It is possible that this age will be increased to 67 in the near future as a result of concerns over the financial solvency of Medicare. If you retire early, you may be eligible for insurance through your spouse's employer's plan, or you may need to buy individual insurance to bridge the gap to age 65. Either of these options is likely to be expensive, particularly if you have a known health risk. Another alternative, which was also discussed in Chapter 5, is to extend your employer coverage for eighteen months as allowed under the COBRA legislation. If you are concerned that your Medicare coverage is too limited, there are lots of different Medicare supplement policies. As with other types of individual health insurance, these are likely to be subject to a health examination and to exempt certain conditions such as diabetes.

Prior to COBRA, individuals were more likely to wait to retire until they were eligible for Medicare. Researchers who have examined these trends suggest that current policies that facilitate continued health coverage will make early retirement more likely. Nevertheless, for those with significant health needs, either for themselves or a dependent, it may be advisable to continue working to age 65 to ensure continued health coverage.

Long-Term Care

What is long-term care? It includes both medical and custodial care for conditions that impair your ability to care for yourself. Statistically, 40 percent of those over the age of 65, and a larger percentage of women, will spend some time in a nursing home. This percentage is increasing rapidly as more people live into their eighties. This is of particular concern for women, because they make up most of the over-eighty population. The annual cost of a nursing home in 1999 ranged from $40,000 to $100,000 (the average was $56,000), and barely any of this cost is covered under traditional health insurance. Medicare does not cover nursing home care at all. Total expenditures

Illustration by Kristopher S. Bajtelsmit

on long-term care in the United States now top $100 billion per year, and nearly one-third of this cost is being covered by Medicaid, a state welfare program for the poor.

It is advisable to look carefully at your parents' long-term care coverage (insurance and accumulated wealth from which these costs can be paid) as well as your own. Women are three times more likely than men to end up providing home health care and personal assistance for their aging parents. So it is in your best interest to be sure that your parents are prepared for this potential expense. The Family Caregiver Alliance (*www.caregiver.org*) and the National Family Caregivers Association (*www.nfacares.org*) are both good sources of information on these issues.

According to the Health Insurance Association of America, nearly 5 million people purchased long-term care policies in the last decade alone, resulting in a market that is increasing at a rate of more than 20 percent per year. In general, it is recommended that families consider purchasing long-term care insurance if they have assets in excess of $75,000, excluding their home and a car, and income of at least $25,000 for singles and $35,000 for couples. Those with lower assets will quickly qualify for state assistance through Medicaid and are probably not as concerned with leaving an estate to their heirs. However, Medicaid assistance is not available until the patient's assets are down to $2,000. For couples, if only one is in long-term care, the total allowed assets is $81,900 plus the family home.

In considering different long-term care policies, here are a few important features to compare:

- *Financial health of the insurer:* You want the insurer to be around when you need the benefit.

- *Daily benefit:* These policies usually pay a dollar amount per day. Will $50 be sufficient, or will long-term care cost you $200 per day? In some areas of the country (e.g., the Northeast), nursing home care is much more expensive than in other areas.

- *Waiting period:* Most of these plans will not pay until the person has been in the nursing care facility for a minimum number of days, usually sixty to ninety.

- *Inflation protection:* Does the daily amount increase annually with inflation? Keep in mind that the facility providing the care is likely to increase its rates each year.

- *Coverage:* Does the plan cover all types of care (including home care and adult day care) or only nursing home care? Are certain conditions (e.g., Alzheimer's disease) excluded?

- *Length of coverage:* Many plans limit coverage to a specified number of years, and those with unlimited or lifetime benefits will be significantly more expensive.

- *Premium structure:* Are the premiums the same for the life of the policy, or do they increase as you get older?

- *Claims process:* How do you collect? Most insurers will require that you submit bills for reimbursement. What percentage of claims is paid?

You can expect this insurance to be fairly expensive. The average annual premium for a 65-year-old ranges from $1,000 to $2,300, depending on the terms of the policy. For a 79-year-old, the average will be several times higher, as much as $7,000 per year. But compared to the $50,000 annual cost of nursing home care, this may be a small price to pay.

Summary

If you have read this chapter and completed the worksheets, you now know:

- How much wealth you need to have accumulated by the time you retire

- How much you can expect from Social Security (assuming that there are no substantial changes in the program before you retire)

- The most likely Social Security reforms to expect

- The amount of annual savings necessary to meet your retirement wealth goal

- The importance of knowing your retiree health insurance coverage

- The potential expense of long-term care

This chapter may have exposed a scary truth to you—it won't be easy to save enough to provide for a comfortable retirement, particularly if you are already halfway there and you haven't saved much yet. You will probably need to cut back on other expenditures in order to channel funds to this important goal. It is important to consider retirement plans when choosing employers, since employer contributions help your retirement savings to accumulate.

CHAPTER 15

Estate Planning Isn't Just for the Rich

You need to read this chapter if:

- ✔ You do not understand why estate planning is an essential component of your financial plan.

- ✔ You (or your spouse) do not have a will.

- ✔ You don't understand how trusts can help to reduce estate taxes.

- ✔ You have a family-owned business that doesn't have liquid assets.

- ✔ You would like to protect your assets from creditors.

- ✔ You don't know how to pick an estate planning professional.

The Only Certain Things in Life Are Death and Taxes

This chapter is all about death and taxes—preparing for the first and avoiding the second. So perhaps the old adage isn't totally true. Certainly, we are all going to die. It will probably not be tomorrow, but it is inevitable. However, it is not always true that a huge portion of your estate must go to the tax collector. When you die, estate taxes can take a big bite out of your hard-earned savings, leaving less for your survivors. But appropriate planning can significantly reduce the tax impact.

At the time of this writing, Congress has made some extensive changes to the estate tax laws, although these changes will be phased in gradually through 2009, at which time the estate tax is reinstated in its current form. Since we cannot predict when we will die (and it could be tomorrow), estate planning should always be done taking into consideration the current law and then adjusted as the new rules become effective over time.

In my opinion, the two primary purposes of estate planning are to maximize the resources available to your survivors and to reduce the hassles associated with settling your estate. Both of these goals require a little advance planning and the willingness to face an unpleasant but inevitable reality—your own death or that of your spouse.

Estate planning is a complex topic, and there are many books devoted to explaining the details. After reading one short chapter, you will not become an expert by any means. I have included some additional resources in the appendix should you feel the need for more detail. The point of this chapter is to help you to understand why estate planning is an essential component of your overall financial plan and to encourage you to take the first steps toward developing a plan that will protect you and your family from unnecessary expense. Once you understand the basics, you should consult an estate-planning professional to help you deal with the legal issues, particularly if you are a person with greater wealth.

Why Do You Need an Estate Plan?

The best way to help you understand the necessity for estate planning is to give you a few examples of what can happen if you do not have an estate plan.

Your Children Depend on You to Be Prepared

Example: Susan is the single mother of a teenage daughter, Christine, having divorced her abusive husband several years ago. Her ex-husband does not provide any financial or emotional support for Christine. The day-to-day stresses of working full-time and keeping up with Christine's activities have left Susan little time for financial planning. She has a $500,000 term life insurance policy and $25,000 saved for Christine's college expenses. She also has $300,000 in her 401(k) plan, home equity of $100,000, and $100,000 in other assets, so she feels that Christine will be taken care of if something should happen to her. Susan dies unexpectedly in a car accident, and no one can find evidence that she ever executed a will.

This is a worst-case scenario. If you have a child and you die without a will, the state will decide who will be the guardian of your child. A likely choice will be the child's birth father. Or she might be given to relatives she barely knows who live in another state. In addition, if you do not have a will, the assets of your estate, after taxes, will pass according to the rules of "intestate succession" (which just means passing the assets without a will) in your state. If you are married, this usually means that your child and your husband will each be given a share. If you are unmarried, your parents or siblings may be entitled to a portion. In any event, a teenage girl will now have responsibility for a substantial amount of money that will be managed by a state-appointed guardian until she reaches majority (which may be age 18 in some states), at which time she will have control. Do you really want to give an 18-year-old that kind of responsibility?

What about taxes? In this case, Susan's estate will be barely over the current exemption amount, so there will not be substantial taxes owed, but the costs of settling the estate will be much higher than if Susan had done a little advance planning.

Be Sure That Your Spouse Has Taken Care of Business

Example: Fred and Wilma have been married for many years, and Fred has just made the decision to retire from his job as *a university professor at age 60. Unexpectedly, Fred dies of a heart attack while jogging in the local park. Wilma, who has been a homemaker all their married life, finds that Fred has no valid will; has recently reduced his life insurance to $50,000; has not selected the survivorship option for benefits from his university pension; and has most of the family savings accounts in his name, the exception being the primary checking account, which has a $2,000 balance. The bulk of his estate is his pension and the equity in the family home.*

You should rightfully be asking "What was he thinking???" In this true story, Wilma had to rely on the financial help of her grown children until the estate could be settled, which took almost a year. All the bank accounts that were in Fred's name were frozen until the estate could be probated. She was eventually able to receive Social Security survivor benefits, but because Fred failed to choose the survivorship option, his pension benefits were due only until his death and did not continue to be payable to his surviving spouse. Fred probably thought that he would live longer than Wilma and therefore was willing to take that risk in return for the higher benefits payable without the survivorship option. Under current law, spouses must sign a document indicating that they understand that this decision has been made.

Family Businesses May Not Have the Money to Pay the Estate Taxes

Example: Marissa owns and operates a convenience store with the help of her three grown sons. She dies with a simple will that leaves all her interest in the company to her children equally upon her death. The total value of her estate is $3,000,000. The estate taxes, after her exemption and the family-business exemption, are $645,000. Since the business does not have enough liquid assets to cover this, the tax liability will seriously impair her children's ability to keep the business in the family.

Although the Taxpayer Relief Act of 1997 included a provision that allows family businesses a larger exemption, the lack of liquid assets in these situations makes payment of *any* estate taxes a problem. A simple solution to this problem would have been for Marissa to buy life insurance, naming her children as beneficiaries, and place it in a trust that would bypass the estate (and thus not be taxable). Her children could then use the proceeds of the policy to pay the estate taxes due upon her death.

The estate tax repeal passed by Congress in 2001 allows a much larger estate to be transferred without paying estate taxes, thereby reducing the likelihood that family businesses will experience this problem.

Deterrents to Estate Planning

If you are like most women, estate planning is a subject that you haven't thought much about before and would rather not think about. Why is that? Here are a few reasons that women have offered to me for avoiding this issue. See if any of them hit home for you:

- I don't like to think about negative things like death.

- I don't understand all the legal terms and complex contractual arrangements.

- I find it hard to trust an estate planner to do what's best for me and not just what makes him or her a fee.

- I don't like to deal with lawyers; I feel that they patronize me.

- It's hard to talk to my spouse and children about money issues.

- I don't have many assets, so what's the point?

- I don't have time right now to think about that.

Do any of these excuses sound familiar? If so, you aren't alone. Many people delay thinking about these issues until it is too late, to their detriment or the detriment of their heirs. Perhaps the most seductive of all excuses for busy women is the last one. None of us has much extra time. But you need to ask yourself whether the benefits of having those few extra minutes are worth the potential costs.

Whatever the stage you are at in your life, it is wise to become informed about your options and to set in place a plan that can evolve as you mature.

What's the Point?

In the introduction to this chapter, I told you that the two main reasons for estate planning are to simplify the settlement of the estate and to avoid paying unnecessary taxes. Interestingly, if we are talking about *your* estate, neither of these will have a direct impact on *you*, because you will be dead. If you have loved ones, you are probably interested in minimizing the negative impact that your death may have on them. However, you should keep in mind that, if you are married, your husband is likely to die before you do, so the planning you do now is most likely to benefit *you* as his primary beneficiary. Table 15-1 summarizes the primary and secondary benefits of estate planning.

Let's assume that at least some of the benefits of estate planning are goals that you would like to accomplish. And let's also assume that you can overcome the emotional hurdles that have prevented you from facing this topic until now. In the remainder of this chapter,

Table 15-1 Benefits of Estate Planning

1. Being able to sleep at night
2. Protecting your minor children, parents, and spouse
3. Reducing estate taxes
4. Providing liquidity so that taxes due can be paid
5. Protecting your assets from creditors and lawsuits
6. Distributing your assets according to your wishes upon your death
7. Simplifying the settlement of your estate
8. Reducing the costs of settling your estate

I explain the basic components of an estate plan (see Table 15-2) and what you need to do to get your plan under way. Once you understand the terminology and the purpose of these components, you will be able to consult an estate-planning professional without feeling overwhelmed.

You Need to Have a Will

Even though all states have rules that stipulate how an estate is to be divided among heirs in the event that a person dies without a will, it is still advisable to have a valid will. If you have minor dependent children, it is absolutely necessary so that you can specify a guardian and direct the management of your assets for your children's benefit. If you would prefer to specify the distribution of your assets rather than have them divided according to statute (which will normally give some of them to your children, rather than all of them to your husband), then you need to have a will. In addition, if you do not have a will, your surviving spouse and children will incur greater expenses. Even something as simple as ensuring that a family heirloom goes to the person you have promised it to must be specified. You cannot count on verbal promises made while you are living.

You have probably all seen a movie or read a book that involved a last will and testament. Sometimes the issue is mental capacity or duress in the making of the will (as in the case of Howard Hughes). A particularly interesting story is John Grisham's novel *The Testament,* in which a wealthy man with lots of money-grubbing relatives

---

Table 15-2 Basic Components of an Estate Plan

1. Execute a valid last will and testament.
2. Prepare a plan for minimizing the impact of taxes on your estate.
3. Keep life insurance outside of your estate.
4. Develop a gifting plan.
5. Be sure that assets are titled appropriately.
6. Consider using trusts as a means of reducing future tax impact.

executes a holographic will (just before killing himself) in which he cancels his previous will and names a previously secret illegitimate daughter as his sole heir. A holographic will is one that is completely handwritten and signed by the maker; it does not have to be witnessed if it can be shown that the person actually wrote it and if it meets the other requirements for a valid will. This is a very limited exception to the requirements that wills be typed and witnessed.

Although you do not need to have an attorney draw up a will for it to be valid, and there are lots of self-help books that provide samples for you to follow in writing one, I highly recommend that you spend the money to have your will professionally drawn up. It's not very expensive, especially if you just need a simple will—probably no more than $200. And the attorney can ensure that the will has met all the requirements in your state. If your circumstances are more complex, the attorney can ensure that your goals for your estate plan will be adequately addressed through your will. Later in this chapter, I provide some pointers on selecting the appropriate professional help.

The requirements for a valid will are outlined in Table 15-3. As with other contracts, legal capacity (age of majority) and mental capacity to make a contract ("being of sound mind and body") are

---

Table 15-3 Requirements for a Valid Will

In order to be valid in most states, a will must meet the following criteria:

1. The maker of the will must be of legal age (usually 18).
2. The maker must have the mental capacity to make a will:
    a. Must understand the nature and extent of her or his assets
    b. Must understand whom she or he is willing the estate to
    c. Must understand how she or he is distributing it
3. The maker of the will must be intending for the document to be her or his will.
4. The will must be in writing and (with some limited exceptions) typed or printed.
5. The will must be dated.
6. The will must be signed in the presence of two witnesses who are not relatives or named beneficiaries.
7. The will must name at least one executor.

required. When people make or change their wills late in life, there may be challenges to the wills if there is some question of senility. As long as the person understands the nature of what she or he is doing, the will is likely to be upheld. However, to avoid fraud, the will must be in writing and cannot be made under duress or undue influence.

If you want your daughter to have your engagement ring when you die, you cannot assume that she will get it unless you specify in your will that she should get it. You would be surprised how many people are buried with valuable jewelry for sentimental reasons. Family members are also reluctant to reveal that the deceased promised something to them for fear of sounding greedy. I don't know about you, but I am very certain that I will *not* need my jewelry anymore after I'm dead.

Because people may write several wills during the course of a lifetime as their circumstances change, the will must be dated and must indicate that it is the maker's "last" will or that it is an addendum, or codicil, to a previous will.

Specific Bequests

I strongly recommend that you be fairly specific about personal belongings that you would like to have divided among your children. If you don't, then one of two equally problematic outcomes will result. First, your children may fight over your stuff. Some of the most heated family disputes arise out of the distribution of assets. If you remain silent, you may be assuming that everyone will just divide up your stuff fairly, but this is unlikely to happen. You are doing your heirs no favors by failing to make the tough decisions for them. The emotional stress of dealing with a loss and wanting to have something to remember that person by will cause even the most even-tempered people to act irrationally. In the case of one family I know, the relatives descended on Grandma's house after her death and took whatever they wanted. Unfortunately, the closest relatives didn't live nearby and got there after most of the family photos and memorabilia had already disappeared. Something tells me that that would not have been Grandma's preference.

The second possible outcome is that no one takes anything. My own family provides a good example of this. My mother passed away three years ago after an extended battle with ovarian cancer, leaving everything to my father. She had a large collection of costume jewelry that she had verbally said she wanted to split among my two younger sisters and myself. But she never actually said how or when to do it, and nothing was said about it in her will. My sisters and I live in three different states and rarely are in one place at the same time. When we are together, the typical pandemonium of family gatherings makes it difficult to find time to talk, let alone divide up our mother's jewelry. So even though I know my father has a vision of us sitting down together to do this, it is unlikely to ever happen. All three of us would like to have something of my mother's to remember her by, and none of us has a great deal of preference as to what. But still it sits there, and we feel awkward even bringing up the subject.

The lesson in this is that you need to take the responsibility for making specific bequests, not only to be sure the things get to the person you want to have them, but also to reduce the family conflicts that might result later.

Federal Estate and Gift Tax

Since one of the primary goals of estate planning is to reduce the burden of estate taxes on your estate and on the estates of your heirs, you should familiarize yourself with the basic rules.

This section assumes that you are subject to taxes in effect in 2001. While I have noted the changes that will be phased in over the next several years, you should plan for current rather than future tax rules.

Estate Tax Exemptions

The Taxpayer Relief Act of 1997 included provisions that increased the level of wealth that is exempt from estate tax gradually to $1,000,000 over the next several years. In 2001, the first $675,000 of the estate net assets for each spouse is exempt from taxation.

Under the terms of the 2001 estate tax repeal, the exemption will increase to $1,000,000 in 2002, $1,500,000 in 2004, $2,000,000 in 2006, and $3,500,000 in 2009. The tax will be completely repealed for those dying in 2010, but current tax rules will go back into effect in 2011 unless further legislative action is taken.

Although these exemptions may seem large, keep in mind that baby boomers have been accumulating significant amounts of wealth in their retirement plans over the last couple of decades and that they still have many years of life expectancy. I hope to have well over the current exemption amount by the time I die. And I would really prefer not to give half of it to the government, particularly since I will have already paid income taxes on all but my retirement plan assets.

To reduce the impact of estate taxes on surviving spouses, there is an unlimited marital deduction for jointly held property. All that this means is that the government is willing to wait for both spouses to die before collecting the tax. Suppose your husband dies and you inherit all his wealth. Using the unlimited marital deduction, you owe no estate tax. When you die, however, the portion of his estate that you still own will now pass to your heirs, presumably your children, and they will be subject to the tax if your assets are greater than the exemption amount. This may be a problem for you sooner than you think in the event that you inherit substantial wealth from your parents before you die. This "generation-skipping" tax is also repealed after 2009.

How Much Tax Will Be Payable on Your Estate?

To estimate the potential impact of estate taxes on your specific situation, you can use Table 15-4 to calculate your adjusted gross estate and the tax that would be due on it.

Keep in mind that your estate will probably keep growing for some years. Real estate values generally rise, and your mortgage is gradually being paid off. Your retirement account and other savings accounts are still increasing in value. When you calculate your net worth using the worksheet in Chapter 2, you may find that your net wealth is nowhere near $675,000. However, you will need to adjust for items that affect an estate but are not part of your current net

Table 15-4 Estimated Estate Tax Calculation

1. Your net worth (from Table 2-3) $_____
2. Future value factor (from Table 15-5) _____
3. Future value of estate (multiply #1 by #2) _____
4. Plus proceeds from life insurance _____
5. Minus estate deductions _____
   —Funeral expenses _____
   —Executor's fee _____
   —Legal fees _____
   —Court fees _____
   —Other expenses of administering the estate _____
6. Adjusted gross estate (AGE) (#3 − #4 + #5) _____
7. Minus unlimited marital deduction _____
8. Minus unlimited charitable deduction _____
9. Taxable estate (#6 − #7 − #8) _____
10. Tentative tax owed (Table 15-6) _____
11. Minus tax credits (Table 15-7) _____
12. Taxes due on estate (#10 − #11) _____

worth, and you also need to adjust for future growth in the value of your estate.

Adjustments to Net Worth to Arrive at Adjusted Gross Estate

Your adjusted gross estate (AGE) is your net worth as you calculated it in Chapter 2, Table 2-3, adjusted to future value (by multiplying by the appropriate interest factor in Table 15.5), plus the net proceeds from any life insurance that is subject to estate tax, minus funeral expenses (estimate at $10,000) and the administrative costs of settling the estate. As an alternative to using the tables in this chapter, you can use the net worth and estate tax calculators at *http://www. smartmoney.com/estate*.

To arrive at the taxable estate value, you then subtract the unlimited marital deduction and any charitable deductions. For the sake of argument, let's assume that your husband dies before you, so that

Table 15-5 Adjusting Your Estate to Future Value
(Multiply your current estate by the factor below for your life
expectancy and annual after-tax appreciation.)

Life Expectancy	Annual After-Tax Increase in Estate Value			
	2%	4%	6%	8%
10	1.2189	1.4802	1.7908	2.1589
15	1.3459	1.8009	2.3966	3.1722
20	1.4859	2.1911	3.2071	4.6609
25	1.6106	2.6658	4.2919	6.8485
30	1.8114	3.2434	5.7435	10.0627
35	1.9999	3.9461	7.6861	14.7853
40	2.2081	4.8010	10.2857	21.7245
45	2.4379	5.8412	13.7646	31.9204
50	2.6916	7.1067	18.4201	46.9016

you are leaving all your combined wealth to your children. Calculate the tentative tax from Table 15-6 and subtract the tax credit from Table 15-7. If you have a family-owned business, you may be entitled to another $625,000 exemption under current law for family business property in the estate.

If you have projected that some taxes will be due on your estate, it is now time to think about how estate planning can help you reduce this burden on your heirs.

Give Your Money Away Before You Die

Early Gifts to Your Heirs

If you have sufficient assets for your own needs and you anticipate that you will leave a fairly large estate when you die, then gifting may be advisable. You (and your spouse) are each allowed to give $10,000 (increasing with inflation in each year after 1999) in cash or property to any number of individuals each year without incurring any tax to you or the person receiving the gift. If you give more than $10,000, you will be subject to tax unless you choose to use some of your allowed estate and gift tax credit (Table 15.7). Gifts of less than $10,000 do not require the filing of a special tax return.

Table 15-6 2001 Federal Estate and Gift Tax Rates

Taxable Estate			Tax Owed Equals	Plus %	On Amount Over
$ 0 to	$	10,000	$ 0	18%	$ 0
10,001 to		20,000	1,800	20%	10,000
20,001 to		40,000	3,800	22%	20,000
40,001 to		60,000	8,200	24%	40,000
60,001 to		80,000	13,000	26%	60,000
80,001 to		100,000	18,200	28%	80,000
100,001 to		150,000	23,800	30%	100,000
150,001 to		250,000	38,800	32%	150,000
250,001 to		500,000	70,800	34%	250,000
500,001 to		750,000	155,800	37%	500,000
750,001 to		1,000,000	248,300	39%	750,000
1,000,001 to		1,250,000	345,800	41%	1,000,000
1,250,001 to		1,500,000	448,300	43%	1,250,000
1,500,001 to		2,000,000	555,800	45%	1,500,000
2,000,001 to		2,500,000	780,800	49%	2,000,000
2,500,001 to		3,000,000	1,025,800	53%	2,500,000
3,000,001 to		10,000,000	1,290,800	55%	3,000,000
10,000,001 to		21,040,000	5,140,800	60%	10,000,000
21,040,001 and		higher	125,764,800	55%	21,040,000

Table 15-7 2001 Estate and Gift Tax Credits

Year of Death	Tax Credit Amount	Effective Estate Exclusion
2001	$220,550	$ 675,000
2002	$229,800	$ 700,000
2003	$229,800	$ 700,000
2004	$287,300	$ 850,000
2005	$326,300	$ 950,000
2006	$345,800	$1,000,000

Example: Margaret, a widow, is 65 years old and has an estate with an estimated value of $2,200,000. She has two grown daughters, both of whom have children. She plans to leave her estate to her two daughters equally and would like to minimize the impact of estate taxes on her heirs. She decides to begin giving her daughters and their spouses each $10,000 an-

*nually (for a total of $40,000 per year). Within five years, she
will be able to reduce her estate to the allowed $2,000,000 ex-
emption (effective 2006).*

Another terrific gift tax exclusion is the unlimited annual exclusion for payment of medical expenses or tuition directly to the educational institution or medical provider. This is a way of reducing
your estate without the worry that your gifts will be used for frivolous
purposes.

If you have property in your estate, such as real estate or securities, you may want to consider gifting those assets that you think will
have the greatest appreciation in the future. The advantage of this is
that all of the appreciated value is removed from your estate. Property that has already appreciated significantly in value may be better
left in the estate. If property has appreciated significantly since the
time that you purchased it, selling it would generate a significant
capital gains tax liability. But if it passes to your heirs on your death,
they are entitled to a "stepped-up basis," so that it is valued at market value. If they sell it, the capital gain is the difference between the
value of the property at your death and its value at the date of sale,
which will mean that little or no capital gains tax will be due.

For people dying after 2010, this will no longer be the case and
their heirs are likely to be subject to substantial capital gains taxes if
they choose to sell inherited assets that have appreciated a lot in
value.

Making gifts to minors is a little more complex and will definitely
require professional help. Under the Uniform Gifts to Minors Act or
the Uniform Transfers to Minors Act (depending on your state of resi-
dence), you can set up a custodial account to which gifts can be
made for the benefit of a minor. The primary disadvantages are related to the age at which the child gains control over the money,
which may be as young as eighteen in some states.

Gifts to Charities

Your estate is allowed an unlimited charitable deduction, so if you
decide to leave everything to your favorite charity, there will be no

estate taxes due, no matter how large your estate is. Or you may want to leave a portion of your estate to charity while still providing for your children and grandchildren.

If you have more than enough wealth for your needs, you should consider making charitable gifts while you are still living rather than waiting until you die. Although you do not pay estate tax on the amounts willed to charities, the additional advantage of gifting during your lifetime is that you get a current income tax deduction as long as the donation does not exceed 50 percent of your adjusted gross income. In addition, the charity will have the use of the property or cash sooner. The best way to leverage a lifetime gift is to give away property that has appreciated significantly, such as shares of stock that were bought at much lower than current market prices.

> *Example: Katie owns $5,000 of Wal-Mart stock for which she originally paid $500. She would like to make a $5,000 donation to her church. Should she (a) give the church $5,000 cash or (b) give the church the stock directly?*

In either case, Katie will get the $5,000 deduction on her income taxes and reduce the size of her future estate. By giving the stock, she avoids paying capital gains tax on all of the appreciation. If she would still like to be a Wal-Mart shareholder, a better alternative would be to give the church the stock and then use the $5,000 cash to buy more Wal-Mart stock. In that case, she can still participate in future increases in the value of the stock, but she will have a much lower income tax obligation should she need to sell the stock in the future.

Credit Shelter Trust

Although the unlimited marital deduction sounds like a great deal, it actually can work to the detriment of your heirs. Instead of thinking only about minimizing taxes to your spouse, you should think about the ultimate taxes that will be paid on the total estate by the heirs of the last to survive.

*Example: John and Mary have total wealth of $2,000,000.
John dies in 2001 and leaves his half to Mary. She uses the
unlimited marital deduction and pays no estate tax. Mary dies
in 2004 and leaves everything to her children, Stephen and
Sharon. The estate can use only Mary's exemption of
$1,500,000, so Stephen and Sharon will end up paying estate
tax on $500,000 of the inherited wealth.*

In this example, if Mary dies earlier than 2006, note that her heirs
will owe even more tax, since the applicable exemption amount will
be lower.

Although these instruments are likely to decline in usage under
the new law, a commonly recommended method for avoiding a big
tax burden on the next generation is to establish a credit shelter or
family trust. The basic idea of this type of arrangement is that each
spouse specifies in his or her will that some of his or her property
will go to the trust at his or her death (specifically, an amount equal
to the allowable exemption), rather than directly to the spouse. The
survivor, who is also the trustee of the trust, can use the money in
the trust for support during his or her lifetime, and the remainder
goes to the children at the survivor's death without being included in
the estate of the trustee. In the previous example, if John had willed
$1,000,000 to such a trust, upon Mary's death, her estate of
$1,000,000 would go to their children tax free, as would the remain-
der of the trust assets.

In order to achieve this outcome, Mary and John will need to
be sure that they do not hold all of their assets jointly with right of
survivorship. In that type of ownership, the surviving joint tenant
automatically owns the asset at the death of the other joint tenant.
Instead, at least some assets will need to be held as tenants in common (which means that you each own exactly half and can control
that half through your will) so that a portion can pass to the trust.

Even when you have not specifically designated a trust, you can
achieve a similar outcome (reducing taxes for the next generation)
by disclaiming a portion of your inheritance from your spouse. In
Mary's case, she could have chosen to disclaim some or all of the

$1,000,000 from her deceased husband as long as she did it within nine months of his death. The effect of this decision is that the law will apply as if Mary had died first, so the money will pass to the next in line according to his will, provided that the assets are not jointly held. Of course, if your next in line are minors, your will would need to have a trust arrangement or custodial provision.

Revocable Living Trusts

Another type of trust arrangement is one that is created during your lifetime. You place all of your assets in the trust (retitling them in the name of the trust) and manage it during your lifetime. Upon your death, all the trust assets pass directly to the beneficiaries without going through probate, although they will still be subject to estate taxation. The primary advantage of doing this is to avoid probate, but since the probate process is not always very onerous, the expense may not be worth the savings. If you have property in several states, there may be more advantage, since your will would otherwise have to go through probate in several different jurisdictions.

Other types of trust arrangements are also possible, so it is important to consult a qualified professional for advice on which would be most appropriate for your needs.

Using Life Insurance in Estate Planning

In Chapter 6, I discussed life insurance mainly as a tool for providing income to your survivors. In estate planning, in addition to increasing the size of your estate at a relatively low cost when you are young, life insurance can also provide a means of paying estate taxes that would otherwise require liquidation of family assets.

Survivor Life Insurance

Since surviving spouses will owe no estate tax during their lifetime, the type of life insurance that is most helpful for estate planning is survivorship life insurance. This type of permanent insurance (as opposed to term life) pays out on the death of the second spouse and is therefore significantly cheaper than purchasing life insurance on both lives individually. You can fund your required death benefit with a lower premium, or, alternatively, you can increase the death benefit level for your heirs.

Irrevocable Life Insurance Trusts

Normally, the proceeds of life insurance are subject to estate tax, so it is likely that your estate-planning professional will recommend that you remove the life insurance from your taxable estate by putting it in an irrevocable life insurance trust if your estate is expected to exceed the tax exemption amount. In this type of arrangement, the trust is created and you gift the insurance premiums to the trust for the benefit of your heirs, subject to gift tax limitations. Thus, the maximum amount of life insurance that you can buy without being subject to gift tax is whatever amount can be purchased with a premium of $10,000 (plus inflation) per year per beneficiary. As you learned in Chapter 6, the earlier you begin your premium payments for this insurance, the lower the annual premiums.

Life insurance that you previously owned and later transferred to the trust will still be deemed part of your estate for three years after the transfer. Therefore, it may be preferable to have the trust purchase the policy rather than transfer an existing policy.

Working With an Estate-Planning Professional

I suspect that after reading this chapter, you clearly understand the necessity of getting professional help for estate planning. The uncertain future of estate and gift taxation makes it difficult for individuals to decide on and implement a plan that will keep pace with statutory change without help. More than in any other area of your financial plan, you will benefit from professional expertise. Although many of the suggestions that I have made in earlier chapters regarding the selection of financial advisers also apply here, a few specifics related to estate planning are different and should be noted.

Not Just Any Lawyer Will Do

Many law schools do not require that every student take an estate-planning course. Both estate planning and taxation are highly specialized fields that require additional study and practical experience. You should be sure that the attorney you select has limited his or her practice to this area of specialization. Not only will you get better advice, but generally it will end up being cheaper, since someone who has more experience will take less time to complete tasks than a generalist, who may be charging you for the time it takes him or her to bone up on the subject matter.

Sources of Information

Attorney-provided: Most professionals will provide a brochure or résumé upon request. Look for years of experience, evidence that the attorney is primarily specializing in estate planning, and evidence that she or he keeps current.

Library: Check the *Law Directory* at the local library for the ratings of particular local estate-planning attorneys.

Professional associations: The local bar association will be able to give you a list of all the attorneys in the area who specialize in estate planning. You can also check with the American College of Trust and Estate Counsel (ACTEC) at (301) 398-1888 or with a local Estate Planning Council chapter for names of members in your area. Neither of these sources will vouch for the credentials or experience of its members, however, so you will still need to check references

Friends: If you have friends or colleagues who have previously used an estate-planning attorney, this may be a good place to start. You should still check into the qualifications of the attorney rather than assuming that your friend did so. You would be surprised how many people will go to a general practitioner because he or she is a friend rather than attempting to find a more qualified person.

Certifications: There are several different certifications that you might find among estate-planning professionals. Certified Financial

Planners (CFPs) must have three years' experience in financial planning and must pass a difficult certification exam. They are subject to a code of ethics and are required to have several hours of continuing education credits every year. An attorney with that designation will also be qualified to give you advice on your overall financial plan. Accredited Estate Planners (AEPs) must have five years' experience in estate planning and complete education requirements in that specialized area. They are also subject to continuing education requirements.

Interview the Candidates

You will usually be allowed an initial free interview with the attorney. This will give you a good idea of whether you will be able to work effectively together to achieve your estate-planning goals. Do not feel compelled to continue working with a person with whom you do not feel comfortable. The purpose of this interview is for you to make that decision. When couples interview attorneys together, the woman sometimes feels that the attorney tends to focus more on what her husband is saying, perhaps on the assumption that the man is the financial decision maker. (This problem is not limited to male attorneys.)

At this meeting, you should get a clear idea of how the attorney will charge for his or her services. This may be an hourly charge or a flat fee (e.g., for preparation of a will). If you are seeing the attorney to settle the estate of a loved one, it is not uncommon to be charged a percentage of the value of the estate. Ask for a clear statement of what is included in the charges and what items will be extra.

Reduce the Attorney Costs

It's a fact of life—women like to talk. However, if you are paying on an hourly basis for consultation with an attorney, chatting can get to be very expensive, so you need to keep a tight rein on your innate need to get to know the attorney personally. Every minute that you spend talking about nonestate topics is still costing you, so stay focused. The biggest mistake that people make is to go to an attorney without having carefully thought out what they want to do. You should already have thought through the most important issues, such as who gets the money when and who gets guardianship of the kids.

If you have done your homework, you can get a lot accomplished in a short time. Reading this book and doing the worksheets will have helped you to be better prepared for the meeting with the attorney. You should bring all relevant documents and lists with you to the meeting to maximize what can be accomplished there. This will include your most recent tax return(s); your will(s); a list of assets and liabilities; and copies of life insurance policies, deeds, mortgages, and any other legal documents affecting your estate. Information on your retirement plan, business interests, and real property interests as well as personal information (including date of birth and Social Security number) for you and members of your household who are beneficiaries under your will or insurance should also be made available.

Summary

If you have read this chapter and followed the worksheets, you now should know:

- The benefits of estate planning

- The basic elements of an estate plan

- The requirements for a valid will

- How to estimate your future estate tax

- How to minimize the impact of estate taxes on your heirs through the use of lifetime gifts, creation of trusts, and the purchase of life insurance

- How to select an estate-planning attorney

The bad news is that we all will die someday. The good news is that we don't need to die broke. By reading this book, developing some financial goals, and taking steps toward achieving those goals, you are making it more likely that you will have some assets for your heirs to worry about in the future. The other good news is that we do not need to burden our survivors with unnecessary financial and administrative hassles.

At least for the near future, it seems unlikely that estate taxes will be a serious problem for your heirs. With adequate planning and a valid will in place, you can ensure that your estate is handled according to your wishes.

CHAPTER 16

Some Closing Thoughts on the Financial Future of Women

You're on the Way to Financial Freedom!

When you began reading this book, I told you that, with a little more financial know-how and a small investment of time, you could achieve your financial freedom. If you're the typical busy woman, you may have skimmed a few chapters and skipped to the end, but that's okay—even if you only read a chapter or two of this book, you will have taken something from it that will be worth the cover price many times over. Every little bit of financial education takes you that much closer to achieving your financial objectives.

My goal in writing this book was to condense a wealth of information into a short enough space that a busy woman could get the basics without investing a huge amount of time. Maybe you used this book to develop a budget, or to better understand how to buy a home or a car. Or perhaps you are now working on a plan to reduce your credit or to increase your savings for college or retirement. Maybe you simply learned that you need to buy some more life insurance.

No matter what you take from this book, you will have achieved a degree of financial freedom. And I will feel that I have accomplished something.

In this book, I have repeatedly referred to the growing body of research on women and their finances. The basic conclusions should now be familiar to you. On average:

- Women have less income than men.

- Women have less accumulated wealth than men.

- Women live longer than men and thus need to save more to fund a longer retirement.

- Women are more conservative investors than men, which makes it more difficult for them to accumulate sufficient wealth.

- Women are less likely than men to have life and health insurance.

- Most women will eventually be widowed or divorced and therefore cannot rely on a man to take care of them.

This all sounds pretty grim, doesn't it? And I forgot to mention the most important problem: Women are *very* busy. They are mothers, spouses, working professionals, and homemakers. So it's no wonder that women have often found that they don't have much time to learn what they need to know about their finances.

But there's good news. Just as you have taken the time to read all or part of this book, other women across the nation are also recognizing the need to take charge of their finances. Over the years, I have spoken with many women about their finances. Without exception, they say that they *know* they need to know more. And little by little, they are collectively taking action to learn more. Furthermore, there has never been a better time in history to be seeking help. The Internet is the great equalizer, providing access and information to everyone, regardless of financial circumstances or gender. Financial professionals, employers, and retirement plan managers understand the special needs of women and are making great strides in providing useful and female-friendly information. The deluge of information, in and of itself, can become a problem, since it is difficult to separate information that is useful and practical from that which is not. Nevertheless, our success is in the statistics—in nearly all dimensions of income and wealth, women's finances have been improving steadily. It should come as no big surprise to find out that the youngest cohorts of women are doing the best.

We Have the Power

When my boys were young, there was a TV cartoon in which the superhero turned on her super strength by holding up her sword and shouting, "I have the power!" There have been many occasions in my life when I wished I had that sword. But even without it, "I have the power!" should be the mantra for baby boom women and their daughters. I cannot tell you how very thankful I am that I was born in an era where women have the same opportunities as men. In the last few decades, we have won the vote, we have taken control of our bodies, and we have earned our right to equal opportunity in education and in the workplace. It was barely a generation ago that there were actually scientists who thought that women were not capable of understanding math and science because their brains were smaller!

There are still a few frontiers left to explore and conquer, and some of them will take more time, such as persistent wage inequality and unequal division of responsibilities for child care and housework. But there are others that are currently within your power to change. All women have the ability to understand their financial circumstances, to set financial goals, to make wise choices about household purchases and borrowing, and to prepare for their future financial needs. We owe it to ourselves, and to our daughters, to take advantage of the opportunities that are given to us.

APPENDIX

Additional Resources

General

Women's Financial Network is a financial institution created by women for women that offers various products and services designed for women investors. It sponsors a web site at *http://www. wfn.com* that includes valuable tools for financial planning.

Women's Institute for Financial Education at *http://wife.org* provides articles, book recommendations, and educational resources.

Comprehensive financial planning sites include *http://www. moneycentral.msn.com* and *http://www.smartmoney.com*.

Investment Madness: How Psychology Affects Your Investing . . . and What to Do About It, by John Nofsinger (Financial Times, Prentice Hall, 2001). Here is a terrific summary of behavioral finance and its impact on investing—not just for women.

Psychological Aspects of Women's Attitudes Toward Money

Prince Charming Isn't Coming: How Women Get Smart About Money, by Barbara Stanny (New York: Penguin Books, 1997). This book uncovers the myths and facts related to women and money and focuses on encouraging women to rely on themselves, rather than a man in their life, to manage their financial future.

Credit Management

http://www.financenter.com/compare/cards?compare.fcs. This site allows you to compare credit card terms.

http://www.debtfreeforme.com/calcs/index.htm. This on-line calculator will help you determine how long it will take to pay back your debt.

http://www.consumercredit.com/. The web site for American Consumer Credit Counseling Service. This service offers advice on debt consolidation and credit management.

http://www.cccsintl.org. The web site for the Consumer Credit Counseling Service, a nonprofit organization with local branches all over the country that provides free and low-cost counseling. This organization will help you create a budget and repayment plan and can also help you make payment arrangements with your creditors.

Retirement Planning

The American Association of Retired Persons (AARP) has many resources that you should take advantage of. For women going back to work after a time out, check out *Returning to the Job Market: A Woman's Guide to Employment Planning*. In addition, the AARP's web site, *http://www.aarp.org*, is very useful and includes coverage of many of the topics discussed in this book.

Your 401(k) Plan, by Mark L. Schwanbeck (New York: Irwin Professional Publishing, 1994), provides a good overview of characteristics of 401(k) pension plans, basics of investing, and pension-planning issues.

Straight Talk About Social Security, by Robert Ball (New York: Century Foundation, 1998), is written by a former commissioner of the Social Security Administration. It explains the financing problems of the program and analyzes the potential fixes.

The Social Security Administration has a useful web site at *http://ssa.gov* and also provides free pamphlets, "Understanding Social Security" (SSA 05-10024) and "What Every Woman Should Know" (SSA 05-10127) upon request (800-772-1213). The calculator at *http://ssa.*

gov/OACT/COLA/benefitEx.html will allow you to estimate your future benefits.

Social Security Benefits Handbook, 2nd ed., by Stanley Tomkiel III (Naperville, IL: Sphinx Publishing, 1998), is a comprehensive guide to determining your benefit eligibility and making claims for retirement, disability, and health benefits under Social Security. Although much of this information is also available directly from the Social Security Administration or through its web site, the book is a convenient resource.

Health Insurance

www.nationalpartnership.org. This is the official web site for the National Partnership for Women and Families. Of particular interest in this area is the page "Health Insurance 101," which explains health insurance terminology.

www.kff.org. The Henry J. Kaiser Family Foundation web site includes a report from the Kaiser Commission on Medicaid and the Uninsured. Other pages detail important information about the health-care marketplace, Medicaid, and women's health policy.

www.census.gov/hhes/hlthins/hlthin98. This site provides a report from the Census Bureau on the health insurance coverage of the U.S. population in 1998 based on the Current Population Survey.

www.fwhc.org. This is the Feminist Women's Health Center web site.

www.familiesusa.org. This is a good source of information on managed-care plans and issues related to insurance coverage for women.

Life Insurance

Your Life Insurance Options, by Alan Lavine (New York: John Wiley & Sons, 1993) (part of the Institute for Certified Financial Planners Personal Wealth Building Series) provides detailed information on different types of life insurance.

http://www.smartmoney.com/insurance/life/. This site includes an on-line calculator for estimating your life insurance needs.

http://www.insurance.yahoo.com. Yahoo's Insurance Center is a portal that links to lots of other insurance sites and includes educational information as well.

Web sites that provide insurance quotes:

http://www.insweb.com

http://www.quotesmith.com

http://www.insurerate.com

http://www.financecenter.com/compare/insurance_compare.fcs

Investments

Investing 101, by Kathy Kristof (Bloomberg Press, 2000), is a simple and straightforward primer on investing and personal finance.

Stocks for the Long Run, 2/e, by Jeremy Siegel and Peter Bernstein (New York: McGraw-Hill, 1998), provides a convincing argument that stocks are actually the safest investment for the long run.

http://www.armchairmillionaire.com. A web site designed specifically for novice women investors.

http://www.womenswire.com/money. A web site sponsored by the financial news service Bloomberg. It includes an on-line portfolio tracker and an advisory service.

http://www.womensinvest.about.com/money/womensinvest/. A web site for women investors. It includes interesting articles, summaries of recent research, and links to other related sites.

http://www.better-investing.org/clubs/. This web site explains what an investment club is and suggests steps for starting one.

Sites providing easy access to current stock and bond prices and market news include *http://www.quicken.com* and *http://www.yahoo.com,* both of which also allow you to set up and track a personal portfolio on-line.

College Planning and Saving

http://www.banksite.com/calc/tuition. This is a tuition savings calculator.

http://www.savingforcollege.com. This provides an Internet guide to Section 529 plans across the country.

http://www.fool.com/school/taxes/1998/taxes981016.htm. Roy Lewis, "The Hope Scholarship Credit," October 16, 1998.

http://www.fool.com/school/taxes/1998/taxes981023.htm. Roy Lewis, "The Lifetime Learning Credit," October 23, 1998.

http://www.fool.com/school/taxes/1998/taxes981030.htm. Roy Lewis, "Education IRA," October 30, 1998.

http://www.finaid.org. This site provides a variety of information on financial aid.

http://www.fastweb.com. This site allows you to search for available scholarships.

Real Estate

http://smartmoney.com/home/. This site provides on-line worksheets for home purchases and financing choices. It also provides tax tips, a checklist for selling your home, recommendations for home improvements, and a mortgage rate quote service.

Car Buying

The Car Buyer's Art, by Darrell Parrish (1998); available from Book Express, P.O. Box 1249, Bellflower, CA 90706; (562) 867-3723. This book provides detailed information about the process of buying a car and how to be a good negotiator.

Used Cars: How to Buy One, by Darrell Parrish (1998); available from Book Express, P.O. Box 1249, Bellflower, CA 90706; (562) 867-3723. This is similar to the previous book, but it focuses only on used cars.

http://www.edmunds.com. A terrific all-purpose car buyers' site. It gives information on new and used car prices, trade-in values, vehicle options, automobile insurance, and much more.

http://www.money.com. This site includes a "Money 101" on-line tutorial on buying a car.

http://www.carbuyingtips.com. This site includes lots of advice on buying cars, including pricing, negotiation strategies, and financing information.

Elder Care

http://www.ltcinsurance.com/ltc101.html. This site gives a tutorial on long-term care and how to prepare for it.

http://www.smartmoney.com/eldercare/. This site includes a worksheet to assess your need for long-term care and also provides information on cost and financing.

Estate Planning

"Federal Estate and Gift Taxes," IRS Publication 148, is free.

The Women's Estate Planning Guide, by Zoe M. Hicks (Chicago: Contemporary Books, 1998).

http://www.smartmoney.com/estate/. This site includes estate-planning worksheets, tax-saving tips, and general information.

Index